The BEST *of* *Especially* *for* Mormons

*Y*our all-time favorite LDS stories and thoughts gleaned from Volumes 1 through 5 of the original best-selling *Especially for Mormons.*

Stan & Sharon Miller and Sherm & Peg Fugal

The phrase, *Especially for Mormons*, is the copyrighted, trademarked property of Stan Miller; used with permission

The *Best of Especially for Mormons* is the copyrighted and trademarked property of Especially for Mormons, Inc.

Selections in The *Best of Especially for Mormons* were selected from *Especially for Mormons, Volumes 1-5*; selections were made by Stan and Sharon Miller and Sherm and Peg Fugal; selections were edited by Peg Fugal

Every reasonable effort was made to seek reprint permission from known authors of selections included herein when originally published in *Especially for Mormons, Volumes 1-5*

Special thanks to Smith-Sligting Partners for design and format; to Jayson Fugal for formatting and art direction; and to PLBF, Inc. and Covenant Communications, Inc. for advertising and marketing

The Best of Especially for Mormons is published by:
Especially for Mormons, Inc.
Box 1516
American Fork, UT 84003-6516
(801) 772-0440; 0990 fax
especiallyformormons.com

The Best of Especially for Mormons is distributed by:
Covenant Communications, Inc.
920 East State Road/Suite F
P.O. Box 416
American Fork, UT 84003-0416
(801) 756-9966; 1049 fax

ISBN 1-57734-763-3

Copyright 2000, Especially for Mormons, Inc.
First printing: August, 2000

Dedicated to Sherm, whose idea it was to produce *The Best of* edition

Special thanks to our many readers of nearly thirty years whose support have made *Especially for Mormons* one of the top-twenty best-selling books in LDS publishing history, and one of only a handful of LDS books to ever sell more than a million copies

The Story of Especially for Mormons

Everyone loves a story. I'm convinced of that. After all, life is a story. A never-ending story.

I grew up in Mesa, Arizona in the '50s. It was a quiet town, filled with wonderful people, most of us Mormons. My family lived in the Mesa 11th Ward, which encompassed the Mesa Arizona Temple.

Even in those days, the lovely winter weather in Mesa attracted many people who spent their golden years serving in the temple. Many of those temple workers lived in our ward.

Sometime around the age of seven or eight, I experienced something in sacrament meeting that made a profound impression on my young life. I heard a story. An inspirational story. A story I could understand. And relate to. A story that was easier to listen to and remember than the usual sermons.

After church, I said to my mother, "That was a good meeting," which surprised her. Normally, children do not comment on sacrament meeting because normally children do not pay attention during sacrament meeting.

"What made it so good?" she asked. And I repeated the story which had also impressed her. And so began my love of inspirational stories.

As a young teenager, I began collecting inspirational stories. At first it was just a hobby that took a more serious turn when I was assigned a topic to speak on in church and could not find just the right story to illustrate my point. I vowed that would never happen again, and my hobby turned into a quest.

Whenever I heard an inspirational thought, poem, or story in church or seminary, I would not rest until I had a copy of it. Because there were no photocopiers in those days, I had to hand-type each piece. I also began tearing pieces out of magazines and newspapers. Somewhere along the way, I acquired an old filing cabinet and began filling it. I used items from my collection many times for talks, devotionals at seminary, family home evening, or to help a friend through a trying time.

In 1965, I received a call to serve in the Eastern Atlantic States Mission headquartered in Washington, D.C. Knowing missionaries were occasionally called upon to speak, I went through my filing cabinet pulling out quite a few of my favorite stories and organizing them by subject in an expanding accordion folio which I carried into the mission field with me.

The first area I was assigned to was the Mount Vernon Ward in Alexandria, Virginia. The first Sunday, my companion and I arrived early for sacrament meeting where we were met in the foyer by the bishop who said, "Our speaker couldn't be here today, so Elder uhhhhh, what's your name?"

"Miller," I replied.

"Okay, Elder Miller, you speak first and Elder Reeder can conclude." With that he turned around and walked away.

I was panic-stricken. My materials were in our apartment and there was no time to retrieve them. I had my scriptures with me, but was not as comfortable using them as I would someday become.

I don't recall what I spoke about that day. I probably gave the same sort of sermon I never listened to as a kid. The following preparation day I bought a big three-ring binder, a set of alphabetical tab dividers, a three-hole punch, and I started organizing. I kept the binder in the car and a couple of my favorite stories tucked in my scriptures for emergencies. I used the binder often in meetings with other missionaries and members. I called my collection *Especially for Mormons.*

In 1967, one of my missionary buddies, who had been eyeing my collection, asked if he could copy it. Xerox had recently introduced its first photocopier and the public library had one. Elder Martin borrowed my binder for a week and returned it at our next meeting, proudly announcing that he had copied every page at a cost of more than $30, a huge sum in those days. That was the first time it occurred to me that others might find the same joy in reading inspirational material that I had always found.

After my mission, I returned to BYU and married in 1970. My wife, Sharon, was a secretary in one of the campus offices and brought her own electric typewriter into our family. I dug out my collection and announced that I wanted to turn it into a book, naive enough to think that I could actually do that.

Over the course of several months Sharon typed everything onto 417 pages and I took it to my friend, Mignon Julian, who was an order processor and estimator for BYU Printing Services.

She looked everything over, spent some time writing and calculating, and handed me a bid for $130 to print 500 copies. That was a lot of money to us but, after prayerfully considering it, we gave her the go-ahead, thinking we would give away some as Christmas presents, save some for posterity, and try to sell the remainder to recoup the printing costs.

Upon delivery I took a copy of my newly published book to the BYU Bookstore where a gracious woman named Gladys Palfreyman, manager of the general book department, looked it over with skepticism, commenting, "I don't know why all you returned missionaries think everyone likes this sort of thing." I must have looked crestfallen, so she offered to take four copies on consignment—which meant I wouldn't get paid unless the books sold. The next day she called and ordered four more.

Within two weeks, 200 copies had sold and Gladys began calling daily with orders. Then a devastating thing happened.

I received the printing bill from BYU Printing Services—$1,300—ten times the amount bid. I didn't sleep that night. The next morning I was at Mignon's office when she arrived and pointed out the error in the bill. She assured me it was correct. I handed her the written bid for $130. She looked at the bid, then the bill, then the bid, then turned ashen and dashed out of the office, returning with Frank Haymore, the general manager, who was terribly upset.

"Stan, you can't hold us to this bid. You had to know it was wrong. She forgot a zero. The correct price is $1,300."

Then I turned ashen and hastened to explain that I would never have spent that amount of money because I didn't have it. As it turned out, they reduced the bill a little and extended the payment terms a lot, and I stumbled into the world of self-publishing.

To this day I bless that sweet woman who left off the zero. Had it not been for her error, there might never have been an *Especially for Mormons*. Because of her, more than a million copies of this collection are now gracing the bookshelves of LDS homes throughout the world.

I was in a fix. I had a debt to pay. I also had faith in my product. And faith in my market. I also had a collection of thoughts, poetry, and prose not written by me. It was the work of many people, most of whom I didn't know. I did not have permission to reprint anything. I was merely trying to share my collection with others.

With the help of my neighbor and lawyer, Dale Jeffs, we spent a few months writing letters seeking permissions. Surprisingly, most people were thrilled to think I would want to include their story in my collection. After nearly a year of effort, we went back to press with a revised edition which continued to sell like hotcakes at the BYU Bookstore. But there were other bookstores to contact.

I visited the presidents of the two largest LDS publishers, Deseret Book and Bookcraft, and asked for a list of all the LDS bookstores. They laughed at me. Unbeknownst to me, that information was costly, closely guarded, and never shared.

All was not lost. Marvin Wallin, the president of Bookcraft (who would later become a great friend and mentor), had received inquiries about our book and offered to add it to his catalog which was, unfortunately, not going to press for several months. We were on our own.

A couple of weeks later, we borrowed a trailer and headed north with a few hundred books in tow. In every town we stopped and looked in the phone book for the local LDS bookstore. That first weekend we traveled as far as Idaho Falls, making a half dozen stops along the way, and selling a few books at each stop. The following weekend we drove in a different direction with the same results. That summer we vacationed in both Arizona and California where we found a dozen more bookstores. We had a grand time and made some good friends, many of whom remain friends today.

And then a miracle happened. Orders started pouring in. Business was booming! Over the next couple of years, we sold several hundred thousand books.

I was working fulltime at BYU at the time, which meant I spent my evenings and weekends packing boxes and typing orders and invoices. My UPS man and I became fast friends.

Somewhere along the line Bookcraft added us to their catalog and began buying thousands of books at a time.

Early in 1973 Bookcraft asked when we were going to publish Volume Two. The thought had never entered my mind. By Christmas, people were buying Volume Two as enthusiastically as they had purchased the original.

Though I was busier than ever, I began collecting materials for a third volume, aided by people offering their own inspirational stories, which might not otherwise have ever been published.

In 1975 we turned the printing and distribution of *Especially for Mormons* over to Bookcraft, promising Volume Three by late summer of 1976 for the upcoming Christmas season. However, I had a new Church calling, and a new business, and missed the deadline by months.

I remember going into Marvin's office the Monday morning before Thanksgiving with the completed manuscript and my apologies, hoping Bookcraft could get it out in time for Valentine's Day. Though he was grateful to finally have the manuscript, he was also sorry that we had missed the Christmas season.

Five days later, I happened into the Seventies Mission Book Store in Provo, where I instinctively wandered over to the table which held my books—and, lo and behold, there was Volume Three. I asked the manager when he had received it. "Yesterday," he said, "and I've already sold quite a few." I was dumbfounded.

I hurried home and called Marvin to ask how he had published a book of that size that fast. He said, "I wanted to surprise you, so I told the printers and binders to work around the clock."

And then an interesting thing happened. I ran out of material to compile. When the publisher called for Volume Four, Peg Fugal, a friend, business associate, and local writer, was sitting in my office. Just as I was about to confess that I didn't have enough material to compile a fourth volume, Peg leaned across my desk and whispered, "I do."

With that, Volume Four was produced, with an added bonus: an index to all four volumes, a suggestion made by Peg (who is also a marketing genius). Content aside, the index made Volume Four a best-seller, which demanded a Volume Five. Once again the Fugals stepped in and offered to help, along with my sister Julianne, and Volume Five was born.

There have been more than thirty printings of Volume One alone. All together, there have been more than a hundred printings of the combined volumes, earning *Especially for Mormons* a distinction few LDS books have ever held: an estimated million copies sold. In fact, *Especially for Mormons* is one of the top twenty best-selling books in LDS publishing history, a mark of distinction in which we take great pride.

As we approach our thirtieth year in print, we decided to do something special for our loyal readers: produce a brand new special hardcover leather edition of *The Best of Especially for Mormons,* which you now hold in your hands. Less expensive and cumbersome than our previous five paperback volumes, and infinitely better designed, edited, and bound, we think it will become your favorite.

Keep a hanky handy as you read through the stories you love best from all five volumes, then pass it along, or better yet, share another copy with a friend. And then watch for a whole collectible library to follow, including *Christmas Especially for Mormons, Especially for Mormon Missionaries, Poetry Especially for Mormons,* and so on.

Feel free, as well, to submit your own inspirational stories for inclusion in an upcoming, *All New Especially for Mormons,* by visiting our website, or faxing or writing to us (details below).

I want to thank the thousands of you who have offered suggestions and gratitude over the years. I'm especially grateful to my wife, Sharon, to Sherm and Peg Fugal, our new publisher, and to Carolyn Olsen and Cory Maxwell at Bookcraft who always believed in the magic of an inspirational story.

With much love,
Stan Miller
Co-Compiler
August, 2000

Especially for Mormons, Inc.
Box 1516
American Fork, UT 84003-6516
(801) 772-0440, 0990 fax
www.especiallyformormons.com

The Best of Especially for Mormons

W hy *The Best of*? Several reasons. First of all, with each volume now priced at almost $20, a complete set of all five volumes of *Especially for Mormons* now costs close to $100.

Secondly, it's a new millennium, which demands a new effort.

Thirdly, *Especially for Mormons* is approaching its thirtieth year in print, which demands some sort of commemorative effort.

Fourthly, *Especially for Mormons* has entered the ranks of one of the top-twenty, best-selling books in LDS publishing history, and one of only a handful of LDS books to ever sell more than a million copies—which demands a hard-bound leather, commemorative *The Best of* edition.

Like you, we have been using *Especially for Mormons* for years in our talks and lessons and family home evenings and letters to missionaries. We have our beloved pieces that we use over and over again—which are probably the same pieces you love and use over and over again, too. Making the cut was another story.

Stan and Sharon took Volumes 1 and 2, Sherm took Volumes 3 and 4, and I took Volume 5. Each of us read every thought, poem, and story in our volumes, circling our most beloved ones, and crossing out the others—a task that literally took weeks—and left us with three times the material we needed and wanted.

I had the unenviable task of making the final cut, which nearly killed me. Not only did it takes days and weeks of reading, cutting, editing, and cutting some more, the task gave me tendonitis and completely consumed my life.

Maybe we put too much effort into it. But when the cover reads *The Best of,* then we want the contents to reflect exactly that: the very best thoughts and stories from our entire collection, the ones we love the most, the ones you love the most, the ones that move people the most, the ones that best illustrate who we are and what we believe.

You may not realize this, but the original five volumes of *Especially for Mormons* were hand-typed and printed as typed, errors and all, with no editing. *The Best of* edition demanded a greater effort. Every piece has been read, re-read, and edited to read well for generations. That's what took the most time, that's what makes this brand new edition so valuable.

Enjoy it, and look for future titles to enhance your new leather library of *Especially for Mormons.*

Peg Fugal
Co-Compiler & Editor
August, 2000

Table of Contents

America

It seems a little ridiculous now, but this country was originally founded as a protest against taxation.

❧

The Meaning of the Pledge of Allegiance

When you pledge allegiance to the flag, you promise loyalty and devotion to your nation. Each word has a deep meaning: "I pledge allegiance" (I promise to be true) "to the flag" (to the sign our country) "of the United States of America" (a country made up of fifty states, each with certain rights of its own) "and to the Republic" (a country where the people elect others to make laws for them) "for which it stands" (the flag means the country), "one nation under God" (a country whose people believe in a supreme being), "indivisible" (the country cannot be split into parts), "with liberty and justice" (with freedom and fairness) "for all" (for each person in this country, both you and me).

❧

All the Lord's Work is Planned

The work to be done by John the Baptist, by the ancient Twelve, by Columbus, by the signers of the Declaration of Independence, and by the framers of the Constitution of the United States was all known and arranged for in advance. And all these are but illustrations and patterns, for all of the Lord's work is planned and prepared in advance, and those who are called and chosen to do the work receive their commission and ordination from him, first in the pre-existence and then, if they remain true and faithful, again here in mortality.

—Bruce R. McConkie

❧

Fall of Civilization

It's appalling that since the dawn of history no less than 22 civilizations have risen and fallen. When you look for and classify the reasons, they are monotonous in their similarity:

1. They lost their religious convictions and flouted basic morality

2. They became obsessed with sex

3. They debased their money of its intrinsic value and let inflation run rampant

4. Honest work ceased to be a virtue

5. Respect for law disintegrated, and violence became an accepted method of achieving individual and group desires

6. They reached the point where the citizens were no longer willing to be soldiers and fight for the defense of their nation and their heritage; they resorted to paid mercenaries or tried to buy off their attackers

—Kenneth McFarland

God Sends a Baby

When a wrong wants righting, or a truth wants preaching, or a continent wants discovering, God sends a baby into the world to do it.

What mother, looking down with tenderness upon her chubby infant, does not envision her child as the President of the Church or the leader of her nation.

As he is nestled in her arms, she sees him a statesman, a leader, a prophet. Some dreams do come true.

One mother gives us a Shakespeare, another a Michelangelo, and another an Abraham Lincoln, and still another a Joseph Smith.

When theologians are reeling and stumbling; when lips are pretending and hearts are wandering; and people are 'running to and fro, seeking the word of the Lord and cannot find it'; when clouds or error need dissipating, and spiritual darkness needs penetrating, and heavens need opening, a little infant is born.

—*Spencer W. Kimball*

❧

Mystery Guest in Philadelphia

Thomas Jefferson tells that on the day of our nation's birth in the little hall in Philadelphia, debate had raged for hours. The men gathered there were honorable men, hard-pressed by a king who had flouted the very laws they were willing to obey. Even so, to sign a Declaration of Independence was such an irretrievable act that the walls resounded with the words "treason, the gallows, the headman's ax", and the issue remained in doubt.

Then a man rose and spoke. Jefferson described him as not a young man, but one who had to summon all his energy for an impassioned plea. He cited the grievances that had brought them to this moment and finally, his voice failing, he said, "They may turn every tree into a gallows, every home into a grave, and yet the words of that parchment can never die. To the mechanic in the workshop, they will speak hope; to the slave in the mines, freedom. Sign that parchment. Sign if the next moment the noose is around your neck, for that parchment will be the textbook of freedom, the Bible of the rights of man forever." He fell back, exhausted.

The 56 delegates, swept up by his eloquence, rushed forward and signed a document destined to be as immortal as a work of man can be.

When they turned to thank him for his timely oratory, he was not to be found, nor could any be found who knew who he was or how he had come in or gone out through the locked and guarded doors.

Fifty-six men, a little band so unique, we have never seen their like since, had pledged their lives, their fortunes and their sacred honor.

—*Ronald Reagan*

Rights and Obligations

America is a unique land of many rights and obligations.

Americans have the right to go to a church, synagogue, or temple, or not to go—and an obligation to respect this right in others.

Americans have the right to say what they think individually, or collectively—and an obligation to hold their tongues when it will hurt their country.

Americans have the right to select those in public office—and those in public office have an obligation to serve with honesty, integrity, wisdom, and selflessness.

Americans have the right of protection for their lives, homes, and property—and an obligation to respect the laws of the nation.

Americans have the right to enjoy the greatest progress made by any nation on earth—and an obligation to do an honest day's work to contribute to that progress.

Americans have the right to enjoy the abundance of this nation—and an obligation to share that abundance with those less fortunate.

Americans have many rights—and many obligations.

❧

The Price They Paid

Have you ever wondered what happened to those men who signed the Declaration of Independence? Five signers were captured by the British as traitors, and tortured before they died. Twelve had their homes ransacked and burned. Two lost their sons in the Revolutionary Army, another had two sons captured. Nine of the fifty-six fought and died from wounds or the hardships of the Revolutionary War.

What kind of men were they? Twenty-four were lawyers and jurists. Eleven were merchants. Nine were farmers and large plantation owners, men of means, well-educated.

But they signed the Declaration of Independence knowing full well that the penalty would be death if they were captured. They signed and they pledged their lives, their fortunes, and their sacred honor.

Carter Braxton of Virginia, a wealthy planter and trader, saw his ships swept from the seas by the British navy; he sold his home and properties to pay his debts, and died in rags.

Thomas McKean was so hounded by the British that he was forced to move his family almost constantly; he served in the Congress without pay, and his family was kept in hiding; his possessions were taken from him, and poverty was his reward.

Vandals or soldiers or both looted the properties of Ellery, Clymer, Hall, Walton, Gwinnett, Heyward, Ruttledge, and Middleton.

At the Battle of Yorktown, Thomas Nelson, Jr. noted that the British General Cornwallis had taken over the Nelson home for his headquarters; the owner quietly urged General

George Washington to open fire, which was done; the home was destroyed, and Nelson died bankrupt.

Francis Lewis had his home and properties destroyed; the enemy jailed his wife, and she died within a few months.

John Hart was driven from his wife's bedside as she was dying; their thirteen children fled for their lives; his fields and his grist mill were laid waste; for more than a year, he lived in forests and caves, returning home after the war to find his wife dead, his children vanished; a few weeks later he died from exhaustion and a broken heart.

Norris and Livingston suffered a similar fate.

Such were the stories and sacrifices of the American Revolution. These were not wild-eyed, rabble-rousing ruffians. These were soft-spoken men of means and education. They had security, but they valued liberty more. Standing tall, straight, and unwavering, they pledged, "For the support of this declaration, with a firm reliance on the protection of the Divine Providence, we mutually pledge to each other, our lives, our fortunes, and our sacred honor."

They gave us an independent America. Can we keep it?

The Battle Hymn of the Republic

During the Civil War, there was a serious problem with desertion.

President Lincoln called for 75,000 volunteer troops for a period of ninety days. He got his volunteers, but four years later, they were still fighting.

They had been away from their wives, children, families, homes, and work for four years, so they did what one would expect in those circumstances: they gave up. The Union army was worn out and despondent: they deserted by the hundreds; many were shot for desertion.

At this particular time, Julia Ward Howe wrote, "The Battle Hymn of the Republic." It was said that this song was the equivalent of 100,000 troops. The last stanza reads:

> *In the beauty of the lilies, Christ was born across the sea,*
> *With a glory in His bosom that transfigures you and me;*
> *As he died to make men holy, let us die to make men free,*
> *While God is marching on.*

These same weary soldiers became different overnight. Their vision had been restored, their perspective to life had changed, their will to win had returned.

Bible

Bible Facts

The Bible contains 3,566,480 letters; 733,746 words; 31,163 verses; 1,189 chapters; and 66 books.

The longest chapter is Psalms 119. The longest verse is Esther 8:9. The shortest verse is John 11:35. The middle verse is Psalms 118:8. The longest name is in Isaiah 8.

The word "and" appears 46, 227 times. The word "Jehovah" appears 6,855 times. The name of God is not mentioned in the book of Esther.

Isaiah 37 and 2 Kings 19 are alike. Ezra 7:21 contains the alphabet. The finest reading is Acts 26.

The Bible contains two testaments: the Old is law, the New is love. The Old is the bud, the New is the bloom. In the Old, man is reaching up for God; in the New, God is reaching down for man. In the Old, man is in the valley, but can see the sun shining on the mountain tops; in the New, he is on the mountain-top, basking in the sunlight of God's infinite love.

❧

Fate of the Original Twelve Apostles

1. Matthew—slain by sword in Ethiopia, approx. 60 AD

2. Mark—dragged to death through the streets of Alexandria, then burned, approx. 74 AD

3. Luke—hanged from an olive tree in Greece

4. John—banished to the Isle of Patmos, 96 AD (Rev. 1:9), still walks the earth

5. Peter—crucified head down in Rome, 66 AD

6. James (son of Zebedee)—beheaded in Jerusalem by sword (Acts 12:1-9)

7. Phillip—crucified at Heirapole Phryga, 52 AD

8. James, the lesser (son of Alphaeus)—thrown from the pinnacle, then beaten to death, 60 AD

9. Bartholomew—beaten, crucified, beheaded by command of a king, 52 AD

10. Andrew—preached until he expired, 74 AD

11. Thomas—ran through by a lance at Corehandal, East Indies, 52 AD

12. Jude—shot to death, 76 AD

13. Simon—crucified in Persia, 74 AD

14. Mathias—stoned, then beheaded in Ethiopia, 70 AD

15. Barnabus—stoned to death by James at Salancan, approx. 73 AD

16. Paul—beheaded by Herod of Nero, 66 AD

17. Judas Iscariot—committed suicide by hanging himself, 34 AD (Acts 1:18)

18. Thaddeus—shot to death by arrows, 72 AD

—John Fox Ricks

❧

The Village that Lives by the Bible

It was early in 1945 when, as a correspondent with the U.S. forces beating out their bloody victory on Okinawa, I first came upon Shimabuku, the strangest and most inspiring community I ever saw. Huddled beneath its groves of banyan and twisted pine trees, this remote village of some 1,000 souls was in the path of the American advance and so received a severe shelling.

But when an advance patrol swept up to the village compound, the GIs stopped dead in their tracks. Barring their way were two little old men; they bowed low and began to speak. The battle-hardened sergeant, wary of enemy tricks, held up his hand, and summoned a Nisei interpreter.

The interpreter shook his head. "I don't get it. Seems we're being welcomed—as fellow Christians. One says he's the mayor of the village, the other's the schoolmaster. That's a Bible the older one has in his hand. They seem to be asking for just one thing—a picture of Jesus."

The sergeant spat reflectively on the ground, then grunted, "Better call the chaplain."

The chaplain came, and with him a brace of correspondents. Guided by the two old men—Mojun Nakarnura, the mayor, and Shosei Kina, the schoolmaster—we cautiously toured the compound. We'd seen other Okinawa villages, uniformly down-at-the-heels and despairing; by contrast, this one shone like a diamond in a dung heap. Everywhere we were greeted by smiles and dignified bows. Proudly the two old men showed us their spotless homes, their terraced fields, fertile and neat, their storehouses and granaries, their prized sugar mill.

Gravely the old men talked on, and the interpreter said, "They've met only one American before, long ago. Because he was a Christian, they assume we are, too—though they can't quite understand why we came in shooting."

Piecemeal, the incredible story came out. Thirty years before, an American missionary on his way to Japan had paused at Shimabuku. He'd stayed only long enough to make a pair of converts (these same two men), teach them a couple of hymns, leave them a Japanese translation of the Bible, and exhort them to live by it. They'd had no contact with any Christian since. Yet during those 30 years, guided by the Bible, they had managed to create a Christian democracy at its purest.

How had it happened? Picking their way through the Bible, the two converts had found not only an inspiring person on whom to pattern a life, but sound precepts on which to base their society. They'd adopted the Ten Commandments as Shimabuku's legal code; the Sermon on the Mount as their guide to social conduct. In Kina's school, the Bible was the chief literature; it was read daily by all students, and major passages were memorized. In Nakamura's village government, the precepts of the Bible were law.

Nurtured on this book, a whole generation of Shimabukans had drawn from it their ideas of human dignity and of the rights and responsibilities of citizenship. The result was plain to see. Shimabuku for years had had no jail, no brothel, no drunkenness, no divorce; there was a high level of health and happiness.

Next day, the tide of battle swept us on. But a few days later, during a lull, I requisitioned a jeep and a Japanese-speaking driver and went back to Shimabuku. Over the winding roads outside the village, huge truck convoys and endless lines of American troops moved dustily; behind them lumbered armored tanks, heavy artillery. But inside, Shimabuku was an oasis of serenity.

Once again I strolled through the quiet village streets, soaking up Shimabuku's calm. There was a sound of singing. We followed it and came to Nakamura's house where a curious religious service was under way. Having no knowledge of churchly forms or ritual, the Shimabukans had developed their own. There was much Bible reading by Kina, repeated in sing-song fashion by the worshippers. Then came hymn singing. The tunes of the two hymns the missionary had taught—"Fairest Lord Jesus" and "All Hail the Power of Jesus' Name"—had naturally suffered some changes, but they were recognizable. Swept up in the hearty spirit of "All Hail the Power", we joined in.

After many prayers, voiced spontaneously by people in the crowd, there was a discussion of community problems. With each question, Kina turned quickly to some Bible passage to find the answer. The book's imitation-leather cover was cracked and worn, its pages stained and dog-eared from 30 years' constant use. Kina held it with the reverent care one would use in handling the original Magna Carta.

The service over, we waited as the crowd moved out, and my driver whispered hoarsely, "So this is what comes out of only a Bible and a couple of old guys who wanted to live like Jesus!" Then, with a glance at a shell hole, he murmured, "Maybe we're using the wrong kind of weapons to make the world over!"

Time had dimmed the Shimabukan's memory of the missionary; neither Kina nor Nakamura could recall his name. They did remember his parting statement, "Study this book well. It will give you a strong faith. And when faith is strong, everything is strong."

Now, in 1945, explosive changes lay ahead, and Shimabuku would need strong faith indeed. A few days after I left the village, thousands of refugees poured in, bloating the little hamlet to ten times its normal population. At first, the villagers were stunned by the enormous influx; but they rose to the challenge when Nakamura looked up the appropriate Biblical passage and repeated to them, "I was a stranger, and ye took me in."

A few weeks later an even more severe shock came—the U.S. High Command, needing a staging area for the invasion of Japan, ordered Shimabuku bulldozed out of existence and its people moved to the arid north. The villagers were taken out by army trucks, with only such possessions as they could carry—and not until eight months later were they allowed to return—to find their idyllic little village nothing but rubble.

Patiently, Kina and Nakamura, with the help of sympathetic U.S. officials, led the villagers in building the new Shimabuku. During the reconstruction, the Bible passage most read was Nehemiah's moving account of his rebuilding of Jerusalem, "The God of Heaven, he will prepare us, therefore we his servants will arise and build."

Recently, haunted by my war-time memories, I went back to Okinawa to see how it had fared since "civilization", in the form of the American occupation, came up like thunder to engulf it. I found Okinawa unrecognizable. Where once little villages slumbered in isolation, GI housing developments now crowd the island's green slopes. Lacing the island are crowded four-lane highways lined with modern shopping centers, supermarkets, and endless miles of army warehouses. Adjacent to the huge air bases and other installations are officers' clubs, movie theaters, golf courses, bathing beaches, and radio and TV stations.

I looked for little Shimabuku, once so remote that strangers seldom came, and I found it surrounded by "progress". Today the tiny village is hedged in on one side by a multi-lane highway buzzing with traffic, and on the other by a plush golf course. From every side modernity's more noisome accompaniments intrude upon it. A few hundred yards down the highway is Koza, a big "recreational area" catering to GIs, blazing with neon lights, crowded with honky-tonks, bars, and night clubs.

Yet these influences have not tainted Shimabuku. Physically surrounded, it remains spiritually remote from the honky-tonks. Its life is still centered on the Bible. Most important in keeping it so is the lovely little church the villagers have erected with their own hands. It includes a separate Sunday School building and social hall for young people, with a seven-day-a-week program that makes Christianity the core of Shimabuku's society.

For keeping Shimabuku's rare spirit intact, the village's two grand old men take no credit. As Nakamura told me quietly, "You see, the missionary was right: if faith is strong, everything is strong."

As he spoke, my jeep driver of 1945 was beside me in memory again. I could hear him whispering his amazement at what had come out of "only a Bible and a couple of old guys who wanted to live like Jesus." And somehow his impulsive observation struck me with fresh cogency: "Maybe we're using the wrong kind of weapons to make the world over!"

—*Clarence W. Hall*

Character

Thought is action in rehearsal.

—*Freud*

Character is a victory, not a gift.

The wind of anger blows out the lamp of intelligence.

Courage is not the absence of fear; it is the mastery of it.

Character is not built in an emergency—merely exhibited.

No matter what you do, someone always knew you would.

Nothing sets one out of the devil's reach so much as humility.

To profit from good advice requires more wisdom than to give it.

The people who object to rules are people who don't obey the rules.

—*N. Eldon Tanner*

It is impossible to rise higher as leaders than we rise as individuals.

—*Sterling W. Sill*

The high-minded man must care more for the truth than for what people think.

—*Aristotle*

Man's mind stretched to a new idea never goes back to its original dimensions.

—*Oliver Wendell Holmes*

Whenever you violate a principle, you get a short-term gain, but a long-term loss.
—*Rodney Turner*

❧

The greatest battles of life are fought out daily in the silent chambers of the soul.
—*David O. McKay*

❧

Self-discipline is doing what you know you should do when you don't want to do it.
—*N. Eldon Tanner*

❧

Reputation through a thousand years may depend on the conduct of a single moment.

❧

We are always in the forge or on the anvil; by trials, God is shaping us for higher things.
—*Henry Ward Beecher*

❧

To err is human—but when the eraser wears out before the pencil does, you're overdoing it.

❧

The man who does not read good books has no advantage over the man who can't read them.
—*Mark Twain*

❧

It is considered a good thing to look wise, especially when not overburdened with information.
—*J. Golden Kimball*

❧

Reputation is what men and women think of us; character is what God and the angels know of us.
—*Thomas Paine*

❧

Ability will enable a man to get to the top, but character is the only thing that will keep him there.

❧

Sign over an arch leading to a university campus: "You are not what you are, but what you think you are."

❧

Lord, when we are wrong, make us willing to change. And when we are right, make us easy to live with.

—*Peter Marshall*

❧

The first milestone to being a good citizen is learning how to disagree without being disagreeable.

❧

There are two things we should learn to forget: the good we have done to others, and the evil they have done to us.

❧

Flabbiness of character, more than flabbiness of muscle, lies at the root of most of the problems facing American youth.

—*David O. McKay*

❧

Man will never reach his destiny until he realizes there is as much dignity in tilling the soil as there is in writing a poem.

—*Booker T. Washington*

❧

Character is the aim of true education; science, history, and literature are but means to accomplish this desired end.

—*David O. McKay*

❧

Unless the way we live draws us closer to Heavenly Father and to our fellow men, there will be an enormous emptiness in our lives.

—*Spencer W. Kimball*

❧

If you are right, take the humble side—and you will help the other fellow; if you are wrong, take the humble side—and you will help yourself.

❧

Self-pity is easily the most destructive of the non-pharmaceutical narcotics; it is addictive, gives momentary pleasure, and separates the victim from reality.

—*John W. Gardner*

It is better for the development of character and contentment to do certain things badly for yourself than to have them done better for you by someone else.

༂

Character is like chiseling a statue: one has to knock off huge hunks of selfishness, which requires self-discipline; only then does character begin to emerge.
—*Fulton J. Sheen*

༂

Be grateful for your problems, because if you didn't have them, you wouldn't be here, and if they were less difficult, we would get someone with less ability to take your place.
—*Sign in executive lounge*

༂

People are like stained glass windows: they glow and sparkle when it is sunny and bright; but when the sun goes down their true beauty is revealed only if there is a light from within.

༂

Shakespeare, Leonardo da Vinci, Benjamin Franklin, and Lincoln never saw a movie, heard a radio, or looked at television. They had "loneliness" and knew what to do with it. They were not afraid of being lonely because they knew that was when the creative mood in them would mark.
—*Carl Sandburg*

༂

Ten Reasons Why I Swear

1. It pleases Mother so much

2. It is a fine mark of manliness

3. It proves I have self-control

4. It indicates how clearly my mind operates

5. It makes my conversation so pleasing to everyone

6. It leaves no doubt in anybody's mind about my good breeding

7. It impresses people that I have more than an ordinary education

8. It is an unmistakable sign of culture and refinement

9. It makes me a very desirable personality among children and women and in respectable society

10. It is my way of honoring God who said, "Thou shalt not take the name of the Lord, thy God, in vain."

Character of the Saints

Why were the Saints saints? Because they were cheerful when it was difficult to be cheerful; patient when it was difficult to be patient; and because they pushed on when they wanted to stand still, kept silent when they wanted to talk, and were agreeable when they wanted to be disagreeable. That was all. It was quite simple, and it always will be.

The Ten Commandments

The Ten Commandments are not rules to obey as a personal favor to God. They are the fundamental principles without which mankind cannot live together. They make of those who keep them faithfully strong, wholesome, confident, dedicated men and women. This is because the commandments come from the same divine hand that fashioned our human nature.

—*Cecil B. DeMille*

An Abstainer

The story is told of a boy who was a total abstainer, and who was about to be apprenticed to a trade. The foreman of the place offered him a glass of beer, but the lad refused, saying he never drank such stuff. Somewhat irritated, the foreman said angrily, "We have no teetotalers in this place!"

"You'll have one if you have me," said the lad.

More irritated than ever, the foreman cried, "Look here, boy, you must have this beer inside or outside!"

"Well," answered the little fellow, "you can please yourself, sir. I came here this morning with a clean jacket and a clean character. You can soil my jacket if you like, but you cannot soil my character."

—*David O. McKay*

Character vs. Intelligence and Education

Recently I became acquainted with an organization named Mensa. It is for geniuses and near geniuses. To be eligible for membership, one must have an IQ that is in the top two per cent of the nation.

I read through seventy pages of names of members in the United States and did not recognize a single one. I cannot recall having seen any name there as the author of a book or article, a public official or statesman, a noted educator or scientist, or an industrial leader. This is not a scientific conclusion, but I do venture the suspicion that high intelligence does not always result in distinguished achievement.

There were many people in this nation with greater intelligence and greater education than Washington and Lincoln at the times they served so ably as to be described as our greatest presidents. There are a million and a half people in our country today who are endowed intellectually more highly than either Washington or Lincoln. Neither of them had a college education. Washington's formal education stopped when he was fifteen years old. Lincoln once figured that, all told, he had spent about one year in school.

What is it, then, that prepares us for high achievement? It is possible that character has more to do with what we make out of our lives than does intelligence or education. A study of geniuses in the United States conducted some years back concluded that people who "achieve eminence are characterized not only by high intellectual traits, but also by persistence of motive and effort, confidence in their abilities, and great strength or force of character."

—*Robert W. Moon*

The North Side of the Mountain

A ship-building company ad read: "All of our timber comes for the north side of the mountain."

Why the north side? What does that have to do with timber?

The best timber grows on the north side of the mountain because of the rigors of Mother Nature. The snow is deeper and the cold is colder, the winds are stiffer, and the warmth is not so warm, as on the south side of the mountain. The very harshness of the weather is a contributing factor to the toughness of the timber.

Human character is not much different from timber. How often the best in personality grows on the north side of the mountain. We grumble about our hardships and difficulties, yet those very difficulties help us to grow and become nature persons. Each can look at his own life and see that the times when he made the greatest personal progress was probably when life had him on "the north side of the mountain".

—*Edmond H. Babbitt*

The Wedge of Discouragement

A Chinese legend describes how the Father of Sin decided to have a sale and dispose of all the tools he owned to anyone who would pay his price.

The implements were laid out in a row for inspection. Among them were tools labeled: Malice, Hatred, Envy, Jealousy, and Deceit. Every one had a price tag on it. Apart from the others lay a harmless looking wedge-shaped tool, very worn from use, that was priced a great deal higher than any of the rest.

One of the buyers asked the Devil what it was. "That," he said, "is discouragement, and it's in fine shape."

"But why have you priced it so high?"

"Because it's more useful than any of the others. I can pry open and get inside a man's conscience with that wedge when I couldn't get near him with any other. And, believe me, once I get inside, I can use that man to whatever suits me best. Of course, you'll notice it's a little worn; that's because I use it with nearly everybody, for very few of you mortals know that it belongs to me."

However the price was so high that this particular tool was never sold.

The Devil still owns it, and is still using it today.

❧

The Duke and His Subject

More than a century ago, the nobility of England, in their colorful finery, were on a fox hunt. They came to a closed gate, where nearby sat a ragged youngster.

"Open the gate, lad," said the leader of the hunt.

"No, this property belongs to my father, and he desires it left shut."

"Open the gate, lad. Do you know who I am?"

"No, sir.

"I am the Duke of Wellington."

"The Duke of Wellington, this nation's hero, would not ask me to disobey my father."

And the riders of the hunt silently rode on.

❧

The Two Models

A great artist who was engaged to paint a mural for a great cathedral in an old Sicilian town. The subject was to be the life of Christ. For many years the artist labored diligently, and finally the painting was finished except for the most important figures, the Christ Child and Judas Iscariot. He searched far and wide for models for these two figures.

One day while walking in an old part of the city, he came upon some children playing in the street. Among them was a twelve-year-old boy whose face stirred the painter's heart. It was the face of an angel—a very dirty one, perhaps, but the face he needed.

The artist took the child home with him, and day after day the boy sat patiently until the face of the Christ Child was finished.

But the painter failed to find a model for Judas. For years, haunted by the fear that his masterpiece would remain unfinished, he continued his search.

One afternoon in a tavern, the painter saw a gaunt and tattered figure stagger across the threshold and fall to the floor, begging for a glass of wine. The painter lifted him up and looked into a face that startled him. It seemed to bear the mark of every sin of man.

"Come with me, " the painter said, "I will give you wine, food, and clothing." Here at last was his model for Judas! For many days and parts of many nights, the painter worked feverishly to complete his masterpiece.

As the work went on, a change came over the model. A strange tension replaced the stuporous languor, and his bloodshot eyes were fixed with horror on the painted likeness of himself. One day, perceiving his agitation, the painter paused saying, "My son, I'd like to help you. What troubles you so?"

The model sobbed and buried his face in his hands. After a long moment he lifted pleading eyes to the old painter's face. "Do you not remember me? Years ago I was your model for the Christ Child!"

—*Sterling Provost*

Chastity

A mind engrossed in sex is good for little else.

To be carnally minded is to be spiritually dead.

—*David O. McKay*

It is easier to suppress the first desire than to satisfy all that follow it.

—*Benjamin Franklin*

To educate a man in mind and not in morals is to educate a menace to society.

—*Theodore Roosevelt*

When we learn that physical gratification is only incident to, and not the compelling force of, love itself, we have made a supreme discovery.

He who is morally unclean sins against himself. No one can sin and really feel good about it. Some part of him constantly protests, and he is therefore at war with himself, and war is always destructive.

—*Hugh B. Brown*

Two Flowers

Girls, the flower by the roadside that catches the dust of every traveler is not the one to be admired, and is seldom, if ever, plucked; but the one blooming way up on the hillside, protected by a perpendicular cliff, is the flower with the virgin perfume, and the one the boys will almost risk his life to possess.

—*David O. McKay*

Narrowing the Breach

When a person tells an unclean story he imbeds impurity deeper in his own mind; he breaks down his own resistance to evil; he talks himself into the idea that the smutty thing he talks about isn't so bad after all and he narrows the breach between the unclean thought and the unclean deed. He sets up an acceptance in his own mind of the type of filth he discusses and lays a foundation for sinful acts. He builds a barrier against his own reception of the Spirit of God and its guidance.

—*Editor, Church News*

❧

After Midnight

If you can't find anything else to do, go home. Limit your "parking", no matter where it might be. Say good night, and mean it. Set a decently reasonable hour, and stick to it. When the hour is late, the body might be so full of fatigue that poisons, that clear thinking will fade out very rapidly. Most mistakes of youth—if not all—are made after midnight.

❧

Self-Mastery

There are some things that never become old-fashioned. The sweetness of a baby is one. The virtue and chastity of manhood is another. Youth is the time to lay the foundation for our homes. There are those who tell you that suppression is wrong, but self-mastery, not indulgence, is the virtue that contributes to the virility of manhood and to the beauty of womanhood.

❧

A Beauty Every Girl Has

There is a beauty every girl has—a gift from God, as pure as the sunlight, and as sacred as life. It is a beauty all men love, a virtue that wins all men's souls. That beauty is chastity. Chastity without skin beauty may enkindle the soul; skin beauty without chastity can kindle only the eye. Chastity enshrined in the mold of true womanhood will hold true love eternally.

—*David O. McKay*

The Devil's Ground

We have no right to go near temptation, or in fact to do or say a thing that we cannot honestly ask the blessings of the Lord upon, neither to visit any place where we would be ashamed to take our sister or sweetheart. The Good Spirit will not go with us on to the Devil's ground, and if we are standing alone upon the ground belonging to the adversary of men's souls, he may have the power to trip us up and destroy us. The only safe ground is so far from danger as it is possible to get. Virtue is more valuable than life. Never allow yourself to go out of curiosity to see any of the undercrust in this world. We can't handle dirty things and keep our hands clean.

—*Heber J. Grant*

The Meaning of a Kiss

A kiss is a sacred way of expressing love, deep affection, admiration, and respect. It is not a way of saying "good night". It is not a way of saying, "thank you for a good time". And especially, it is not a way to get a thrill or to entertain each other. Respect and admiration must be a part of the love you feel for a person before a kiss will mean anything. Naturally, you can't feel love, respect, and admiration for every person you date and so, naturally, you don't kiss every person you date. In fact, there are very few who will merit enough respect for you to kiss. We are taught to practice moderation in all things. If, after dating one person for awhile, your love and respect for him grows, then a kiss is the best way to show your love for him. But it will remain a sweet expression of love only if you remember that a kiss is sacred. To remain sacred, it must be given in the right atmosphere, with the proper attitude, kept in small doses, and it must not be an every-date occurrence. A kiss brings a couple closer together; it helps their love and respect for each other grow, if it is used the way it is meant to be used, and in the attitude of love and purity.

Chastity and the Five Different Facets of Our Nature

Chastity: I suppose you've had that word come at you from many different angles. It's an important word, for the concept behind it carries with it the purity, integrity, cleanness of spirit and soul that allows every chaste young woman to stand before the world in the brightness of day with a clear conscience, free spirit, and peaceful thoughts. It brings that true happiness I spoke about. But what is it really—how does is apply to the real world? Here are my thoughts…

God is our Father; we are his children. There are five different facets of our nature that make life full—physical, emotional, mental, social, and spiritual. There is little limit to our potential. And the Lord has said that we are that we might have joy—in all its fullness. This is true also with the life-giving, fulfilling experience of making love.

Many people today seem to be settling for just two or three of these facets. It's amazing to me when all five are available to everyone. It is possible to enjoy all five, and it is what I wish for you. Here's how it works:

Physical: The physical is easy to come by—sort of like hitting a pressure point with a hammer; anyone with a central nervous system intact will respond. It's a quick stimulus that can work in many instances between two people anywhere. It's biological.

Emotional: To enjoy an emotional involvement as well, you need to find someone who cares for you and for whom you care, at least for now. This can be achieved through casual relationships. It can produce an electric, if not lasting, encounter. But there is more than the mere physical and emotional experience that has furnished eloquence for the poet and fortunes for the film maker—there is also a mental need to be filled.

Mental: To achieve the fulfillment of your intellectual need, you will need to have an alliance that your mind can sanction as well as your heart. You will need to find someone you would choose in the cold calculations of daylight, someone your brain says is right, not just someone who stirs you physically and emotionally. I once heard a marriage counselor say to a group, "If you and your fiance can spend a whole day together without once making any physical contact—and have a good time—you are probably in love, not just infatuated."

Social: But being human and part of a society, you can expect even more from marriage. You can enjoy a relationship that is honored and accepted and smiled on by those you care about. You can kiss in the sunlight, have a genuine place, and walk with your head high. It's easy to flaunt society in the abstract, to say, "I don't care what people think." But we do; we all do. We care what people we care about think. And society, with its traditions and mores, has furnished us an honorable, workable setting for much that is good, including lovemaking. There isn't a setting to compare with marriage for generating deep, meaningful, long-lasting, and devoted partnerships that make the world in which they exist better for their being.

Spiritual: Finally, as a child of God, you have every right to expect your love to comprise not only the best of these capacities—the impact of the physical, the thrill of the emotional, the assurance of the mental, and the comfort of the social—but you can expect as well the overriding bliss of spiritual confirmation of the most blessed and sacred of any human involvement. To have your Father in Heaven's approval, to feel his pleasure, to know his blessing in that beautiful act, together with those human and potent feelings—this is to know what love and lovemaking are really all about.

—*David O. McKay*

Dating Standards

If you want to keep your standards high while dating, rehearse these dozen questions in your mind:

1. Would you want your own children to do the same things you do?

2. Boys, would you like some other boy to treat your sister like you treat girls?

3. Where should you "draw the line"? Where would you like the person you are to marry to have drawn the line during his or her high school dating days?

4. Does the one you are to marry have a right to know what kind of life you have led? Suppose you decide to live carelessly for a while, then shape up and marry a wonderful person. When the topic of marriage comes up, that person asks how morally clean you have kept yourself. If you haven't kept your standards high, how will you explain yourself? (Stop right now, and think about exactly how you would say it.)

5. Make up your mind before the situations arise which moral standards you will keep on a date; then, regardless of what temptations arise, your decision is made. You are in control.

6. Who has a better chance to build a marriage based on trust, loyalty, and happiness—those who keep themselves morally clean, or those who refuse to wait until marriage to display affection?

7. Review often your goals of marriage, home, and future—and decide what you must and must not do to attain them.

8. Can you spend your dollar a penny at a time? How much of your dollar is left when you have spent all but the last few pennies? Can you spend virtue in the same way?

9. Is it true that "no one will know"? You know. Your Father in Heaven knows. The other person involved knows. The devil knows.

10. No one goes to hell in one jump.

11. It is a long road back.

12. When a young man or a young lady starts to shop for a mate, where will you be found—all sparkling clean in the showroom, or a little grimy in the used car lot?

Christ

God so loved the world that he did not send a committee.
                                        —*Winston Churchill*

❧

An Empty Tomb

In 1956, a guide in the Holy Land led the late Elder Adam S. Bennion to the tomb which belonged to Joseph of Arimathaea in the days when Jesus lived, and in which Jesus was entombed after his crucifixion. As the guide stood there, he said, "There are many tombs of great men to be found all over the earth, but this one is different from any of the others: this one is empty!"

                                        —*Harold B. Lee*

❧

The Legend of the First Robin

A small brown bird looked down from a tree and saw a man standing beneath a heavy wooden cross. A crown of thorns encircled his head and cruelly pierced the skin. Moved by his suffering, the little bird followed along with the crowd surrounding the man, and suddenly swooped down and pulled one of the thorns from the man's forehead. The man lifted his eyes to the little bird and smiled a silent "thank you". As the bird flew on, a drop of blood fell from the thorn and stained his breast a bright crimson. Ever since that day, the humble robin wears a symbol of his mercy for that suffering man—our Lord and Savior.

❧

The Sheep and the Goats

The trumpet was blown and the heavenly arch-angel made an announcement, "The sheep will now be separated from the goats. The sheep will stand on the right hand of the throne and the goats on the left. Those on the right shall be welcomed into the Kingdom, those on the left shall be accursed and flung into everlasting fire."

"Is there any appeal from this sentence?"

A brief pause in heaven.

Then one forward stepped with lifted hands, in which nail-prints were visible.

"The goats," he said, "the goats are also mine."

❧

No Hands But Ours

Shortly after the culmination of the Second World War, a devastated city in England began its heart-breaking and wearying work of restoration. In the old city square had stood a large statue of Jesus Christ, with his hands outspread in an attitude of invitation. On the pedestal were carved the words, "Come unto me."

In the process of the restoration of the statue, with the aid of master artists and sculptors, the figure eventually was reassembled, except for the hands, of which no fragments could be discovered anywhere in the surrounding rubble. Someone made the suggestion that the artists would have to fashion new hands.

Later came a public protest, couched in the words, "No, leave him without hands!" So today, in the public square of that English city, the restored statue of Christ stands without hands, and on its base are carved the words, "Christ has no hands but ours!"

One Solitary Life

Here is a man who was born in an obscure village, the child of a peasant woman. He grew up in another obscure village. He worked in a carpenter shop until he was 30, and then for years he was an itinerant preacher.

He never wrote a book. He never held any office. He never went to college. He never put his foot inside a big city. He never traveled 200 miles from the place of his birth. He never did one of the things that accompany greatness. He had no credentials but himself. He had nothing to do within this world except the naked power of his divine manhood.

While still a young man, the tide of popular opinion turned against him. His friends ran away. One of them denied him; another betrayed him. He was turned over to his enemies. He went through the mockery of a trial. He was nailed on the cross between two thieves. His executors gambled for the one piece of property he had on earth while he was dying, and that was his coat. When he was dead, he was taken down and laid in a borrowed grave through the pity of a friend.

Nineteen wide centuries have come and gone, and today he is the center of the human race, and the leader of the column of progress. I am far within the mark when I say that all the armies of the world that ever marched, and that ever were built, and all the navies that were ever built, and all the parliaments that ever sat, and all the kings that ever reigned, put together, have not affected the life of man upon this earth as did that one solitary life.

—*Jim Bishop*

He Took My Whopping For Me

Years ago there was a certain school in the mountains of Virginia which no teacher could handle. The boys were so rough that the teachers resigned.

A young, grey-eyed teacher applied, and the old director scanned him, then said, "Young feller, do you know what you are asking? An awful beatin'. Every teacher we have had for years has had to take it."

He replied, "I'll risk it."

Finally he appeared for duty. One big fellow, Tom, whispered, "I won't need any help, I can lick him myself."

The teacher said, "Good morning, boys, we have come to conduct school." They yelled at the top of their voices. "Now, I want a good school, but confess I do not know how unless you help me. Suppose we have a few rules. You tell me and I will write them on the blackboard."

One fellow yelled, "No stealin'."

Another yelled, "On time." Finally ten rules appeared.

"Now," said the teacher, "a law is no good unless there is a penalty attached. What shall we do with the one who breaks them?"

"Beat him across the back ten times without his coat on."

"That is pretty severe, boys. Are you ready to stand by it?" Another yell, and the teacher said, "School come to order."

In a day or so, "Big Tom" found his lunch was stolen. Upon inquiry, the thief was located—a hungry fellow about ten. The next morning the teacher announced, "We have found a thief and he must be punished accordin' to your rule—ten stripes across the back! Jim, come up here."

The little fellow, trembling, came up slowly with a big coat fastened up to the neck and pleaded, "Teacher, you can lick me as hard as you like, but please don't make me take my coat off."

"Take that coat off, you helped make the rules!"

"Oh, teacher, don't make me." He began to unbutton, and what did the teacher behold—lo, the lad had no shirt on, but strings for braces over his bony little body.

"How can I whip this child?" thought he. "But I must do something if I keep this rule." Everything was quiet as death. "How come you came without a shirt, Jim?"

He replied, "My father died and Mother is very poor. I have only one shirt to my name, and she is washing that today and I wore my brother's coat to keep warm."

The teacher, with rod in hand, hesitated. Just then "Big Tom" jumped to his feet and said, "Teacher, if you don't mind, I will take Jim's licking for him."

"Very well, there is a certain law that one can become a substitute for another. Are you all agreed?" Off came Tom's coat, and after five hard strokes the rod broke. The teacher bowed his head in his hands, and thought, "How can I finish this awful task?"

Then he heard the entire school sobbing, and what did he see? Little Jim had reached up and caught Tom with both arms around the neck. "Tom, I was awful hungry. I'll love you till I die for taking my licking for me! Yes, I'll love you forever."

Friend, you have broken many rules and deserve eternal punishment—but Jesus Christ took your scourging for you, died in your stead, and now offers to clothe you in his garments of salvation. Will you not fall at his feet and tell him you will love and follow him forever? The wages of sin is death, but the gift of God is eternal life through Jesus Christ, our Lord.

—Rev. A.C. Dixon

Where Jesus Walked

George was lonely as he walked down the high school halls. Lonely even with eleven hundred students crowded into the brick corridors, which between classes seemed narrow.

George walked with a shuffle, and his shoulders seemed drooped, as if the weight of some burden unshared with others would crush him into the hardwood floors that glistened beneath his worn and scuffed shoes.

He didn't glance up when a group of giggling, laughing girls approached. George didn't need to. He knew it was one of the many in-groups of the high school.

"Pretty," he thought, "but repulsed by students like me."

It wasn't that George wasn't handsome; it just never really showed through his home cut hair, patched Levis, and frayed shirt. As the girls passed by, George heard one of them say, "You would think he would at least comb his hair."

Lost in thought, George wasn't ready for the jarring blow that slammed him into the lockers on the north side of the hall, and the foot that simultaneously knocked his legs from under him. He felt only the burning sensation that slowly climbed up his back as he sat on the floor looking up into the faces of three of the school's best football players. Standing between the other two was Jim—Jim, the only friend George had. Now he stood looking down at George and laughing. The bell rang. As the three football players left, one turned and said, "Tomorrow at lunch we'll settle this."

With an intense ache in his shoulder and a burning pain in his back, George started to get up. With more force than the agony which now wracked his body, the words "Tomorrow at lunch we'll settle this" hammered in his mind.

That night the soup and half dried bread went almost untouched in spite of the emptiness in his stomach. "Tomorrow, tomorrow," was all George could think of as the crisp fall air slid down the mountain and filtered into their antiquated house to chill George as he lay on his old frame bed with only a light blanket for a covering. "Tomorrow."

Clouds hung gray in the sky that morning as George walked down the lane to catch the school bus. Sitting at the back of the bus were Jim and the boy who had said, "Tomorrow at lunch we'll settle this."

It was hard for George to think of school. The lunch bell rang and he left shop. George was careful to keep his eyes open as he walked toward the library, instead of toward the cafeteria.

The firm grip of a hand settled on his shoulder and spun him around. There before him stood his persecutors.

"Do you think you can say that about me?" the voice pierced his ears.

"Say what?" he thought.

"Jim said you…"

How much time had passed George didn't know. He remembered seeing a large fist speeding through the air, hearing the thud and then voices.

The taste of blood was salty in his mouth, and a warm trickle pulsed from his swollen lips. One eye wouldn't open and his side jumped with pain every time he moved.

Some students stared; others whispered in hushed tones; someone sneered, "They finally got him."

No one tried to help. After what seemed an endless passing of time, the principal came.

The principal moved him to the nurse's office, and with the care and concern of one who thought he might have prevented this incident, he attended to George's needs.

All afternoon George laid on the cot in the nurse's office. That night after school when George got on the bus, Jim turned his head, not wanting to look at George.

Only five students were in the bus as it rounded the Hanksville corner. Coming around the corner on the wrong side of the road was a large cattle truck.

There was a metal-mashing crash, screams, a wild careening as the bus shot out over the guard rail and down into the ravine.

Only the sliding of some small rocks through the brush could be heard as the bus lay on its side, like some huge yellow beast mortally wounded. The bus driver and three students including Jim climbed up and out through the door.

Gas fumes filled the air and spread, seeping through the stricken bus. Fire broke out. Before long, the whole bus would blow up.

George dragged himself into an upright position. His whole body hurt, and with every stab of pain he thought of the football players and Jim.

As he lifted himself to try to climb through a window, his foot struck something. Leaning down, he saw the football player, blood scarlet on his brow. The heat of the fire was intense and the hot air snatched George's breath away.

Crying with pain, George lifted his tormentor's arms. Exerting all his strength, he pushed him up through the window. Someone said, "I've got him." There was another explosion. George slipped backward, then it hit. The yellow of the bus blended with the yellow ball of fire that burst against the afternoon sky.

Great sobs burst in Jim's chest as he ran through the oak brush.

—*John P. Sanders*

A Second Coming

If there should be a Second Coming, would there not soon be a second crucifixion? And this time, not by the Romans or the Jews, but by those who proudly call themselves Christians?

I wonder how we today would regard and treat this man with his strange and frightening and impractical doctrines of human behavior and relationships.

Would we believe and follow, any more than the masses of people in his day believed and followed?

Would not the militarists among us assail him as a cowardly pacifist because he urges us to resist evil?

Would not the nationalists among us attack him as a dangerous internationalist because he tells us we are all of one flesh?

Would not the wealthy among us castigate him as a trouble-making radical because he bars the rich from entering the kingdom of heaven?

Would not the liberals among us dismiss him as a dreaming vagabond because he advises us to take no thought for the morrow, to lay up no treasures on earth?

Would not the ecclesiastics among us denounce him as a ranting heretic because he cuts through the core of ritual and commands us only to love God and our neighbors?

Would not the sentimentalists among us deride him as a cynic because he warns us that the way to salvation is narrow and difficult?

Would not the Puritans among us despise and reject him because he eats and drinks with publicans and sinners, preferring the company of wine-bibbers and harlots to that of respectable church members?

Would not the sensual among us scorn him because he fasts for forty days in the desert, neglecting the needs of the body?

Would not the proud and important among us laugh at him when he instructs the twelve disciples that he who would be first should be the one to take the role of the least and serve all?

Would not the worldly-wise and educated among us be aghast to hear that we cannot be saved except we become as children, and that a little child shall lead us?

Would not each of us in his own way find some part of this man's saying and doing to be so threatening to our ways of life, so much at odds with our rooted beliefs, that we could not tolerate him for long?

I wonder. I wonder if we are any more prepared for the Second Coming than we would have been for the first.

—*Sydney J. Harris*

The Parallel Lives of Jesus and Joseph

His father, Joseph, was a poor man who made his living through the honest toil of his callused hands. His birth brought no special notice from the religious leaders of the day. Why should it? They had not anticipated such a prophet would be born at this time.

He grew up in obscurity, receiving only the common education given the back country people of that day. But he learned about life. He walked in the fields and saw the sparrow and the hawk, the wheat and the tares, the flowers blooming in the meadow and the barren earth. And he wondered about God and about man and his responsibility to both.

He learned line upon line and precept upon precept. In his early youth, he confounded the ministers of his day, telling them things which they thought impossible for a mere child to know. Then he was left alone to ponder the wonders he had learned.

The heavens were opened unto him and he received a divine commission which prompted him to restore to the earth the gospel which was as old as the earth itself.

He gathered about him a few disciples; not the learned and scholarly men, but simple folk like himself. He commissioned his disciples with the same authority he had and told them to go forth and teach others. He ordained them with the same priesthood he held that they might bind on earth and in heaven.

He devoted himself entirely to his ministry. The ordinary pursuits of men held no attraction to him for he had a mission to perform. He never acquired wealth, he scarcely had a place he could call home.

People loved him. All kinds of people loved him: the saint, the sinner, the strong, the weak.

He loved people. It was said of him that he could be no prophet for he was too much of a social being. He liked company and would invite the poor ones from the street to come and dine with him.

He was hated and persecuted. Some of his own disciples turned away and he was betrayed into the hands of enemies. When he was in his thirties he sealed his mission with his blood rather than deny that he was God's anointed.

Even before the mobs formed, he had said that he would be killed.

On a day in late December, those who believed his words remember the occasion of his birth and thank God for his life and mission.

He was Jesus Christ.

The same also might be said about his Prophet Joseph Smith.

Here, however, the parallelism ends, for Jesus was divine, the Son of God; Joseph was but a man, chosen of God.

—*Kenneth J. Brown*

Mary

The girl wiped a tear from her eye and wondered for perhaps the hundredth time that day what his reaction would be. She had known and kept her secret for two weeks now, and she could no longer keep it from him. He told her he would be coming to see her today, anytime now; she must compose herself.

The weather was certainly no help. It had been hot, very hot, even for April. The spring rains were few and far between; then, when it did rain, it became humid: clothes stuck to your body and homes were too stifling to be cooped up in.

Today was really no different except that she had to tell him. She told her mother and father three days before. Her remembrance of those first few anxious moments of the revelation caused her to tremble. They had been very understanding, but then, her parents were who she could always rely upon and trust for support and backing.

It had been hot that day, too, but last night it rained and now the atmosphere was a thick, heavy mantle. It certainly didn't help ease the apprehension that was gripping her. The sun was blasting in the cloudless sky with its flames seeming to scorch the plants and dry, brown earth as she watched out the door for her beloved.

The girl's mind raced over what she had to say and how she should say it. She was in a quandary over whether to blurt it out or to lead up to it gradually. Should she be hesitant and shy about it, or bold and straight forward?

I'll wait and see him then, depending on his mood, I'll tell him, she thought. Or perhaps...there he is, at the corner. She hurried back into the sparsely furnished room and sat down so she wouldn't appear to be too anxious to meet him.

The young man who rounded the corner on his way to see his girl was light-hearted. The morning had been successful. He received two work orders for his particular skill of carpentry and had feelers out for three more. Now he was to see his girl. They would be married soon and, now that he was starting to do well financially, he was looking forward with an eager heart to marriage to this young woman who had captured his heart.

She is lovely, he thought. What more could a man want than a beautiful, considerate, understanding wife and financial security? His heart quickened as he neared her door, and he thought briefly of the greeting kiss he would receive.

There she was seated, looking like a beautiful statue carved in pure white marble. She rose to greet him with arms opened wide to embrace him. Their greetings tumbled forth words of affection and endearment between two young people whose love and forthcoming marriage seemed made in heaven.

Suddenly, without realizing what she was doing, the girl found herself saying, "I have something to tell you, something vitally important to both of us."

"What is it, my love?" he asked. "Sit down, here, beside me,"

They sat, the young woman and the young man, side by side, quietly for a long minute in silence. Without raising her eyes from the floor, the girl, her heart pounding an irregular rhythm, slowly said, "I'm going to become a mother."

"Of course you are, many times. We're going to have a large family."

"No, no. You don't understand," she said. He won't understand what I must say, she thought; he will be angry. After a pause to rephrase her statement she continued. "No, I'm going to have a child very soon. I'm pregnant now."

The silence that settled over the room was alive with tension and, as yet, unanswered questions. The young man stared unflinching into the brilliance that poured through the opened door. He suddenly felt the oppressive heat that poured through surrounding him. Funny, how he hadn't noticed it before. The sweat was running down his forehead in a trickle that caused him to wrinkle the folds of flesh over his eyes and rub the irritating perspiration out of his eyes. His mind raced ahead to future actions to be taken. Fleetingly, he asked himself if he should walk through the door never to return, or perhaps he should tenderly put his arm around her and reassure her that everything was all right. The law said that he could publicly ridicule and shame her.

"What happened? How could you let this happen to you?"

She heard and felt the hurt in his voice. What could she say that would sooth this young, dynamic man she loved so much? Trying to put herself in his place, she could easily imagine the shock and indignation of learning of the pregnancy of his fiancée—especially knowing that the child was not his own. Blinking back the tears that threatened to burst forth, the girl answered, "It was special, a dear and holy experience. It didn't just happen. It was a planned, wonderful happening. Can you believe that?"

The young man's trust in this special young woman had never before been challenged; he had never had cause to distrust her or have angry words with her. Now this—probably the most shameful thing that could happen—had occurred. He experienced a sudden feeling of shame and ire.

He involuntarily shuddered and rose to his feet. Her eyes didn't leave his figure as he strode about the room, first to the window, then to the door. Her heart seemed to stop, then race ahead as she saw his tall, lean figure pause in the open doorway and look upwards into the cloudless, still sky. His mind was a jumble of ideas and thoughts, crowding each other, each calling to be examined in depth. He was aware that his body was tense. He realized how tired he had become—what a change from the happiness and light-heartedness he had experienced just a few moments before.

A rueful smile crept across his face and he bowed his head, gazing at an insect making his painful way through the dust outside the door. What a simple life animals lead, he thought. They mate only to create and don't know the agony caused by love! This girl had seemingly betrayed him; she had led him to believe one thing, when it was another.

With a deep sigh, he relaxed. The tension ebbed out of his body as he turned to gaze into the shadows of the room. He blinked his eyes to see in the relative darkness. He opened his mouth to speak, but nothing came out; somehow he couldn't bring himself to say what had been on his lips. He felt he must chastise her. But, for some strange reason, he could not stir himself to anger against her. She must have some explanation, a plausible, explainable reason. His heart went out to her as a feeling of calm descended over him.

She was still sitting quietly composed, in the center of the room. As he looked at her figure, so diminutive, he knew for a certainty the course he must follow. Slowly he crossed the few feet separating them and took her hands in his. When she rose at his bidding, he gently put his arm around this strange, exciting young woman and said, "I think I can understand your feelings. It's strange to me and a little frightening, but, I can understand."

The girl's eyes misted and smiled as she nodded to herself and said, "Yes, he said you would understand. I love you."

Suddenly, his heart soaring, he took her in his arms and, smiling down at her up-turned face, he asked, "What shall we call him?"

"Jesus. Jesus. A name fit for the Gods."

❧

To Know Christ

A man passed away and was resurrected and waiting in a room to be interviewed. Another man was ahead of him. The door opened, the first man entered, the door closed. The man on the outside could hear the conversation on the other side of the door. The interviewer began, "Tell me what you know about Jesus Christ."

"He was born of a virgin in Bethlehem. He lived thirty three years, spending the last three as a minister, organizing his church, choosing his Apostles to direct it, giving the gospel to direct our lives."

The interviewer stopped him and said, "Yes, yes, that's all true, but tell me what you know about Christ."

"He was tortured and crucified that we might have eternal life. Three days later he was resurrected that we might return to Heavenly Father."

"Yes, yes, that is true, but tell me what you know about Christ."

The man, a little perplexed, again began, "Well, he restored the gospel in its fullness to the earth through Joseph Smith, reorganized his church, gave us temples wherein we might do work to save our dead. He gave us family prayer and family home evening where we might unite with our families. He gave us the priesthood to heal the sick, and personal ordinances for our salvation and exaltation."

The interviewer again stopped him and said, "All of what you have said to me is true."

The man was then invited to leave the room.

After he left, the door opened and the second man entered. As he approached the interviewer, he fell upon his knees and cried, "My Lord, My God."

⌘

The Gruesome Details of the Crucifixion

The Romans, to whom crucifixion was an exact science, always placed their nails with meticulous accuracy to cause the maximum possible pain. At the crease of the wrist there is a strong muscle over substantial bone structure, and between the bones an open space of about three-eighths of an inch in diameter. The Roman nail passed through here, easily supporting the weight of the body, piercing the great median nerve in the process, and causing the victim terrible agony. Death was caused from tetanic cramp.

Having been scourged and crowned with thorns, he was led to Calvary. There he was stripped, the clothes sticking to the skin with the dried blood of the flogging and taking most of the skin with them. The upright of the cross was already in position. Christ was thrown to the ground and held over the cross piece. The nails were then carefully positioned and driven through with a hard blow of the hammer.

Have you ever had the dentist touch a nerve with his drill? That is only a very small nerve. The wave of pain that followed the piercing of the great median nerve in the wrist is known only to someone who has had an arm or leg cut off. It caused the muscles of the arm, neck, head, and chest to contract and cramp in atrocious agony.

Then the cross piece was lifted and the victim dragged backwards along the ground to where the upright was standing. He was then lifted and the cross piece dropped into the position prepared for it and fixed in place. To prevent the uncontrolled threshing of the legs from tearing the wrists free, a single nail was driven through both feet, pinning them to the cross. The only movement possible was a ceaseless sinuous writhing of the entire body. To ease the terrible pain and to stall off suffocation, the victim could attain a few minutes respite by the dreadful method of straining upwards, literally standing on the nail in his feet. This posture could only be maintained for a short time; he would then slump, exhausted, hanging by the wrists, and the frightful cycle of torture would begin again.

After three hours of ceaseless torment, weakened by the flogging and the strain of the agony in the Garden, Jesus was no longer able to strain upwards and away from the killing agony in his arms and chest. As graphically told in the gospel narrative, death, caused by constriction of the chest muscles stopping the breathing and possibly the heart action as well, finally intervened to end the agony which paid in full for the sins of the world.

—Australian Monthly, 12/49

❧

The Deserter

You wonder at me, a Roman soldier, so far from Jerusalem alone? My friend, you wonder no more than I, myself. The happenings of the past few days have been enough to water the courage of any man. There's the dust of the road upon you as you came down from the hills. You were not in Jerusalem, so you don't know, of course, but the world has been turned upside down.

No, I haven't lost my senses, though it would be no great surprise if I had. I was there, I saw it with my eyes. I saw the darkness settle like the coming of night, though the sun rose high in the heavens. I heard the thunder and felt the earth quake beneath my feet.

I was in the company that took Jesus in. You may have heard of him. A queer fellow who called himself the King of the Jews. Oh, we had great sport. I plaited a crown of thorns on his head and another threw a robe of scarlet about his shoulders. When the mob began to clamor for him, we brought him out, clad in his kingly garments.

I was astounded by the crowd. There's no explaining the queer people or their queer God—no offense to you, of course. This man seemed harmless enough to me. He was silent, even when we stripped him and beat him. But the cry went up, "Crucify him! Crucify him!" I shall always hear that ringing in my ears.

A soldier is used to suffering and death. I've warmed my blade on human blood often enough. But I soon lost my stomach for this business.

There were guards, but there was no need of them as we marched him up the mount of Golgotha. He made no move to escape. It was almost as if he had been born for that very moment.

The cross was so heavy that he stumbled under the load of it. I would have liked to have carried it myself, but I did not. Instead, I helped to stretch out his hands and drive nails through his palms.

And the darkness came. It was different from any darkness I have ever seen, or ever expect to see again. One moment the sun was shining, and the next it was so dark that I could scarcely make out the dying figure on the cross. My stomach crawled within me.

There was a small group of men and women standing off to one side, looking at him with longing eyes as they wept quietly. They must have been relatives—if he had any— and a few followers. But that blood-thirsty mob continued to taunt and rail at him.

"Save yourself," they shouted, "Come down from there!" I'd scarcely have been surprised had he stepped down from that cross and killed them all with his bare hands. His hands! I can still feel the cold sweat upon them—the tendons tightening in his wrists as the spikes tore through his flesh.

Forgive me, friend, if I seem to ramble now and then. My mind is jumbled and twisted until I scarcely know what I'm saying. I've seen brave men die before. I've heard their bitter cursing, their screams of terror. But never have I seen another like this. His face was twisted with pain, and yet he did not so much as lift his voice, excepting near the end. Then he raised his head with an almost super-human effort and loudly called, "Father, forgive them, for they know not what they do."

That stopped them; that struck them dumb. For his voice carried a tone of authority. They stood there, looking silently at one another, wondering, and then the shout went up again.

Don't ask me what happened after that. I only know that I was standing guard when the earthquake came. I tell you sir, the ground shook beneath my feet. There was thunder and the rocks on Golgotha were torn apart. Cracks opened in the ground and buildings trembled on their foundations.

Frightened? I was so frightened at that moment that I realized I had never known fear before. So frightened that I could not reason. I was suddenly overwhelmed with a mad desire to flee. I forgot all training, all loyalty. I wanted only to get as far from that cursed spot as possible.

Don't ask me how I came here, or how long since these things have taken place. It may have been yesterday—the day before—a week ago. I do not know. How can one measure the length of hours when one's very soul is burning?

I know for a truth that this Jesus was the Son of the living God!

You smile, sir, there's nothing in this story about which to smile. There can be no joy in the crucifixion of God himself.

Your hands, kind sir…

Your hands!

They're pierced!

Oh, merciful God…

—*Bernard Palmer*

Death

Death is one of those inexplicable items of life that robs, and in the robbing, gives something in return.

❧

We sometimes congratulate ourselves at the moment of waking from a troubled dream: it may be so the moment after death.

—*Nathaniel Hawthorne*

❧

A Scientist on Eternal Life

In our modern world, many people seem to feel that science has somehow made religion untimely or old-fashioned. But I think science has a real surprise for the skeptics.

Science, for instance, tells us that nothing in nature, not even the tiniest particle, can disappear without a trace.

Think about that for a moment. Once you do, your thoughts about life will never be the same.

Science has found that nothing can disappear without a trace. Nature does not know extinction. All it knows is transformation!

Now, if God applies this fundamental principle to the most minute and insignificant parts of his universe, doesn't it make sense to assume that he applies it also to the masterpiece of his creation—the human soul?

I think it does.

Everything science has taught me—and continues to teach me—strengthens my belief in the continuity of our spiritual existence after death. Nothing disappears without a trace.

—*Dr. Wernher Von Braun*

❧

An Important Mission for Father

And now let me tell you what she did—the finest lesson I have ever heard being taught to children. She planned what will come to be known in her family as a great holy hour. She took the children upstairs, all in a room together. This was on Saturday, seven days after the father had been taken to the hospital. This was the day that, according to their family plans, the father and mother always took the children somewhere for recreational and educational purposes and to solidify their family life.

There, this well-poised woman got a blackboard and placed the names of all the children on the board. She then conducted a class, as had often been done in their home on family nights. She told them that their Father in heaven had a very important mission for someone to perform—that it was of unusual importance, and that he had been looking all over the world for someone to choose for such a mission. Whom would they suggest he call?

One of the youngest children immediately said, "Daddy", and, in that sacred hour, all the others applauded by clapping their hands. In their childish feeling and unsophisticated faith, they were willing that their father be spared for any mission the Lord wanted.

She then told them that their opinion of their father had been shared by their Heavenly Father. In this way, they were told of their father's death.

Death to them was made a glorious and sacred event. It was pictured as a glorious end. Beverly, who right to the last thought that her husband would be healed, had triumphed over her own feelings and resigned herself in peace and tranquility to the will of Heavenly Father. In this glorious way, death to the children was made a living symbol of further opportunity and service for their father, and the beginning of a new and glorious venture for them.

—Told at the funeral service of Beverly Cutler's husband

❧

The House He Lives In

One day when John Quincy Adams was 80 years of age, a friend met him on the streets of Boston.

"How is John Quincy Adams?" this friend asked gaily.

The old man's eyes began to twinkle, and then he spoke slowly, "John Quincy Adams himself is very well, thank you. But the house he lives in is sadly dilapidated. It is tottering on its foundations. The walls are badly shattered, and the roof is worn. The building trembles with every wind, and I think John Quincy Adams will have to move out before very long. But he himself is very well."

And with a wave of his hand the old man walked on.

—James G. Gilkey

Beyond the Horizon

I am standing upon the seashore. A ship at my side spreads her white sails to the morning breeze and starts for the blue ocean. She is an object of beauty and strength, and I stand and watch her until at length she hangs like a speck of white cloud where the sea and sky come down to mingle with each other. Then someone at my side says, "There, she's gone."

Gone where? Gone from my sight, that is all. She is just as large in mast and hull and spar as she was when she left my side, and just as able to bear her load of living weight to the place of destination. Her diminished size is in me, not in her; and just at that moment when someone at my side said, "There, she's gone," there are other eyes watching her coming, and other voices to take the glad shout, "There, she's coming!" And such is dying.

—Story Teller's Scrapbook

My Toddler Taught Me About Death

I had always heard that one could learn many things from children but, not until we had a very precious experience with one of our own, did I realize how true this could be.

This occasion took place when our first child, Alan, was just past two. Alan had learned to talk very early so, by this time, he spoke very clearly and could express himself with a sizeable vocabulary for his age.

Alan's great-aunt, Lida, had just passed away, and I had been worrying about how I was going to tell him about her death.

Mustering all my courage, for I was new at that sort of thing then, I sat Alan on the kitchen stool and drew up a chair, "Alan, honey," I said, "Aunt Lida has gone back to Heavenly Father."

But, before I could say anything more, he asked, "Who took her?"

I stumbled around for an answer, and then I said, "It must have been someone she knew."

Immediately his little face lit up as if he recognized a familiar situation. He said with a happy smile, "Oh, I know what it's like! Grandpa Clark brought me when I came to you. He'll probably take me back when I die."

Alan then proceeded to describe his Grandfather Clark, my father, who had been dead nearly 12 years. He had never even seen a picture of him. He told me how much he loved his grandfather and how good he had been to him. He indicated that my father had helped to teach him and prepare him to come here. He also spoke of Heavenly Father as a definite memory.

Needless to say, this little conversation with Alan that I had been dreading turned out to be one of the sweetest experiences of my life. It left me limp with humility and joy. I no longer felt sorry that my father could not see my children. As each little soul has come along, I have felt that my father probably was better acquainted with the newcomer than was I. This has been a great comfort to me.

Immediately after this occasion, Alan's father talked to him; and Alan repeated the same answers to him. He later told the experience to his Grandmother Clark. For several months, he talked about these things as a happy, natural memory of real experiences. Then, suddenly, the memory was erased, and he did not know what we were talking about when we discussed it.

But, he had taught us some great truths, for which we are most thankful, and he had verified the inspiration in Wordsworth's lines:

> *Our birth is but a sleep and a forgetting;*
> *The Soul that rises with us, our life's Star,*
> *Hath had elsewhere its setting,*
> *And cometh from afar:*
> *Not in entire forgetfulness,*
> *And not in utter nakedness,*
> *But trailing clouds of glory do we come*
> *From God, who is our home:*
> *Heaven lies about us in our infancy!*

—Betty Clark Ruff

Determination

If it is to be, it is up to me.

—E. Wilford Edmar

What is now proved, was once only imagined.

Keep your face to the sunshine and all shadows fall behind.

—Helen Keller

If you believe you can, or if you believe you can't, you're right.

Remember: the man on top of the mountain didn't just fall there.

The determined man finds a way, the other finds an excuse or alibi.

Remember: Everyone who got where he is had to begin from where he was.

—Jim Carlson

Convince a man of what he wants, and he will move heaven and earth to get it.

Anyone who says something is impossible, is always being interrupted by someone doing it.

Don't be afraid to take a big step if one is indicated; you can't cross a chasm in two small jumps.

Men of Determination

What happens to men who refuse to be stopped once they decide where they are going?

Cripple him, and you have Sir Walter Scott.

Put him in prison, and you have John Bunyan.

Bury him in the snow at Valley Forge, and you have George Washington.

Have him born in poverty, and you have Abraham Lincoln.

Give him a speech impediment, lock him in jail, and put him out of office almost in disgrace, and you have Winston Churchill.

Persecute him from town to town, state to state, and finally murder him, and you have Joseph Smith.

❧

Determined to Succeed

From time to time, all of us are called on to listen to tales of woe in which men recount the ill fortune of their ventures. Sometimes these ventures have deserved failure, because they were badly conceived or carelessly managed. Often, however, the result is a disheartening return for men who planned well and worked diligently. To renew the courage of these men, and his own when needed, one executive keeps at hand the biography of a "failure":

Failed at business	'31
Defeated for legislature	'32
Again failed in business	'33
Elected to legislature	'34
Defeated for Speaker	'38
Defeated for Elector	'40
Defeated for Congress	'42
Defeated for Congress	'46
Elected to Congress	'48
Defeated for Senate	'55
Defeated for Vice-President	'56
Defeated for Senate	'58

Here, indeed, is a record that might cause any man to lose faith in himself and hope for his ideals. Fortunately, the man who compiled it lost neither faith nor hope. He tried again. He was Abraham Lincoln, elected in 1860 to serve as President of the United States.

The Determination of Lincoln

Are you having difficulty? Have you lost hope? Take courage from a man who overcame all these feelings, and succeeded.

Death took the life of his mother when he was just nine years of age.

When Abraham Lincoln was but a young man, he ran for the legislature in Illinois, but was badly defeated.

He entered business with a partner who proved to be worthless. After the business failed, he spent seventeen years of his life working to pay the debts that his dishonest partner had left him.

He became engaged to Ann Rutledge, a beautiful girl from New Salem, his first and only true love—and she died. He proposed to Mary Owens a year or two later, and was rejected. After a courtship and one broken engagement with another, he finally married Mary Todd, but was never completely happy in his marriage.

Of Lincoln's four children, all but one died when they were young.

He ran for Congress and was badly defeated.

He tried to get an appointment to the United States Land Office, but was unsuccessful.

He was badly defeated when he became a candidate for the United States Senate. In 1858, he was defeated by Stephen A. Douglas. His associate, Stanton—as well as many others, whom he regarded as friends—publicly ridiculed him.

Through all these losses and disappointments, Abraham Lincoln remained cheerful and carried on with a quiet determination.

He later became the President of the United States, and is today respected among all peoples.

❧

Determined To Do Right

If I were to try to read, much less answer, all the attacks made on me, this shop might as well be closed for any other business. I do the very best I know how—the very best I can; and I mean to keep doing so until the end. If the end brings me out all right, what is said against me won't amount to anything. If the end brings me out wrong, ten angels swearing I was right would make no difference.

—Abraham Lincoln

The Last Lesson

Perhaps the most valuable result of all education is the ability to make yourself do the thing you have to do, when it ought to be done, whether you like it or not; it is the first lesson that ought to be learned, and however early a man's training begins, it is probably the last lesson that he learns thoroughly.

❦

It Must

Nothing ever built arose to touch the skies unless

some man dreamed that it should,

some man believed that it could, and

some man willed that it must.

—*Charles F. Kettering*

❦

Determined To Do More

I will do more than belong—I will participate.

I will do more than care—I will help.

I will do more than believe—I will practice.

I will more than be fair—I will be kind.

I will do more than forgive—I will forget.

I will do more than dream—I will work.

I will do more than teach—I will inspire.

I will do more than earn—I will enrich.

I will do more than give—I will serve.

I will do more than live—I will grow.

I will do more than be friendly—I will be a friend.

I will do more than be a citizen—I will be a patriot.

High Hopes

There was once a man who had an idea that India rubber could be made useful. People laughed at him, but for eleven years he struggled with hardships to make his dream come true. He pawned his clothing and the family jewels to buy food for his children. His neighbors called him insane. But he still insisted that India rubber could be put to practical use. The man was Charles Goodyear, founder of the Goodyear Tire and Rubber Company. Dreams do come true—if you make them!

—Kathryn C. Mertz

Determined To Be the Best

Good is the enemy of best. The thing that most do not realize is that it is not much harder to achieve the second than the first. Rather it is a question of which you expect of yourself, and of your ability to see adversity not as a roadblock but as a challenge of great interest.

Desire is the whole point. And what your mind sees when it looks through the sights of your goals is where your effort will strike.

—Paul H. Dunn

Determined to Focus

In one of the laboratories in Washington, there is a great sun glass that measures three feet across. It is like the "burning glasses" we used to treasure when we were boys, only much larger.

This great glass gathers the rays of the sun that strike its flat surface and focuses them in a single point in space a few feet below. That single spot is hotter than a blow torch. It will melt through a steel plate as easily as a red-hot needle burns through paper.

This terrific heat—it cannot be measured, for it melts all instruments—is just three feet of ordinary sunshine concentrated on a single point. Scattered, these rays are hardly felt, perhaps just pleasantly warm; concentrated, they melt adamant.

The same principle applies to human endeavor. Scattered, a man's energies do not amount to much. Once they are focused on the task at hand, seemingly tremendous difficulties melt like snow on a hot stone.

Get the habit of concentrating when you start to do a thing: throw on all the steam you have and focus every energy on the task at hand. Remember that three feet of sunshine concentrated will burn through anything.

Determined to Fight Discouragement

A man came walking down life's street. Satan said to his little devil with a bitter face, "Go get him for me."

Quickly the imp crossed the street, silently and lightly hopped to the man's shoulder, and whispered in his ear, "You are discouraged."

"No," said the man, "I am not discouraged."

"You are discouraged."

This time, the man replied, "I do not think I am."

More loudly and decidedly the little imp said again, "I tell you, you are discouraged."

The man dropped his head and replied, "Well, I suppose I am."

At that, the imp hopped back to Satan and reported, "I got him. He's discouraged!"

Another man came walking down life's street. Again Satan said to his imp, "Get him for me."

The proud little demon of discouragement repeated his tactics.

The first time he told the man he was discouraged, the man replied emphatically, "No, I am not!"

The second time, the man replied, "I tell you, I am not discouraged!"

The third time, he said, "I am not discouraged. You lie."

The man walked down the street, his head held high, going toward the light.

The imp of discouragement returned to his master crestfallen. "I couldn't get him. Three times I told him he was discouraged. The third time he called me a liar, and that discouraged me!"

❧

Determined to Serve

The first great American B-29 airplane strike, against the enemy of World War II, flown from a land base, was led by an airplane named "City of Los Angeles".

Aboard this aircraft were twelve men—eleven regular crewmen and a colonel, flying as commanding officer. They were to reach a place appointed for meeting, sixty to seventy-five miles off the enemy's mainland, then assume regular fighting formation and fly in on the target—a large number of gasoline tanks.

They reached the appointed place on time, and Colonel Sprouse ordered the dropping of the phosphorous bomb, which was supposed to let off its yellow fumes when it hit the ground as a marker for the dropping of regular bombs.

Sergeant "Red" Irwin skidded this dangerous bomb down the airplane chute as ordered. The act was loaded with death. The flap at the end of the bomb chute had somehow gotten stuck. When the bomb struck it, it exploded ahead of time and burst back into the interior of the airplane, right into the face and chest of Sergeant Irwin.

Dropping to the floor, it began to swiftly burn its way through the thin metal flooring separating it from the incendiary bomb stored in the bomb bay below. In moments, the "City of Los Angeles" and its crew would be blown to bits far out over the ocean in enemy territory.

Sergeant Irwin, terribly wounded, got to his knees, picked up the bomb in his bare hands, cradled it in his arms, and staggered up the passageway. Crashing into the navigator's table, he had to stop and unlatch it with fingers that left burn marks on the hardwood. By now, the airplane was filled with eye-stinging smoke, blinding the pilot, and was wallowing less than three hundred feet above the water.

Irwin staggered into the pilot's compartment, shouting, "Window! Window!" He could not see that it was already open, and his fumbling fingers left burn marks on the metal. He threw the bomb out of the window and collapsed to the deck.

Colonel Sprouse ordered the "City of Los Angeles" back to base in the slim hope that Irwin's life might be saved. Two hours later, they reached Iwo Jima, a small island in the Pacific. Irwin's flesh was still smoking with embedded phosphorous when he was removed from the plane by comrades who had to hide their faces from his awful wounds.

Sergeant Irwin lived to receive the Medal of Honor, his nation's highest honor for extreme bravery, and he survived nearly fifty plastic surgeries that helped restore him to a somewhat normal life. He lived to marry and to become a father.

With him, there lived eleven other men, who, but for his almost unbelievable courage, would be dead. Eleven men, spared to their lives, work, and families through the decision and courageous act of one man!

⁓

The $5 Lawn

No one in our small Utah town knew where the Countess had come from; her careful precise English indicated that she was not a native American. From the size of her house and staff, we knew that she must be wealthy, but she never entertained, and she made it clear that when she was at home she was completely inaccessible. Only when she stepped outdoors did she become at all a public figure, and then chiefly to the small fry of the town, who lived in awe of her.

The Countess always carried a cane, not only for support, but as a means of chastising any youngster she thought needed disciplining. And at one time or another, most of the youngsters in our neighborhood seemed to display that need. By running fast and staying alert, I had managed to keep out of her reach. But one day, when I was about thirteen, as I was short-cutting through her hedge, she got close enough to rap my head with the stick.

"Young man, I want to talk to you," she said. I was expecting a lecture on the evils of trespassing, but as she looked at me, half smiling, she seemed to change her mind.

"Don't you live in that green house with the yellow trees in the next block?"

"Yes, Ma'am."

"Do you take care of your lawn? Water it? Clip it? Mow it?

"Yes, Ma'am."

"Good, I've lost my gardener. Be at my house Thursday morning at seven, and don't tell me you have something else to do; I've seen you slouching on Thursdays."

When the Countess gave an order, it was carried out. I didn't dare not come.

I went over the whole lawn three times with a mower before she was satisfied, and then she had me down on all fours looking for weeds until my knees were as green as the grass. She finally called me up to the porch.

"Well, young man, how much do you want for your day's work?"

"I don't know—50 cents maybe."

"Is that what you figure you're worth?"

"Yes'm. About that."

"Very well, here's the 50 cents you say you're worth, and here's the $1.50 that I earned for you by pushing you. Now, I'm going to tell you something about how you and I are going to work together. There are as many ways to mow a lawn as there are people, and they may be worth anywhere from a penny to $5. Let's say that a $3 job would be just about what you have done today, except that you would do it all by yourself. A $4 job would be so perfect that you'd have to be something of a fool to spend that much time on a lawn. A $5 lawn is—well, it's impossible, so we'll forget about that. Now then, each week I'm going to pay you according to your own evaluation of your work."

I left with my $2, richer than I remembered being in my whole life, and determined that I would get $4 out of her the next time. But I failed to reach even the $3 mark. My will began to falter the second time around her yard.

"Two dollars again, eh? That kind of job puts you right on the edge of being dismissed, young man."

"Yes'm, but I'll do better next week."

And somehow I did. The last time around the lawn I was exhausted, but I found I could spur myself on. In the exhilaration of that new feeling, I had no hesitation in asking the Countess for $3.

Each Thursday for the next few weeks, I became more acquainted with her lawn, places where the ground was a little high or a little low, places where it needed to be clipped short or left long on the edges to make a more satisfying curve along the garden. Then I became more aware of just what a $4 lawn would consist of. And each week I would resolve to do just that kind of job. But, by the time I had my $3-$3.50 mark, I was too tired to remember even having had the ambition to go beyond that point.

"You look like a good, consistent $3.50 man," she would say as she handed me the money.

"I guess so," I would say, too happy at the sight of the money to remember that I had shot for something higher.

"Well, don't feel too bad," she would comfort me. "After all, there are only a handful of people in the world who could do a $4 job."

And her words were a comfort to me at first, but then, without my noticing too much what was happening, her comfort became an irritant that made me resolve to do that $4 job, even if it killed me. In the fever of my resolve, I could see myself expiring on her lawn, with the Countess leaning over me, handing me the $4 with a tear in her eye, begging my forgiveness for having ever thought I couldn't do it.

It was in the middle of such a fever, on Thursday night when I was trying to forget the day's defeat and get some sleep, that the truth really hit me—so hard that I sat upright, half choking in my excitement. It was the $5 job I had to do, not the $4 one! I had to do the job that no one could do because it was impossible.

I was well acquainted with the difficulties ahead. I had the problem, for example, of doing something about the worm mounds in the lawn. The Countess might not even have noticed them yet, they were so small; but in my bare feet I knew about them and had to do something about them. And I could go on trimming the garden edges with shears, but I knew that a $5 lawn demanded that I line up each edge exactly with a yard stick and then trim it precisely with the edger. And there were other problems that only I and my bare feet knew about.

I started the next Thursday by ironing out the worm mounds with a heavy roller. After two hours of that I was ready to give up for the day. Nine o'clock in the morning and my will was already gone. It was only by accident that I discovered how to regain it. Sitting under a walnut tree for a few minutes after finishing the rolling, I surveyed my job. The lawn looked so good, and felt so good under my feet, I was anxious to get on with the job.

I followed this renewal secret for the rest of the day, reviewing a few minutes every hour or so to regain my perspective. Between reviews, I mowed four times, two times lengthwise, and two times across, until the lawn looked like a green velvet checkerboard. Then I dug around every tree, crumbling the big clods and smoothing the soil with my hands, then finished with the edger, meticulously lining up each stroke so the effect would be perfectly symmetrical. And, I carefully trimmed the grass between the flagstones of the front walk. The shears wore my fingers raw, but the walk never looked better.

Finally, about eight o'clock that evening, it was all completed. I was so proud, I didn't even feel tired when I went up to the door.

"Well, what is it today?" she asked.

"Five dollars," I said, trying for a little calm and sophistication.

"Five dollars? You mean $4, don't you? I told you that a $5 lawn job was impossible."

"Oh, no, it isn't. I just did it."

"Well, young man, the first $5 lawn in history certainly deserves some looking around."

We walked about the lawn together in the light of the evening, and even I was overcome by the impossibility of what I had done.

"Young man," she said putting her hand on my shoulder, "What on earth made you do such a crazy, wonderful thing?"

I didn't know why, but even if I had, I could not have explained it in the excitement of hearing that I had done it.

"I think I know," she continued, "how you felt when this idea first came into your head, this idea of caring for a lawn that I told you was impossible to accomplish. It made you very happy when it first came, then a little frightened; am I right?"

She could see she was right by the startled look on my face.

"I know how you felt, because the same thing happens to almost everyone. They feel this sudden burst in them of wanting to do some great thing. They feel a wonderful happiness. But then it passes because they have said, 'No, I can't do it; it's impossible.' Whenever something in you says, 'It's impossible', remember to take a careful look and see if it isn't really God asking you to grow an inch, or a foot, or a mile, that you may come to a fuller life."

Since that time some twenty-five years ago, when I have felt myself at an end with nothing before me, suddenly with the appearance of the word "impossible", I have experienced with the unexpected life, the leap inside me, and know that the only possible way lay right through the very middle of impossible.

Make a Fool of Yourself!

This is a true story of a teamster who went to a dealer of paper and said, "I want to be a salesman." For ninety days, he pounded the pavement, without a single order. Everyone in the office knew there was no hope for him. Even the merchant, who liked his spirit, determined to let him go.

It happened that the concern was overstocked with certain grades of tinted paper. "If you find any prospects for tinted paper," said the merchant to the salesman, "we are in a position to quote a very low price." The elder salesman paid no attention; they knew well enough that nobody wanted tinted paper. But the poor ex-teamster remembered; he was grasping at any straw.

Eagerly, hopefully, he started out on what was to be his last chance. As he walked, he happened to see an architect in a big office making plans on blue-print paper, and he marched in.

"Do you use much of that blue paper?" he asked. "If you do, I'd like to sell you some."

The architect asked for prices, and the poor fellow went back to the office with a sample, full of hope.

The merchant didn't have the heart to hurt him. He got a price on blue-print paper, though it was entirely out of his line, added a trifling commission, and sent the salesman out again.

The poor fellow came back with an order for a car-load.

Today he is the most successful salesman of that kind of paper, and he has built up a tremendous business. All because he did not know when he was licked, did not know enough to fail!

How much of the world's progress has been made by just such fine, simple fools!

Fools like the Wright Brothers, who persisted in trying to fly, though history was full of men, from Icarus down, who had killed themselves by such foolishness.

Fools like Westinghouse, who imagined that "a train could be stopped by jamming air against wheels."

Fools like Commodore Vanderbilt, the railroad magnate, who scornfully said, "For heaven's sake, give me the young man who has brains enough to make a fool of himself!"

—*Bruce Barton*

Endurance

Private victories precede public victories.

❧

All things are difficult before they are easy.

❧

You can be active in the church without being active in the gospel.

❧

Limitations are self-imposed; no one ever fails without self-consent.

❧

The will to persevere is often the difference between failure and success.
—*David Sarnoff*

❧

All endeavors call for ability to tramp the last mile, shape the last plan, endure the last hour's toil.

❧

Living a good life is like shaving—no matter how well you do it today, you still have to do it again tomorrow.

❧

The reason people fall away from the church is the same reason people fall out of bed: they aren't in it far enough.
—*Jay Osmond*

❧

That which we persist in doing becomes easy to do; not that the nature of the thing has changed, but the ability to do has increased

❧

No one ever collapsed under the burdens of a single day; it is when the burdens of tomorrow are added to it that it becomes unbearable: live one day at a time.

❧

Eternal life means eternal growth; it means endless progression: it is not possible through one outburst of religious zeal to meet the foe, fight the battle, and win the victory once and for all in a single encounter.

—Sterling W. Sill

What Have You Done Today?

From one of the company mills, Charles M. Schwab, the steel magnate, once telegraphed his superior, Andrew Carnegie: "All records broken yesterday."

Instead of a congratulatory message, back came the soul-searching reply: "But what have you done today?"

Stroke by Stroke

It took Michelangelo twelve years—one brush stroke at a time—to paint his Biblical scenes on the ceiling of the Sistine Chapel. It took Brahms twenty years—one note at a time—to compose his First Symphony. It took Edmund Hillary and Tenzing Norgay eighty days—one step at a time—to climb the 29,000 feet of Mount Everest. Stroke by stroke, note by note, step by step, challenge by challenge, prayer by prayer—this is the secret to achievement.

Hands On

Nothing in the world can take the place of persistence and determination.

Talent will not; nothing is more common than unsuccessful men with talent.

Genius will not; un-rewarded genius is a proverb.

Education will not; the world is full of educated derelicts.

Persistence and determination alone are omnipotent.

The watchword "hands on" has solved, and always will solve, the problems of the human race.

—Calvin Coolidge

Stay at Your Post

Puritan lawmakers were in session in Connecticut when an eclipse of the sun occurred. No one in that day knew the cause of such a phenomenon, and being a rather superstitious people, someone suggested they adjourn and hurry home to prepare for what they thought was the end of the world.

One elderly Puritan brother arose and said, "I move that we stay in our places and go on with our job of making laws for this country. If the end of the world is coming, it would make no difference whether we were here or home. I move that lights be brought in and, when the day of judgment comes, we will be found at our post doing our duty."

Forced to Rely on the Scriptures

When John Covey was a mission president in Australia, he visited the island of Sabu in the Philippines, where he discovered the people were very poor. He soon learned that because the people were too poor to purchase Church lesson manuals, they relied solely on the scriptures for all their teaching and learning needs. They also lived the commandments and sought personal revelation.

When President Covey returned to Salt Lake and reported to the prophet, President Kimball asked, "How are the people in Sabu? How are they getting along? Are they living the gospel?"

President Covey replied that there was not enough money for lesson manuals.

"That's not what I asked," President Kimball gently replied. "How are they getting along?"

"Oh, they're getting along very well."

"What are they using?"

"They're using the scriptures in all their meetings to teach all of the lessons."

Thoughtfully, President Kimball exclaimed, "Oh, that more members of the Church did not have enough money to buy lesson manuals!"

The Blacksmith

Though the blacksmith had given his heart to God, he was not prospering materially. In fact, from the time of his conversion forward, more trouble, affliction, and loss were sustained than ever before. Everything seemed to be going wrong.

One day a friend, who was not a Christian, stopped to visit. Sympathizing with the blacksmith in his trials, the friend conjectured, "It seems strange to me that so much affliction should come your way at the very moment when you become an earnest Christian."

The blacksmith didn't answer immediately; he had pondered the same question before. Finally, he replied, "You see the raw iron I have here to make horses shoes? You know what I do with it? I take a piece and heat it in the fire until it is white hot. Then I hammer it unmercifully to shape it into what it should be. Then I plunge it into a pail of cold water to temper it. Then I heat it again and hammer it some more. And I repeat the process until it's finished."

He continued, "Sometimes I find a piece of iron that won't stand up under this treatment. The heat, the hammering, and the cold water are too much for it. I don't know why it fails, but I know it will never make a good horse shoe."

He pointed to a heap of scrap iron near the door. "When I get a piece that cannot take the shape and temper, I throw it on the scrap heap. It'll never be good for anything."

He went on, "I know God has been holding me in the fires of affliction, and I have felt his hammer upon me. And I don't mind, if only he can shape me into what I should be. In my trials, my prayer is this: "Try me in any way you wish, Lord, only don't throw me on the scrap heap."

—Lynell Waterman

The Ten Demandments

1. Demand of yourself a straight and narrow course, neither side-stepping nor stopping along the way. The man of decision cannot be stopped; the man of indecision cannot get started.

2. Demand of yourself no excuses, neither offering alibis, nor blaming the another. Develop those great qualities within yourself, with which you have been endowed.

3. Demand of yourself tolerance. Our most profitable business in life is that of personal growth, and letting others grow, too.

4. Demand of yourself a disposition that is not easily offended. It is best to be a person of action, not a person of reaction to every opposition or misunderstanding.

5. Demand of yourself a day's work for a day's pay. Be a body who is busy, not a busybody.

6. Demand of yourself thrift, and stay out of debt. You owe so much to yourself that you can't afford to owe others.

7. Demand of yourself honest praise for others. Real people need no sugar-coated hosannas, only appreciation for work well done.

8. Demand of yourself a curiosity to gain knowledge, remembering that when you do obtain knowledge, it is only a cup from an ocean of knowledge. Thus we gain humility.

9. Demand of yourself self-control. Those who lead others must first learn to lead themselves.

10. Demand of yourself profit from your failures. Defeat is a destructive force only when you accept it as failure. It will be a turning point in your life if you use it as a stepping stone.

The Accounting

In June, 1965, in his Hotel Utah apartment, President David 0. McKay spoke to a group of brethren from the Physical Facilities Department of the Church. While explaining to them the importance of the work they were engaged in, he paused and recounted the following:

Let me assure you, brethren, that someday you will have a personal priesthood interview with the Savior himself. If you are interested, I will tell you the order in which he will ask you to account for your earthly responsibilities.

First, he will request an accounting of your relationship with your wife. Have you actively been engaged in making her happy, ensuring that her needs as an individual have been met?

Second, he will want an accounting of each of your children—not your stewardship over them, but your personal relationship with each of them.

Third, he will want an accounting of the talents you were given in the pre-existence.

Fourth, he will want an accounting of your Church assignments—not what assignments you had—for in his eyes, the home teacher and the mission president are probably equals—but how you have been of service to your fellow man.

Fifth, he will have no interest in how you earned your living, but he will want to know whether you have been honest in all your dealings.

Sixth, he will ask for an accounting on what you have done to contribute in a positive manner to your community, state, country, and the world.

—*Fred A. Baker*

The Race

A few years ago, along about the first of May, I was out planting a little garden with my youngest boy, who was then just finishing his first year of school.

"Dad, what are you doing on Friday?"

"I don't know, son—why?"

"I want you to come to school with me," he explained. "It's our field day, and we're going to run races; I'm going to be in one of the races, and I want you to come and watch me."

"All right," I said, "I'll be there."

"I won't win the race, Dad; I'll probably come in last. I can't run very fast but, I want you to come and watch me anyway."

I thank Heavenly Father for the lesson taught to me by my little seven-year-old boy that day. I don't know how many boys want their dads to watch them come in last. I don't know how many dads want to see their sons come in last. We'd rather say, "That's my son who made all of the baskets, my boy who made all of the touchdowns, that's me out there."

Well, Friday came, and my little boy was all excited. "Dad, this is the day we've been waiting for! I have to be there at four o'clock." We left at quarter to.

On the way, he said, "Dad, you know, even if I come in last, I'm going to get a prize. Our teacher said she didn't think it was fair that only the winner gets a prize." Again I thanked Heavenly Father for a teacher who can teach my boy how to fail.

We arrived at school and I sat on the bleachers with the other parents, while the children played nearby. Finally, the teacher blew her whistle for the little first-graders. The boys lined up on one side, and the girls lined up on the other. When she blew her whistle, and the girls raced to the other end of the field, where the teacher then presented all of them with an all-day sucker.

Then it was the boys' turn. The whistle blew and they ran. I watched my little boy—his legs going so fast, mostly up and down rather than forward—moving as fast as he could. I watched until he came within ten feet of the goal line. He couldn't contain himself anymore. He turned his head around and looked—was Dad still watching?—and then he stumbled and fell.

The rest of the boys crossed the finish line, while my little boy, on his hands and knees, down in the dirt, crawled across the finish line. The teacher reached down, took hold of his hand, and lifted him up. A smile broke out across his face, and then he received his all-day sucker.

He came to the bleachers where I was sitting, "Dad, did you see me run?"

If I should live to see him become the greatest runner of all time, an Olympic champion of the world, I would never be more humbly grateful than I was that afternoon when I saw him crawl across the goal line—the last one, down in the dirt, on his hands and knees.

That is probably the way I will go out of this old life—missed by a few relatives and a small circle of friends. But if I have run the race of life the best I could, if I have walked the path of life the best I could, even though I cross the finish line on my hands and knees, down in the dirt, I will have a good teacher there who will say, "Well done, my good and faithful servant. The race is not to the swift, nor the battle to the strong, but to him who endureth to the end."

—*Ray F. Smith*

Seven Alone

One day recently, when I was having lunch with some friends, one of the guests had to leave early to drive her thirteen-year-old to a friend's house.

"Can't he ride his bike?" one friend asked. "Or walk?"

"Heavens no," the mother replied. "It's at least a mile."

A minor and commonplace occurrence, surely. And yet, it left us thinking. A mile, she'd said. At least a mile.

In the summer of 1844, in an ox-drawn covered wagon creeping along the rugged Oregon Trail, a pioneer named Sager and his wife became ill and died. With them in the wagon were their seven children: two boys, the oldest thirteen; five girls, the youngest a tiny baby.

The Sager orphans stayed with the wagon train until it reached Fort Hall, a British trading post. There the courage of its leaders faltered. The trail to Oregon seemed too desolate and dangerous. They decided to head southwest to California instead.

But John Sager, age thirteen, remembered what his father had said about the importance of settling Oregon, of holding that territory for the United States. The night the wagon train changed its plans, he wrote a note saying that he and his brother and sisters were going back east with the scout Kit Carson, who happened to be passing through Fort Hall. In the morning, the Sager orphans were gone.

But John Sager was not with Kit Carson, and he was not heading east. Abandoning the heavy wagon, he turned the slow-moving oxen into a pack-train. Driving a cow to furnish milk for the baby, they headed west across the burning plains, seven children, all alone.

Day after day, they crept on under the burning sun. At night, they shivered around a tiny camp fire. The baby became feverish and could not eat. The smaller children wanted to turn back. John urged them on.

Three hundred miles from Fort Hall, sunburned, half-starving, in rags, they came to what is now Boise, Idaho. A kindly trader fed them and tried to persuade them to stay, but John had heard of a missionary-doctor two hundred miles farther on, across the rugged Blue Mountains, who might save his baby sister, so he went on.

The brief summer was ending. As they came to the mountains, it grew very cold. The oxen were dying and had to be abandoned. The eight-year-old girl fell and broke her leg. John packed it in snow to reduce the swelling and put her on the back of the emaciated cow. He made a sling and carried the three-year-old on his back. The baby in his arms weighed almost nothing.

Over the mountains they went, on frost-bitten, bloody feet. By now they were scarecrows, all of them. The cow's hooves were split and broken; she moaned constantly. But they went on, and on, and on, until one day they staggered up to the house where the missionary-doctor lived with his wife.

The kind-hearted woman thought the baby was dead. But after she warmed it and forced a few drops of milk between its blue lips, it uttered a whimpering cry. And John Sager, watching, gave a kind of croak that might have been a laugh.

The doctor and his wife had recently lost their child. They persuaded the Sagers to stay, and eventually adopted them.

That was how John Sager and his brother and sisters came to Oregon. Five hundred trackless miles, alone. And yet, never really alone. The greatness that made America walked with them, every step of the way.

Honore Morrow (from the movie, "Seven Alone")

Leave the Village or Die

Sale Manu and his family were called as missionaries to Satupaitea, Western Samoa, to establish a branch of the Church in that village. The Mormons were hated and persecuted there.

On one occasion, an angry mob, led by a local minister, attacked the Manu family while they were visiting the sick. The family was pushed to the ground, while the minister pushed Sale up against a tree with a machete at his throat and growled, "Why do you steal my sheep (congregation)?"

"Because you do not know the truth and deceive this people," Sale responded.

The minister threatened to kill Sale and his family, but they refused to deny their faith.

The threat was not carried out, but harassment continued, and finally a note from the village high chief arrived: "Leave the village or die."

Sale paddled his outrigger canoe two days and two nights to ask Mission President John Adams what to do. President Adams instructed Sale to pray, and assured him the Lord would answer his prayers.

Two more days and nights were spent upon the waters, returning to his family and praying for guidance. When he returned, Sale gathered his frightened family and said, "It is the Lord's will that we stay on this island and in this village, and, if necessary, to seal our testimonies with our blood."

On December 24, 1945, their gardens were destroyed, their trees felled, and their pineapples uprooted. The village high chief said they must be gone by morning or they would be burned alive.

Christmas morning found the Manu family kneeling in prayer, dressed in their finest clothes. When the mob set fire to their house, the family retreated to the cookhouse, which was also set on fire.

Under the command of the high chief, a huge bonfire was built, and the Manu family was given one last chance to leave the village. Sale stood his ground. "I am here because my church is true and I will never deny it. I am ready to die and seal my testimony with my blood."

The high chief said challenged Sale, "I gave you a chance to save your life and the lives of your family: what do you have to say?"

Sale repeated, "We are ready to die: what are you waiting for?"

The high chief became faint. "Now I know that you are a man of God, and I cannot do this thing," he said. The villagers left one at a time. The huge bonfire burned out.

That evening, the police came and arrested the high chief, the minister, and some forty others. Later, in a packed courtroom, the judge was determined to make an example of the persecutors. To Sale Manu he said, "Whatever you declare to be a just punishment for these man, including years of imprisonment, I will grant you. There will be religious freedom in these islands."

Sale replied, "I forgive them. Let them go home to their families, with the agreement that they leave the Latter-day Saints alone."

The judge decreed: "From this time forth, the Latter-day Saints may preach anywhere on the island, and if they have enough people to build a chapel, they may surely do it."

Within a couple of months, all but a handful of the 900 people living in the village had been baptized.

When they asked Sale where they should build their chapel, he took them to the site of the huge bonfire, where hot coals had burned a mark into the ground. Today, a ward chapel stands on this spot and is one of the largest buildings in Western Samoa.

—*John Lewis Lund*

❧

Tempting Temptation

A man caught a poisonous snake by the neck and held it up to show his companions how clever he was.

Much to his surprise, the snake began to coil around the man's arm and tighten its grip until, in agony, the man was forced to release the serpent's neck, which allowed the snake to strike the man, causing his death.

So it is with man.

Some feel they can go where temptation and danger lurk without getting hurt…play with temptation and not reap the consequences. Such people are commonly surprised.

A young girl had gone to a teacher to confess a moral transgression. "I just don't understand," she said. "I prayed with all my heart that God would keep me from giving in to this temptation, and he let me down."

"Did you know that this type of trouble might come if you continued keeping company with this crowd?" the teacher asked.

"Yes," came her reply.

"Did you make an effort to leave this group and find new friends?"

"No," she responded. "I felt God would cause everything to turn out all right."

Too many of us expect God to direct our destiny with no effort on our own part. James E. Talmage wrote: "The plan of mortality involved the certainty of temptation. The intent of the supplication (from the Lord's prayer) appears to be that we be preserved from temptation beyond our weak powers to withstand; that we be not abandoned to temptation without the divine support that shall be as full a measure of protection as our exercise of choice will allow.

"How inconsistent then to go, as many do, into the places where the temptations to which we are most susceptible are strongest; for the man beset with a passion for strong drink to so pray and then resort to the dramshop; for the man whose desires are lustful to voice such a prayer and then go where lust is kindled; for the dishonest man, though he say the prayer, to then place himself where he knows the opportunity to steal will be found! Can such souls as these be other than hypocrites in asking God to deliver them from the evils they have sought? Temptation will fall in our way without our seeking; and evil will present itself even when we desire most to do right; for deliverance from such we may pray with righteous expectation and assurance."

❧

The Call

Let's paint a picture of what might be...

You have been called in by your Bishop. You assume it is for a new or an additional church calling. You are tired of church work. You don't want the calling you have, let alone another. You'll tell him no. You'll explain why. You'll be convincing. He'll understand. Cut you some slack. You feel better. You leave for the appointment.

The door is ajar, so you walk in.

At first, you feel faint with fear—you'd run away if you dared—for standing where you expected to see the Bishop is Christ.

But the sweet smile on the Savior's face helps you overcome your fear. As he reaches out to take your hands in his, all that was in your mind before you entered the room has faded away.

Then Christ asks if you will help him. He tells you of the great need for service in his kingdom. You feel the nail prints in his hands. He reminds you of his promises to those who serve him.

Through your tears you answer, "If you feel I am worthy, then I'll give my time and energy for you."

Christ can't be in every Bishop's office, but the Bishop is there with the same call...for the same purpose...with the same promise.

A call to serve in the Church of Jesus Christ of Latter-day Saints—in any office—is an opportunity for growth and service and happiness. It could be an invitation to greatness.

⤷

Discerning Between the Spirit and Satan

When you have the Spirit:

You feel happy and calm.

You feel full of light.

Your mind is clear.

Your bosom burns.

You feel generous.

Nobody could offend you.

You feel confident in everything you do.

You wouldn't mind everybody seeing what you are doing.

You feel out-going, anxious to be with people.

You are glad when others succeed.

You want to make others happy; you bring out the best in and say the best of others.

You gladly and willingly perform church ordinances.

You'd like to be in the temple for a while everyday.

You feel you can magnify your church calling.

You feel like praying.

You wish you could keep all the Lord's commandments.

You feel you have control of your appetites and emotions: food and sleep in moderation, sexual restraint, diversion that is wholesome and moderate, calm and controlled speech, no anger, etc.

You're generally just glad to be alive.

When you don't have the Spirit, or Satan is prompting you:

You feel unhappy, depressed, confused, frustrated.

You feel heavy, full of darkness.

Your mind is muddled.

You feel empty, hollow, cold inside.

You feel selfish, possessive, self-centered.

Everything anyone does bothers you.

You are always on the defensive.

You easily become discouraged.

You become secretive, sneaky, evasive.

You want to be alone.

You avoid other people, especially members of your family.

You are envious of what others do and of what they have.

You are critical of others, especially of family members, and of authority.

You feel hesitant, unworthy to perform church ordinances.

You don't want to go to the temple.

You wish you had another church job, or no job at all.

You don't want to pray.

You find the commandments bothersome, restricting, or senseless.

You become a slave to your appetites; your emotions become passionate: over-indulgence in food, sleep, sex, stimulating entertainment, anger, out-spokeness, etc.

You wonder if life is really worth it.

❧

Your Good Name

A number of years ago I was seriously ill. In fact, I think everyone had given up on me except for my wife. With my family, I went to St. George, Utah, to see if the warmer weather would improve my health. We went as far as we could by train, and then continued by wagon, in the bottom of which a bed had been made for me.

In St. George, we arranged for a tent for my health and comfort, with a built-in floor a foot above the ground, and a flap we could roll up the south side for fresh air and sunshine.

I became so weak as to be scarcely able to move. It was a slow and exhausting effort for me even to turn over in bed.

One day, under these conditions, I lost consciousness of my surroundings and thought I had passed to the other side. I found myself standing with my back to a large and beautiful lake, facing a great forest of trees. There was no one in sight, and there was no boat upon the lake, or any other visible means to indicate how I might have arrived there. I realized, or seemed to realize, that I had finished my work in mortality and had gone home.

I began to look around, to see if I could find someone. There was no evidence of anyone's living there, just those great, beautiful trees in front of me, and the wonderful lake behind me.

I began to explore, and soon found a trail through the woods which seemed to have been used little, and was almost obscured by grass. I followed the trail, and after I traveled a considerable distance, I saw a man coming toward me.

I became aware that he was a very large man, and I hurried my steps to reach him, because I recognized him as my grandfather. In mortality, he weighed more than three hundred pounds, so you may know he was a large man. I remember how happy I was to see him coming. I had been given his name and had always been proud of it.

When Grandfather came within a few feet of me, he stopped. His stopping was an invitation for me to stop. Then—and this I would like you to never to forget—he looked at me very earnestly and said, "I would like to know what you have done with my name."

Everything I had ever done passed before me as though it were a flying picture on a screen— everything I had done. Quickly this vivid retrospect came down to the very time I was standing there. My whole life had passed before me. I smiled and looked at my grandfather and said, "I have never done anything with your name of which you need be ashamed."

He stepped forward and took me in his arms, and as he did so, I became conscious again of my earthly surroundings. My pillow was as wet as though water had been poured on it—wet with tears of gratitude that I could answer unashamed.

I have thought of this many times, and I want to tell you that I have been trying, more than ever since that time, to take care of that name. So I want to say to the youth of the Church and of all the world; honor your fathers and your mothers. Honor the names that you bear, because some day you will have the privilege and the obligation of reporting to them (and to your Father in Heaven) what you have done with their name.

—*George Albert Smith*

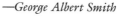

Example

A child went forth and became what he saw.
—Walt Whitman

An ounce of practice is worth a pound of preaching.

If you would lift me, you must be on higher ground.
—Ralph Waldo Emerson

Example is not the main thing in life: it is the only thing.
—Albert Schweitzer

The first great gift we can bestow on others is a good example.
—Morell

Why do you do what you do, when you know what you know?
—Sterling W. Sill

You can teach better with your lives than you can with your lips.

When men speak ill of thee, live so that nobody will believe them.
—Plato

We have committed the Golden Rule to memory: let us now commit it to life.
—Edwin Markham

Be careful how you act: you may be the only standard work people read.

If all Mormons would live their religion, there would be no need of missionaries.

Of all commentaries upon the scriptures, good examples are the best and the liveliest.

—*John Donne*

❧

Advice is like snow: the softer it falls, the longer it dwells upon, and the deeper it sinks into the mind.

—*Coleridge*

❧

He was of that good kind that you are likely to forget while they are present, but remember distinctly after they are gone.

—*0. Henry*

❧

Setting a good example is better than giving advice; good example is a language all can understand, and an argument none can deny.

❧

If you try to improve one person by being a good example, you're improving two; if you try to improve someone without being a good example, you won't improve anybody.

—*James Thorn*

❧

Precept is like the record written in the sand: the tide flows over it and it is gone. Example is like the record written on the rock: the tide recedes and the record remains.

❧

Whatever parent gives his children good instruction, and sets them at the same time a bad example, may be considered as bringing them food in one hand, and poison in the other.

—*Balguy*

❧

There are three ways to effectively teach a child: First is example, Second is by example, and Third is through example.

—*Albert Schweitzer*

Willing to Do Myself

A few words upon the subject of example—and these I speak particularly to my brethren, the Elders of Israel, yet they will apply to all classes of mankind. It is a rule with me, and always has been, to request nothing of the people that I am not willing to do myself, to require no obedience of them that I am unwilling to yield. Experience has taught me that example is the best method of preaching to any people.

—Brigham Young

❧

Is There a Latter-day Saint in the House?

Four LDS boys set out from a Utah city on a cross-country trip. They had saved all of their money during the last year of high school for this purpose, and now that graduation was over, they packed their suitcases into the trunk of their car and said good-byes to worrying parents and envious friends.

It was a matter of considerable celebration when they crossed the Utah state line and entered into another state. They pulled up alongside the highway and got out to see how it felt to be in new surroundings. A certain thrill of excitement was noted by each of the young travelers, and the sense of adventure led them to great speculation.

They had agreed to send their parents a post card every other day to indicate their whereabouts, and had promised to send a collect telegram if they ran into any trouble.

One of the boys commented that it felt really good to be on his own and not be under the necessity of getting advance approval from someone for every move he made. Another suggested that they must act like seasoned travelers and not impress others as country boys on their first junket away from home.

As a follow-up, this same boy proposed to his friends that they forget all about being Mormons for the duration of their adventure. Asked, "Why?" by three puzzled boys, he said that they could now afford to "let their hair down" and sample some of the excitement enjoyed by other people not of the Mormon Church. "Anyway, " he argued, "what difference will it make—nobody out here in the world knows us, or cares anything about our Church connections."

The thrill of the new experience weighed their judgment, and the group made an agreement to give it a try. They decided to announce themselves to the world as students from the east who had been to school in Utah for a short time. Their Utah license plates made this strategy necessary.

Nightfall on the first day of the journey found them at a famous tourist attraction spot and they made arrangements for camping near the resort. After dinner, they gathered at the large hotel for the night's entertainment. No sooner had they arrived than one of the boys suggested that they begin here and now sampling the things they had been so long denied by strict parents and teachers.

The first thing that caught their eyes was a large neon sign at the far end of the lounge. It read, "Bar—Beer and Cocktails". Thinking it a moderate nod in the direction of "sinning just a wee bit", they agreed to go into the bar and each order a glass of beer. There was a nervous air about them as they entered the gaudily lighted bar and surveyed the counters loaded with intriguing bottles of liquor. The boy who had been delegated to give the order lost his voice on the first try and had to swallow hard to get out an understandable, "Four glasses of beer, please."

What the beer lacked in taste, the atmosphere and thrill more than made it up. They grew bolder and began to talk of the next adventure they would undertake. The talk was growing racy when suddenly a well-dressed man entered the bar and walked straight toward their table. The look on the stranger's face and the determined pace at which he walked left the boys completely unnerved.

When the man reached the table at which the boys were sitting, he extended his hand to one and said, "I beg your pardon, but aren't you George Redford's son from Utah?"

The boy was speechless and terrified. His fingers froze around the base of the glass of beer and he answered in a wavering voice, "Why, yes, sir, I am. "

"I thought I recognized you when you came in the lobby of the hotel," the stranger continued. "I am Henry Paulsen, vice-president of the company your dad works for, and I met you and your mother last winter at a company dinner at a hotel in Salt Lake. I have never forgotten how you explained your Mormon priesthood to one of our other executives who asked you what it meant to be a Mormon boy. I must say I was a little surprised to see you head for the bar, but I suppose that with Mormons, as well as non-Mormons, boys will be boys when they're off the roost."

These boys had heard a sermon they would never hear duplicated in the pulpit. They were sick, ashamed, and crestfallen. As they left their half-filled glasses and walked out through the hotel lobby, they had the feeling that everyone was looking at them.

No one of us knows when and where we will hear the call, "Is there a Latter-day Saint in the house?"

Faith

One scriptural proof is worth ten thousand opinions.
—Brigham Young

A friend once wrote, "Give me your faith, not your doubts."

I would rather walk with God in the dark, than go alone in the light.
—Mary Gardiner Brajharel

Faith is not a sense, nor sight, nor reason, but taking God at his work.
—A. B. Evans

I believe in Christ as I believe in the rising sun—not that I can see it, but that by it I can see everything.

A belief is not something you carry around, but a conviction is something that carries you around. How strong are your convictions?

Faith without works is like a bird without wings: though it may hop with its companions here on earth, it will never fly with them in the heavens.

All the strength and force of man comes from his faith in things unseen; he who believes is strong; he who doubts is weak; strong convictions precede great actions.
—James F. Clarke

I believe in the sun even when it's not shining.

I believe in love even when I'm alone.

I believe in God even when he's silent.

God grant me the serenity to accept the things I cannot change,

the courage to change the things I can,

and the wisdom to know the difference.

❧

Better Than a Light

I said to the man who stood at the gate of the year, "Give me a light that I may tread safely into the unknown."

The man replied, "Go forth in the darkness and put your hand into the hand of God, which shall be to you better than a light and safer than a known way."

❧

If

Do you sometimes think, "If I could just see Christ. If I could meet him. If I could talk to him personally, then this life would be easier."

But you have seen him. You have met him. You have talked to him personally.

This knowledge, believed in faith, can make life easier.

❧

Hope

The best kind of self-help in the area of building hope in the soul is to consider "hope is like the sun, which, as we journey toward it, casts the shadow of our burden behind us."

This, too, will pass, the scriptures say, and that goes for the delightful moments as well as the trying ones.

Hope sweetens the memory of experiences well loved. It tempers our troubles to our growth and our strength. It befriends us in dark hours, excites us in bright ones. It lends promise to the future and purpose to the past. It turns discouragement to determination.
—*Samuel Smiles*

❧

Two Oars

A man hired a boy to row him across a lake.

About half way across, he noticed a "W" painted on one oar and an "F" on the other. Upon inquiring as to the significance of these letters, he was told, "F" stands for "faith" and "W" stands for "work".

"If I row just with faith, then I go in circles to my left. If I row just with works, then I go in circles to my right. In order to go straight ahead, I have to use both of oars," the boy explained.

In our lives the same principles apply. If we use faith alone, or works alone, we will go in circles. We must use both faith and works in order to make a straight course through life.

⚬⚬

Are You There?

More than half a century ago I was standing at a little railway station in Cardston, Alberta, Canada. I was leaving on a mission to England. My precious mother stood there with me and held my hand, and this is what she said:

"Hugh, my son, when you were a little tot, you often had bad dreams—nightmares—and you would often call out to me as I slept in the next room. In your fright, you would say, 'Mother, are you there?' I always said, 'Yes, my son, I am here. Just turn over and go to sleep. Everything is all right.'

"My boy, five thousand miles, a continent, and an ocean will soon separate us. You are not only going to call out and have bad dreams at night, but many times in the daytime you are going to call out.

"Now, my son, when you are in trouble and face difficulties, when you meet temptations, and when you are confused and do not know which way to go, call out and say, 'Father, are you there?' I promise you he will always answer you, and you need not fear."

Through intervening years, countless occasions have arisen where men could not help me. I felt alone; I had nightmares with my eyes wide open. I have taken the advice of my mother. I have said, "Father, are you there?" He has not spoken to me audibly; he has not appeared to me personally; but he has always answered me. There has come into my heart a quiet peace that has enabled me to know that I could, figuratively, turn over and go to sleep.

—*Hugh B. Brown*

⚬⚬

I Am Immortal

Discouragement is one of Satan's most effective tools: I must not let him use it on me.

I believe that God created me to be happy, to enjoy the blessings of life, to be useful to my fellow beings, and an honor to my church.

I believe that the trials which beset me today are but the fiery tests by which my character is strengthened, ennobled, and made worthy to enjoy the higher things of life which I believe are in store for me.

I believe that my soul is worth too much to be crushed by defeat: I will rise above it.

I believe that I am the architect of my own fate; therefore, I will master my circumstances and surroundings, and not be a slave to them.

I will not yield to discouragements: I will trample them under foot and make them serve as stepping-stones to success.

I will conquer my obstacles and turn them into opportunities.

My failures of today will help to guide me on to victory on the morrow.

The morrow will bring new strength, new hopes, new opportunities and new beginnings; I will be ready to meet it with a brave heart, a calm mind and an undaunted spirit.

In all things, I will do my best, and leave the rest to the infinite.

I will not waste my mental energies by useless worry: I will learn to dominate my restless thoughts and look on the bright side of things.

I will face the world bravely; I will not be a coward; I will assert my God-given birthright; for I am immortal, and nothing can overcome me.

🙠

Trials of Faith

Brigham Young pointed out that the intensity of Christ's suffering was induced by the withdrawal from him of the Father's Spirit:

"…at the very moment…when the crisis came…the Father withdrew…His spirit, and cast a veil over him. That is what made him sweat blood. He then pled with the Father not to forsake him. 'No,' says the Father, 'you must have your trials, as well as others.'" (Journal of Discourses, Volume 3, page 206)

Just as Jesus had to endure affliction to prove himself, so must all men endure affliction to prove themselves.

Brigham Young observed that the prophet (Joseph Smith) was more perfect in thirty-eight years, with the severe tribulation through which he passed, than he would have been in a thousand years without it.

For after much tribulation come the blessings. (D&C 58:2-4)
—*Marion G. Romney*

🙠

Master of the Universe

Sir Isaac Newton, the British scientist, once had a skillful mechanic make him a miniature replica of our solar system, with balls representing the planets geared together by cogs and belts so as to move in harmony when cranked. Later, Newton was visited by a scientist friend who did not believe in God.

As Newton sat reading in his study with his mechanism on a large table near him, his friend stepped in. Scientist that he was, he recognized at a glance what was before him. Stepping up to it, he slowly turned the crank, and with undisguised admiration watched the heavenly bodies all move in their relative speed in their individual orbits. Standing off a few feet he exclaimed, "My! What an exquisite thing this is! Who made it?" Without looking up from his book, Newton answered, "Nobody."

Quickly turning to Newton, the infidel said, "Evidently you did not understand the question. I asked who made this?" Looking up now Newton solemnly assured him that nobody made it, but that the aggregation of matter so much admired had just happened to assume the form it was in. But the astonished infidel replied with some heat, "You must think I am a fool! Of course somebody made it, and he is a genius, and I'd like to know who he is."

Laying aside his book, Newton arose and laid a hand on his friend's shoulder. "This thing is but a puny imitation of a much grander system whose laws you know, and I am not able to convince you that this mere toy is without a designer and maker; yet you profess to believe that the great original from which the design is taken has come into being without either designer or maker! Now tell me by what sort of reasoning do you reach such an incongruous conclusion?"

I Had to Play

It was the day of the big game—the big rivalry between two competitive teams and towns.

There was great hope of winning because of a fellow named Tom. Coach and students alike have placed their confidence in him.

The height of their hopes is equaled only by the depth of their despair when a message arrives that Tom's father has died. The Coach has the double duty of telling the boy the news of his loss, while simultaneously swallowing his own despair. He stifles the urge to play the game first and break the news later.

The coach found it easier to break the news than to look into the dry eyes of the boy. While the boy had never talked much about his dad, he had said enough to indicate that there was a closeness. Yet, here he was taking the news like a weather report.

When he finally spoke, his response shocked the coach. "I'll go right after the game," he said.

The coach thought he knew boys, but he'd never run into such callousness, and he did not know what to think or how to respond.

Assuming the boy was too grief-stricken to be thinking straight, the coach finally said, "You don't have to play, Tom; the game's not that important."

"It is to me," Tom said, before dashing off to dress.

That night the game was gloriously won, pretty much by Tom alone. The other players, stunned by this new side of their star, tried, but their hearts weren't in it. What they lacked, Tom had. He played like one possessed. It was as if the news had released a caged being, given birth to a different person. How he played! Only those among the spectators who didn't know of Tom's loss were with him. Even the cheerleaders gave only perfunctory cheers.

After the win, Tom's fellow players showered and left quickly, one or two mumbling a word of sympathy as they exited.

When the Coach came to confront Tom, to talk to him about over-devotion to the game, he found him toweling rhythmically to a whistled tune.

"Why? Why did you play the game, Tom?" the coach demanded. "At first I thought maybe it was for me, but it wasn't. Your father is dead, Tom, and I am ashamed of you, and of myself."

The boy looked at his coach long without a word. Then he answered, "Coach, I'm a senior. It's my last game. I had to play . This was the first time my dad ever saw me play. I had to play like I never played before."

The boy stopped and the coach looked at him, not understanding. There was a barely perceptible break in the boy's voice when he explained, "My father was blind."

~

And a Little Child

There's a story, which I understand is true, about a small farming community in the southwest, which demonstrates an interesting and important point.

It seems that this community had been suffering for a long time from a serious drought. Their crops and cattle faced certain destruction along with their economy if the needed rains continued to stay away. Finally, the situation became so serious that drastic measures were called for and the entire population was called upon to collect at the small local church to pray for rain.

On the appointed day, the thirty or forty families of the area dutifully showed up at the church. The sky was a blazing sheet of brass without a cloud in sight. The heat was almost more than a person could stand. Dust devils could be seen whirling across the fields and the group looked upon the dreary scene through squinted eyes as they trooped into the church, depressed and silent.

Inside, led by the local preacher, they fell silent and each in his own way prayed for the cooling, life-giving rain that could save them. An hour passed. Outside, there was a change in the wind, and over the distant mountains to the west a long, heavy line of clouds began to darken the sky. The worshippers inside the little church were unaware of this and continued their silent prayers until, suddenly, their heads raised at the distant sound of thunder. They held their breath until the sound came again, this time unmistakable, the distant crack of heavy, business-like thunder.

They ran out into the churchyard and filled their lungs with the sweetest smelling air on earth, the smell of fresh, cool water falling on dry, parched earth. And soon the fast moving storm reached them and the rain fell in torrents. They jumped up and down and shouted and hugged one another; they danced in circles and thanked God for the saving rain. And then, suddenly, they all fell silent. There was only the sound of the booming thunder and the cascading rain as they all stood and looked at one little seven-year-old girl who was smiling from ear to ear and watching the rain from beneath the shelter of a tiny umbrella.

Out of the entire assembly, she had been the only one who, in her simple, childish faith, had expected the rain to be delivered, and had, in her womanly wisdom, provided herself with an umbrella. The dripping adults looked at each other, and then they splashed back into the church for a sober thanksgiving service.

—Earl Nightingale

He Got His Hogs

In Winter Quarters, the sufferings of a stricken and homeless people were almost beyond endurance. Winter Quarters has been called by some, the "Valley Forge of Mormondom".

Day after day, the burial wagons drove out to the pitiful cemetery with the broken and emaciated remains of Saints whose strength had not been equal to the task imposed upon them.

The usual diet of those driven souls was corn bread, salt bacon, and a little milk. Scurvy, resulting from the lack of vegetables and fresh meat, was making such incursions into the ranks of the pioneers that it was feared before long that all might be sleeping on the hill. It was heartbreaking.

One day, President Brigham Young went to the crude cabin occupied by the family of Lorenzo Young. "Lorenzo," he said, "if you will hitch up your horses and go down into Missouri, the Lord will open the way so that you can bring us some hogs and give this people fresh meat."

It would have been difficult to imagine anything less likely than the Missourians taking part in any transaction that would benefit the Latter-day Saints.

Nevertheless, Lorenzo Young went. (People didn't ask questions or do what they thought best in those days when they were given assignments.)

Brother Young had only three horses. These he hitched to his wagon and set out.

The first night, he stayed with a wealthy man. A fine horse caught his eye, and he asked his host how much he wanted for him.

"That's Messenger," the man replied, "and he's one of the best animals I have. I'll take one dollar for each mile I've driven him today." He had that day driven Messenger thirty-five miles, and Lorenzo Young gave him thirty-five dollars for the animal.

When Brother Young got to St. Joseph, he found a condition that he had not thought to find any place in Missouri. Whereas he had expected to encounter bitterness and anger, he found friendliness and some show of hospitality. How had this come about?

Some time before, a family of Saints had left Winter Quarters and gone to St. Joseph. One of the girls in the family had obtained employment in a tavern, and had spread word of the sufferings of the pioneers. Her stories had touched the hearts of the people in the community. Some of them even offered to give merchandise to the saints on the plains. Brother Young, however, soon gave them to understand that he wasn't after charity: his was a business trip.

The first thing he did was borrow a thousand dollars from a Jew, and what to you think he did with it? He went out and bought forty acres of unharvested corn. He paid four dollars an acre for the cornfield, and estimated that he would get sixty bushels to the acre. He gathered the corn and put it into bins, then advertised for hogs.

He got his hogs.

It requires a lively imagination to picture what happened after that.

In that county, there are hundreds of miles of oaks, and hogs feed well upon acorns with little trouble and no expense to anyone. When Lorenzo Young asked for hogs, the farmers began to round them up. They came singly, in twos, and in herds. Before long, Brother Young had all the hogs he wanted—1,000 head. They weighed from 150 to 400 pounds each. What do you think he paid for them? The astounding price of seventy-five cents a head!

Thus the Saints got their fresh meat, and were enabled to continue their journey with some assurance of health.

Did the Lord provide any more miraculously for Hagar in the desert, or for the children of Israel in the wilderness, or for the widow to whom he sent the Prophet Elijah?

Let us emulate the faith of our fathers at both Valley Forge and Winter Quarters; let us give as they gave, work as they worked, hope as they hoped. We may then safely trust to the future, that liberty will once more come.

—*J. N. Washburn*

Friendship

I've never met a person I didn't like.

—*Will Rogers*

Friendship: one soul in two bodies.

—*Pythagoras*

Friendship is love without its wings.

—*Byron*

The antidote for fifty enemies is one friend.

—*Aristotle*

There are no strangers, just friends I have never met.

People are lonely because they build walls instead of bridges.

—*Joseph Fort Newton*

A true friend walks in, when the rest of the world walks out.

Better are the blows of a friend, than the false kisses of an enemy.

—*Thomas Becket*

A friend is one who knows all about you, and loves you just the same.

A friend you have to buy, won't be worth what you have to pay for him.

True friendship comes, when silence between two people is comfortable.

—*Dave Tyson Gentry*

Our friends see the best in us, and that very fact calls forth the best from us.
—*Black*

&

A merely fallen enemy may rise again, but the reconciled one is truly vanquished.

&

A warm smile is an invitation to draw up a chair before the log fire of friendship.

&

What wealth it is to have such friends that we cannot think of them without elevation.
—*Henry David Thoreau*

&

Every man should have a fair-sized cemetery in which to bury the faults of his friends.
—*Henry Ward Beecher*

&

Friendship consists in forgetting what one gives, and remembering what one receives.
—*Dumas the Younger*

&

Friendship improves happiness, and abates misery, by doubling our joy, and dividing our grief.

—*Addison*

&

The only way to have a friend is to be a friend; the art of pleasing requires only the desire.

—*Lord Chesterfield*

&

Of all the gifts that a wise providence grants us to make life full and happy, friendship is the most beautiful.

&

Real friends are those who, when you've made a fool of yourself, don't feel that you've done a permanent job.

—*Erwin T. Randall*

&

There are two ways to make friends: one is to do something for people; the other is to let people do something for you.

&

If thou hast a thousand friends, thou hast none to spare; if thou hast a single enemy, thou wilt meet him everywhere.

❧

I am persuaded that he who is capable of being a bitter enemy, can never possess the necessary virtues that constitute a true friend.

❧

To have a good friend is one of the highest delights of life; to be a good friend is one of the noblest and most difficult undertakings.

❧

A friend is someone you can be alone with, and have nothing to do, and not be able to think of anything to say, and be comfortable in the silence.

—*Sheryl Condie*

❧

We take care of our health; we lay up money; we make our roof tight and our clothing sufficient; but who provides wisely that he shall not be wanting in the best property of all—friends?

—*Ralph Waldo Emerson*

❧

Oh, the comfort, the inexpressible comfort of feeling safe with a person—of never having to weigh thoughts nor measure words, but pouring them all right out, chaff and grain together, certain that a faithful hand will take and sift them, keep what is worth keeping, and with a breath of kindness, blow the rest away.

❧

Destroying Enemies

President Abraham Lincoln was once criticized for his attitude toward his enemies.

"Why do you try to make friends of them?" asked an associate. "You should try to destroy them."

"Am I not destroying my enemies," Lincoln gently replied, "when I make them my friends?"

What Is a Friend?

A friend is someone who likes you. Someone with whom you can really be yourself. One who appreciates the good in you, overlooks the bad in you, and brings out the best in you.

With a friend, you can share a laugh, a secret, a viewpoint, a success, or a disappointment—as well as a complete assortment of problems, large and small.

A friend is someone who understands silence as well as words, stands by you, forgives you. One who lifts you up and never lets you down, and who makes you feel it's a pretty nice old world, after all.

How would I know so well? Because you have been such a friend to me.

A blessed thing it is for any man or woman to have a friend—one human soul whom we can trust utterly; who knows the best and the worst of us, and who loves us in spite of all our faults; who will speak the honest truth to us, while the world flatters us to our faces and laughs at us behind our backs; who will give us counsel and reproof in the day of prosperity and self-conceit, but who, again, will comfort and encourage us in the day of difficulty and sorrow, when the world leaves us alone to fight our own battles as we can.

—*Kingsley*

The Significance of Friendship

Six months ago, by appointment from the First Presidency, we attended a mission-wide conference in South Africa. After four glorious days with the wonderful people of that nation and, as we were leaving, many members said, "When you return, please give our best regards and love to our friends all over the world." Little did they realize—and little did I realize at that time—that I would have this kind of an opportunity to extend their love to their friends worldwide.

Since this responsibility has come to me, I have thought a great deal about friends in the gospel of Jesus Christ. I am reminded of that great revelation on priesthood, "You are mine apostles, and even God's high priests; ye are they whom my Father hath given me; ye are my friends." (D&C 84:63.) This verse shows the important blessing of being recognized as the Savior's friend.

I would like to leave this thought with you as we think about friends and the part they should play in our lives as Latter-day Saints. Perhaps this simple illustration will help us realize the need of being friends in the home, in the neighborhood, and in the community.

Several months ago, my wife and I were in our front yard when the newspaper boy came down the street on his bicycle, which was loaded with papers. About twenty or thirty yards behind him was another boy, following on a bicycle. I was not sure at that time what their relationship was, but I did notice they were coming down the street at a pretty good clip.

When the newspaper boy reached our sidewalk, he was traveling too fast to make the approach to our home; as a result, he went one way, the bicycle went another, and the newspapers went everywhere. Noticing the boy had fallen on the lawn and was not hurt, but realizing he would undoubtedly be embarrassed from falling in front of his friend, we moved toward him.

At the sight of this perfect three-point landing, if we may refer to it as that, his companion shouted his pleasure and laughed heartily with complete and full enjoyment at his associate's misfortune.

Trying to relieve the embarrassment of the paper boy, knowing he didn't want help but might want to have his pride repaired a little, I took a few more steps toward him and said, "It's kind of a low blow to have your friend laugh when you've had a bad spill, isn't it?"

He went on picking up the papers without even looking up. Finally, he had the papers back in place, and he got on his bicycle. As he started to pedal away from us, he mumbled, "He isn't my friend: he's my brother."

His words have been ringing through my ears ever since. I sincerely feel that one of the great purposes of family home evening and home teaching is to have family members realize that a brother can be a friend; that a sister can be a friend; and that a father and a mother can be more than parents—they can be friends.

I hope and pray that we might catch the wisdom and inspiration of building a home so that our members in that sacred unit can look upon a father and say, "He is my best friend", or, "My mother is more than my mother; she is my friend". When we realize that parents and family members can be more than blood relations and are in very deed friends, then we will have a glimpse of how our Heavenly Father wants us to live—not only as brothers and sisters, but as very close friends.

—*Marvin J. Ashton*

The Hand-Me-Down Box

When ten-year-old Leigh Baugh got home from school, she found her mother rummaging through a big cardboard box of clothes.

"What are those?" Leigh asked, reaching for a warm molasses cookie cooling on the kitchen counter.

"Those are for dessert, little one," warned her mother, "and this is another box full of hand-me-downs from the Ellers."

Her mother held up a green corduroy jumper and asked, "How do you like this one?"

Leigh reached for a red velveteen party dress with a ruffle of lace at the collar and said, "I like this one better."

"That's lovely, Leigh!" her mother exclaimed. "It hardly shows any wear at all."

"Why do the Ellers give us their hand-me-downs?" Leigh asked, examining a white silk blouse.

Her mother looked up and reached out to stroke Leigh's copper hair, then turned away and sighed, "Because we need them, Leigh."

The Ellers were a rich family who had a large, lovely home in town. They had two daughters just a year older than Leigh and her sister, Tina. The Eller girls went to a private school that required uniforms so, more often than not, they out-grew their other clothes long before they were worn out.

The Baughs were a poor family who lived in a little old farmhouse outside town. Their two daughters had been wearing hand-me-downs for as long as they could remember. Despite their differences, the Baughs and the Ellers were good friends. So, it was with great pleasure that the Ellers gave the Baughs their hand-me-downs, and it was with much gratitude that the Baughs accepted them.

Leigh didn't mind wearing hand-me-downs, particularly the Ellers' hand-me-downs. The Ellers shopped only at the finest stores in the city, and all their clothes were fashionable and well made. Since the Ellers went to a different school, no one in Leigh's school recognized her "new clothes". If anything, her friends marveled that she dressed so well. Leigh never told anyone about the hand-me-down box.

One day in school, Mrs. Kratz, Leigh's fourth-grade teacher, announced, "It's time to decide what you want to be when you grow up." All the children moaned, except Leigh. Leigh had wanted to be a writer ever since she had first learned how to read.

"I want you to tell us what you've decided in a little speech next Wednesday." The children groaned even louder.

"A speech!" Leigh gasped, quietly. She had never spoken in front of a class before. "What will I say?" she wondered. "What will I wear?" she worried.

When Leigh got home from school that day, she tore through the house, frantically calling her mother.

"What's the matter, Leigh?" her mother cried. "Are you hurt?"

Leigh explained breathlessly, "I have to give a speech, and I don't have anything to wear!"

"A speech?" questioned her mother. "Whatever for?"

"I have to talk about what I want to be when I grow up, and I have to do it in front of the whole class! I'll be so nervous! I want to look my best so no one will laugh at me."

Trying not to laugh at what her daughter considered to be a serious problem, Mrs. Baugh stepped down from the ladder where she'd been standing to hang some hand-sewn curtains made of worn-out sheets. "Let's look in that new box of hand-me-downs."

"Not, hand-me-downs," Leigh protested. "Not this time. For once, can't I have a new dress?" she pleaded, eyeing the homemade curtains.

"I don't have the fabric to make you one," offered her mother.

Leigh looked more closely at the sheet curtains and almost stomped her foot before she remembered the punishment for such behavior. Once when her mother had reminded her to do the dishes, Leigh had stomped away in a fit of anger. "If you like stomping so much," her mother had suggested quietly, but firmly, "then you may stomp the entire time you are washing the dishes." Leigh had washed and stomped until she thought her arms and legs would fall off. But she had learned her lesson and decided not to stomp, despite her frustration.

Looking at her still feet, she barely whispered, "Not a hand-me-down dress. Not a homemade dress. A store-bought dress. Like the Ellers wear. Just this once. Please."

Mrs. Baugh knelt before her daughter, placed her hands on Leigh's shoulders, and looked straight into her troubled eyes. "We'll go look on Saturday."

Leigh was triumphant as she hugged her mother. Later that night, Leigh lay awake in bed thinking about her first store-bought dress. "She said 'look'," Leigh reminded herself, "not buy." But I have twelve dollars I have saved in babysitting money, and surely that will buy a dress as nice as the Ellers wear." Then she drifted off to sleep, dreaming about her first trip to one of the fine shops in the city.

But when Saturday came, they didn't go to the city. They went to the next town. They didn't go into a fine shop, either. They went to a factory outlet store that didn't look much different than the local grocery store. Leigh tried hard to conceal her disappointment as her mother lead her to the rack in the corner full of dresses her size. One by one, they pulled dress after dress off the rack and held each up to Leigh, looking for the perfect one for her first speech. The dresses were pretty, but they were all made of cotton. There were no corduroys, velveteens, or silks—just plain old cotton dresses like Leigh used to wear before the Ellers started sending their hand-me-downs. Leigh hesitated to ask, but ventured, "Where are the velveteen dresses, Mother?"

"Oh, Leigh," her mother laughed good-naturedly. "There are no velveteen dresses in here, and if there were, we couldn't afford them."

Leigh wandered to the front of the store and peered out the big plate-glass window to the quaint shop across the street. A little girl in a blue fur coat, hat, and muff was just leaving with her mother, who was laden with ribbon-tied boxes. Leigh turned to the check-out counter in her store and watched the cashier stuff purchases into brown paper bags. Leigh returned to her mother in the back corner.

"Let's go back to the hand-me-down box, Mother," Leigh offered, trying to smile. "I'll save my money until I have enough to buy something better. Maybe in the shop across the street."

Mrs. Baugh looked out at the shop Leigh had seen and consoled, "Maybe someday, Leigh."

It was decided that Leigh would wear the red velveteen dress with the ruffle of white lace at the collar she had first admired in the latest box of hand-me-downs. She tried it on, and was as pleased with how it felt as how it looked. The velveteen seemed to caress her and the red brought out the natural rosiness in her cheeks. Her mother pinned a new hem while Leigh twirled about planning her speech. Leigh had decided to open her speech on her career in writing by talking about how she loved to read.

Leigh practiced her speech aloud one last time while her mother carefully pressed the velveteen dress. Today was the day, and Leigh had never felt more confident in her life.

When she got to school, Leigh carefully removed her coat and patted her dress into place. It was then that she noticed Linnie Lubette staring at her. For years, Leigh had tried to get close to Linnie. Linnie had the best of both worlds. She lived in the country like the Baughs, but was rich like the Ellers. And Leigh very much wanted to be her friend.

"Is that a new dress, Leigh?" Linnie asked, almost mockingly.

"Yes," Leigh answered with confidence. "I got it for my speech today. Are you all ready?"

"Of course," Linnie answered, with even more confidence. "Are you sure that's new?" But before Leigh could respond, Linnie was gone.

Leigh began to panic. The dress was new to her, but it was a hand-me-down from the Ellers. But then, how would Linnie Lubette know that? She finally put it out of her mind to concentrate on her speech.

When Leigh passed Linnie's desk, Linnie grabbed her hand and sneered, "Didn't I see that dress at the church Christmas party?" Leigh pulled away and sat down. Then she remembered. The Ellers and Lubettes belonged to the same church. This velveteen dress might have been Cindy Eller's Christmas party dress. She might have worn it to the church Christmas party. If Linnie had admired it, she might remember it. Leigh suddenly grew very nervous and began fussing with the dress, wishing she could change it into another one right then and there. Suddenly, she heard her name called.

"Why don't you go first, Leigh?" her teacher asked. "We're anxious to hear about your career choice."

Leigh slipped out of her seat and walked slowly to the front of the room. Before she even had a chance to gather her thoughts, her teacher spoke again. "My, don't you look lovely today, Leigh. Is that a new dress?"

Before Leigh could respond, Linnie Lubette chirped, "It's not new. It's a hand-me-down from Cindy Eller."

Leigh was mortified. She'd been found out. Now everyone would know that she wore hand-me-downs. Tears welled up in her eyes and she hung her head to hide them. The room fell silent.

Suddenly, Leigh felt her teacher's arm around her shoulders, pulling her close. "You are so fortunate, Leigh. See this dress I'm wearing? It's a hand-me-down, too."

Leigh looked up for the first time and stared through tear-filled eyes at her teacher's pretty blue floral silk dress. "You see," her teacher turned to explain to the class, "teachers don't make very much money, so I can't afford nice dresses like this. But I have a sister who is a doctor, and she has many beautiful clothes. She shares them with me because she loves me."

Leigh slowly turned her gaze from her teacher to Linnie Lubette, who was shrinking into her seat.

"You are so fortunate, Leigh," her teacher continued, "to have a friend who is kind enough to share her good fortune with you."

Leigh perked up, wiped the tears from her eyes, brushed the skirt of her hand-me-down velveteen dress smooth, and cleared her throat.

"Now, what is it you want to be when you grow up, Leigh?" her teacher asked.

"I want to be like your sister," Leigh answered, smiling.

"A doctor?"

"No," Leigh replied, turning to face the whole class, "someone kind enough to share with others."

Then, instead of talking about her being a writer, Leigh told an enraptured class all about the hand-me-down box.

—*Peg Fugal (originally published in "The Friend", 11/87)*

❧

A Friend to Die For

Darkness filled the corners of the dungeon under the castle. All about on the hard floor lay men who had been arrested by the ruler's soldiers. Most of them had been condemned to death. A hopeless silence filled the room so that the low words of the young man outside the barred door sounded loud and angry.

"What did you do, my good friend, Pythias?" the young man demanded. "What did you do that so displeased the king?"

The prisoner at the door sighed. His hand reached through the narrow bars and touched his friend's arm. Since early childhood, these two had always been together. Now Pythias knew that he was going to leave his friend forever and his heart ached at the thought of this separation.

"I did nothing, Damon," he insisted, "but the King has claimed that I am a rebel. There is nothing that can be done about it."

"Then what can I do for you?" Damon asked. "Shall I go to your home and comfort your parents?"

Neither of the young men had heard the great outer door open. They did not see the ruler as he came near to them.

"I would like to see them myself once more," Pythias' voice was hopeless. "I would come back here and pay with my life if I could only say farewell to them."

A loud laugh startled the two young men. Damon whirled and found himself face to face with his king. Quickly he bowed and waited for the ruler to speak. Again, the king laughed as he looked at the prisoner.

"So you would come back to die if I would let you go to your distant home?" he mocked Pythias and all the prisoners.

"I would come back," Pythias stated simply. "I promise."

"How do I know that you would keep your promise?" the king's eyes narrowed as he watched the man. "You are trying to cheat me. You cannot go."

"Then let me stay in prison in his place," Damon looked straight at the king as he made his request. "He has never broken a promise, but if he does not return, I will die for him on the day that is set for his execution."

The king was amused. This strange request would make a delightful story to tell to his friends. A young man who offered to die for his friend! This was the best jest of the year and he and his courtiers would watch it with interest.

Soon the prison door closed behind Damon, then Pythias was on his way home. The days passed and the day of execution came nearer and nearer. Day by day, the king came to the prison to taunt the foolish young man. Again and again, his cruel laughter rang out.

"If Pythias does not come back, it will not be his fault," Damon stated calmly. "Something must have happened to him."

At last the day for the execution arrived and Pythias had not returned. The king and his courtiers jeered at Damon as he was led from the cell.

"The man who dies for his friend, a false friend," they called out. "We told you that he would not return."

"He will come if he can," Damon said to himself as he walked straight and tall in the line of condemned men. "He will come if..."

"Here he comes! Here he comes!" a soldier ran shouting to the king.

Damon smiled as he saw his friend. Pythias was hardly able to breathe. Storms and misfortunes had beset him all of the way back. He had feared that Damon would die before he could arrive. His face beamed with happiness when he found his friend alive. Quickly he fell into the line of prisoners and pushed Damon aside.

"I came," he panted.

"I knew that you would!"

The king could hardly believe his eyes and ears. Never had he known that there could be such friendship. His heart softened before such a great love. "Go!" he said to the two young men. "Go back to your homes."

Then he turned to his stunned courtiers and added, "I would give all my wealth to have one such friend!"

—A Greek myth adapted by Jewel Varnado

My Friend

I love you not only for what you are, but for what I am when I am with you. I love you not only for what you have made of yourself, but for what you are making of me. I love you for the part of me that you bring out. I love you for putting your hand into my heaped-up heart and passing over all the foolish and frivolous and weak things that you can't help but dimly see there, and for drawing out into the light all of the beautiful, radiant belongings that no one else had looked far enough to find.

I love you for ignoring the possibilities of the fool and the weakling in me, and for laying firm hold on the possibilities of the good in me. I love you for closing your eyes to the discords in me, and for adding to the music in me by worshipful listening. I love you because you are helping me to make of the lumber of my life not a tavern, but a temple, and of the word of my every day not a reproach, but a song.

I love you because you have done more than any creed could have done to make me good, and more than any fate could have done to make me happy. You have done it without a touch, without a word, without a song. You have done it just by being yourself. Perhaps that is what being a friend means after all.

Gratitude

The depth of our gratitude is the depth of our understanding.

∽

Man owes his very existence to a six-inch layer of topsoil, and the fact that it rains.
—*Richard L. Evans*

∽

An Open Letter to Heavenly Father

Most Mighty God:

In these times of trouble and strife, I wish to seek a moment of solitude with thee and thank thee openly for thy marvelous blessings.

First, dear God, I thank thee for the privilege of being born in the promised land of plenty—this great America. I thank thee, 0 God, for inspiring men of great moral stature to lead our ship of state on a peaceful course on a sea of life made treacherous by storms of greed and passion.

I thank thee, 0 God, for goodly parents—parents who have led me through darkness of despair to the brighter glory of thy great work and its manifold blessings. Parents who have fed me, clothed me, and passed on to me the wondrous privilege of being able to say that I am a Mormon.

I thank thee, 0 God, for a sound physical body, an alert, healthy mind, and a humble spirit that may someday return to thee in thy celestial kingdom.

I thank thee, God, for the paragons of faith and obedience that guide thy Church through thy divine revelation and inspiration.

I thank thee for the privilege of being able to take the girl of my choice to thy holy temple, to be united as one, for time and all eternity. For the opportunity of having my children sealed to me, and being able to rear them in thy true Church.

I am grateful, dear God, for everything thou hast placed at my command, for my use and convenience. Life is as a great kaleidoscope when lived in conjunction with thy word—each turn a new day, permeated with peerless, ever-changing patterns of glory and beauty.

Oftimes, O God, it is difficult to realize thy presence amid the hustle and the rush that constitutes today's metropolitan society. At these moments, it is only necessary to repair to the quiet of the home, or the splendor of thy natural creations.

When ere I walk amid lofty pines, or gaze silently at the moon reflected by a black midnight sea, or listen to a coyote in mournful prayer across the desert's plains, then I know of thy presence, dear God, and offer this prayer to thee:

In gratitude, Lord, my head is bowed
In a solemn and gracious prayer.
My spirit soars like a downy cloud
With the knowledge that thou art near.
Stay by me, Lord, when I do seem
From thy straight and narrow to stray,
For I know thou lovest and will redeem
If I but remember to pray.

—*Ronald Acheson*

A Special Type of Soldier

At the request of the First Presidency, I had gone to England as coordinator for the LDS servicemen.

One Saturday afternoon in 1944, I sent a telegram from London to the base chaplain near Liverpool letting him know that I would be in camp the next morning to conduct Mormon Church services at ten o'clock.

When I arrived at that camp, there were seventy-five Mormon boys, all in uniform—and quite a number in battle dress.

The chaplain to whom I had sent the wire proved to be a Baptist minister from the southern United States. He, too, was waiting for my arrival. As these young men ran out to greet me—not because it was I, but because of what I represented—and as they literally threw their arms around me, knowing I was representing their parents as well as the Church, this minister said, "Please, tell me how you do it."

"Do what?"

"Why," he said, "I did not get your wire until late this morning. I made a hurried search. I found there were seventy-six Mormon boys in this camp. I got word to them. Seventy-five of them are here. The other is in the hospital. I have more than six hundred Baptist men in this camp, and if I gave them six months' notice, I could not get a response like that." And then he repeated, "How do you do it?"

I said, "Sir, if you will come inside, perhaps you will see."

We went in to the little chapel. The boys sat down. I asked, "How many here have been on missions?"

I think fully 50 percent raised their hands. I said, "Will you and you and you"—and I pointed to six of them—"please come and administer the sacrament? And will you and you and you"—and I pointed to six others—"please come and sit here and be prepared to speak."

Then I said, "Who can lead music?" A number of hands were raised. "Will you come and lead the music? And who can play this portable organ?" There were several more hands, and one was selected. Then I said, "What would you like to sing, fellows?" With one voice, they replied, "Come, Come Ye Saints!"

We had no hymn books. The boy sounded the chord; they all arose. I have heard "Come, Come Ye Saints" sung in many lands and by many choirs and congregations, and—without in any way reflecting adversely on what we usually hear—I think I have only heard "Come, Come Ye Saints" sung that once when every heart seemed to be bursting. They sang every verse without books. When they came to the last verse, they didn't mute it; they didn't sing it like a dirge—but, throwing back their shoulders, they sang out until I was fearful the walls would burst. "And should we die before our journey's through, happy day, all is well"; I looked at my minister friend, and found him weeping.

Then one of the boys who had been asked to administer the sacrament knelt at the table, bowed his head, and said, "Oh, God, the Eternal Father." He paused for what seemed to be a full minute, and then he proceeded with the rest of the blessing on the bread. At the close of that meeting I sought that boy out. I put my arm around his shoulders, and said, "Son, what's the matter? Why was it so difficult for you to ask the blessing on the bread?"

He paused for a moment and said, rather apologetically, "Well, Brother Brown, it hasn't been two hours since I was over the continent on a bombing mission. As we started to return, I discovered that my tail assembly was partly shot away, that one of my engines was out, that three of my crew were wounded, and that it appeared absolutely impossible that we could reach the shores of England.

"Brother Brown, up there I remembered Primary and Sunday School and MIA and home and church, and up there, when it seemed all hope was lost, I said, 'Oh, God, the Eternal Father, please support this plane until we reach a landing field.' He did just that, and when we landed, I learned of this meeting and I had to run all the way to get here. I didn't have time to change my battle dress, and when I knelt there and again addressed the Lord, I was reminded that I hadn't stopped to say thanks. Brother Brown, I had to pause a little while to tell God how grateful I was."

Well, we went on with our meeting. We sang. Prayers were offered, and these young men, with only a moment's notice, each stood and spoke, preached the gospel of Jesus Christ to their comrades, bore their testimonies, and again I say—with due respect to the various ones with whom I have associated and labored—they were among the finest sermons I ever heard. Then the time was up, and I said, "Fellows, it's time for chow. We must dismiss now, or you will miss your dinner."

With almost one voice, they cried, "We can eat grub any time—let's have a testimony meeting!" So we stayed another hour and a half while every man bore witness to the truthfulness of the restored gospel of Jesus Christ. Each one in turn, and in his own way, said, "I know that God lives. I know that the gospel is restored. I know that Joseph Smith was a prophet of God." Again I looked at my friend, and he was weeping unashamedly.

At the close of that meeting, this minister said to me, "I have been a minister for more than twenty-one years, and this has been the greatest spiritual experience of my life."
—*Hugh B. Brown*

Thank You, Lord

Even though I clutch my blanket and growl when the alarm rings each morning, thank you, Lord, that I can hear. There are those who are deaf.

Even though I huddle in my bed and put off the physical effort of rising, thank you, Lord, that I have the strength to rise. There are many who are bedfast.

Even though the first hour of my day is hectic; when socks are lost, toast is burned, and tempers are short, thank you, Lord, for my family. There are many who are lonely.

Even though our breakfast table never looks like the pictures in the magazines, and the menu is sometimes unbalanced, thank you, Lord, for the food we have. There are many who are hungry.

Even though the routine of my job is often monotonous, thank you, Lord, for the opportunity to work. There are many who have no work.

Even though I grumble and bemoan my fate from day to day, and wish my modest circumstances were not quite so modest, thank you, Lord, for the gift of life.

The Nine and the One

My name is Ruben Ben Zoro. From my dress, you may suppose that I am one of the ancient Jewish people, but I am not. I am a man of old Samaria. I come from a wealthy Samaritan family. And as I grew to man's estate, the blessings were multiplied upon me a thousand-fold when Ruth, the lovely daughter of the priest, became my wife. Two sons were granted us—two beautiful boys.

And then one day, it all came to an end. It was no great calamity, it was simply a small reddish spot upon the flesh of my hand—a spot that would not heal. I hid the spot and spoke of it to no one. But my fear I could not hide. At last because I could not sleep at night, I went to the temple on Mt. Gerizim and showed it there to my father-in-law, the priest.

He greeted me kindly, and with rejoicing, as an old man does to the father of his grandchildren. Then I showed him my hand and the small reddish spot, and a great and overwhelming sorrow came upon him. He hid his face from me.

"I shall go to Ruth," he said, "I shall tell her that unexpected business has detained you and will keep you away from home a fortnight. By then, my son, by then, we shall know."

Fourteen days I spent there, in a lonely little room—fourteen days of mourning, of wild weeping, of desperate praying, that God would spare me this dread thing. But he did not, and before the fortnight had passed, I knew, and so, too, did my father-in-law.

"Will you see Ruth again?" asked my father-in- law, his voice shaking.

"No," I said, "I shall take the path here through the vineyard, and down to the olive orchard, and none shall know of my passing."

I did not notice the flutter of a blue scarf from behind the thick trunk of one of our oldest olive trees, until it was too late. Ruth, weary of my long absence, had come with the children into the sunshine of the orchard. We shrank back, my father-in-law and I, but my son was too quick. His bright eyes caught the movement and he turned and saw us there.

With a joyous shout, "Father, Father," he came running straight for my arms. My father-in-law—oh, may he be blessed—stepped between us, caught the lad up in his arms and carried him away, bewildered now, and struggling.

And Ruth, her face lovely with joy and surprise of my coming, gathered the little one in her arms and rose to come to me. Then, seeing my face, she hesitated, and my heart died within me, as I drew the corner of my robe across my face and cried, in a voice harsh and rough with pain, "Unclean! Unclean!"

The love in her eyes changed to a dawning horror and a great fear as she stood clutching the child tightly to her breast. Then she turned and ran, stumbling along the path among the olive trees. The sound of her great sobbing came to me upon the breeze—and I was left alone—unclean!

I will not weary you with the telling of my suffering of the next few months. You all know the laws of our time concerning the leper—how we were forbidden to enter any town or approach any person, save those afflicted as we ourselves were. There were none to care for our needs; our clothing became ragged and dirty; and we ate what was thrown to us in the streets.

I wandered alone those first months. I could not endure the sight of my fellow sufferers. Then the knowledge that in a short time, a few years, I, too, would be as they—blind perhaps, bony, crippled, wretched, misery without hope. No, it was unbelievable. Surely God would lift His curse and restore me to health and my loved ones as the Prophet Elisha of long ago had healed the leprous Syrian. But I knew there was no Elisha in Samaria or in Israel either, and had not been for hundreds of years.

Then, one day, I joined a small group. There were nine of them, and when they first passed me in the field, I watched them in astonishment. They were hurrying! A leper has no need for haste.

I would have let them pass me by—I still had no desire for their wretched company—had it not been for the last among them. He was old and crippled and leaned upon a staff and, as he tried to run with the others, his staff broke beneath his weight and he fell almost at my feet crying to the others that they should wait. But they did not. In compassion for his trouble, I sprang forward and lifted the old man to his feet.

"May you be rewarded," he sobbed. "Help me—quickly—we must reach the highway! He is there, and we must see him before he passes!"

So we hurried over the hill to the highway. There was a great crowd upon the highway, and here, standing apart from the rest were the eight who had hurried so and their voices were lifted in an agonized cry, "Jesus, Master, have mercy on us! Jesus, Master, have mercy on us!"

Just as we reached them, the man on the highway lifted his hand, and as the voices about him quieted, he called to us, "Go show yourselves unto the priests." Then he turned from us and the multitude closed about him once again.

We stood and looked upon one another. "To the priests?" said one. "What have I to show the priest, save my blinded eye and my leprous skin?"

But the old man who had leaned on me said simply, "I go." And as we went, he leaned no more, but his back straightened, his limbs carried him swiftly and surely, and he went on alone. So, too, the others. They began to run and leap and shout, laughing with each other over the lifting of their curse, and hurrying off to the priests and their loved ones.

And I? I, too, felt the miracle of newborn health within me. A great gratitude for this, my undeserved blessing, welled up within me. For I had not looked for this cleansing. Of Jesus of Nazareth, I had known little and believed less, but I must know more of him. Truly God, this man must be, and I must worship him and thank him and love him.

So I hurried back to the highway. I pushed my way through the crowd, no longer was I unclean. When I reached Jesus, I fell on my face at his feet, and poured out my thanks and my devotion before him.

Jesus looked about him and asked, "Were there not ten cleansed? But where are the nine? There are none found that returned to give glory to God, save this stranger." Then gently he lifted me to my feet. He laid his hand upon me in blessing and said, "Arise, go thy way: thy faith hath made thee whole."

So, because he bade me, I went my way, and was declared clean by the priests of Mt. Gerizim. I did not go to Ruth, nor have I yet seen my growing boys, because my task must be accomplished first.

"Were there not ten cleansed?" Jesus asked. "Should not all give glory to God? But where are the nine?" I must find them!

So I have come to you, this day. Help me. Are there among you some who have received his blessings and have not bowed down in thankfulness? Are there nine, perhaps? Could one of them be you?

—*Dorothy Charlemagne*

My Thanks Comes Easily

My thanks comes easily when my future rises and my will is king, and all the world seems my estate.

My thanks comes easily such times, but today let me reflect upon those thanks I own, which I find express themselves less fluently.

Today let me remember to give thanks for not only for the sunlight, but also for those darker hours that teach me fortitude.

Let me profess today a grateful heart not merely for successes I may know, but also as truly for those failures that teach humility.

Let me express my gratitude for all those petty inner conflicts which, once resolved, bring new serenity, and for all those smaller distressing fears that have their ways of building such hope.

Let me breathe appreciation for all those poignant sights that teach me thoughtfulness, and all those wrongs that teach me fairness, and for each violated trust that leaves loyalty as its lesson.

And let me not forget today to whisper thanks for these:
>*The contempt that teaches pity,*
>*The tear that teaches joy,*
>*The pain that teaches mercy,*
>*And the loneliness that teaches love.*

Now, let me reflect upon these things I owe, and let my thanks come easily today.

Happiness

Joy is not in things, it is in us.

—Richard Wagner

❧

Happiness is neither having nor being, but becoming.

❧

Happiness is not a destination—but a method of travelling.

❧

He who enjoys doing, and enjoys what he has done, is happy.

—Goethe

❧

Much happiness is overlooked because it doesn't cost anything.

❧

The human race has one really effective weapon, and that is laughter.

—Mark Twain

❧

No one has ever injured his eyesight by looking on the bright side of things.

❧

The secret of happiness is not in doing what one likes, but in liking what one has to do.

—James M. Barrie

❧

Happiness is like jam: you can't spread even a little without getting some on yourself.

❧

Happiness doesn't come from doing what we like to do, but from liking what we have to do.

❧

Happiness is a state of mind; Lincoln once said, "We are as happy as we make up our minds to be."

❧

Happiness isn't always doing what you want to do, it's doing what you don't want to do, and being glad you did it.

~

Happiness does not come from doing easy work, but from the satisfaction of achieving a difficult task that demanded our best.

~

Happiness is much like a butterfly. The more you chase it, the more it may elude you; but if you go about other things, it will come and sit on your shoulder.

~

The master secret of happiness is to meet the challenge of each new day with the serene faith that: "All things work together for good to them that love God."

~

You can't pursue happiness and catch it. Happiness comes upon you unaware while you are helping others. The philosophy of happiness is pointedly expressed in the old Hindu proverb: "Help thy brother's boat across, and lo! thine own has reached the shore."

~

Cheerfulness

It costs nothing, but creates much. It enriches those who receive, without impoverishing those who give. It happens in a flash and the memory of it sometimes lasts forever. None are so rich they can get along without it, be it begged, borrowed, or stolen, for it benefits. Yet, it cannot be bought, begged, borrowed, nor stolen, for it is something that is of no earthly good to anyone until it is given away.

~

The Price of Happiness

You ask, "What is the price of happiness?" You will be surprised with the simplicity of the answer. The treasure house of happiness may be unlocked and remain open to those who use the following two keys:

1. Live the gospel of Jesus Christ in its purity and simplicity—not a half-hearted compliance, but an all-out devoted consecration to the great program of salvation and exaltation in an orthodox manner, and

2. Forget yourself and love your companion more than yourself.

If you do these two things, happiness will be yours in great and never-failing abundance.
—*Spencer W. Kimball*

Five Rules For a Happy Life

Many formulas have been given by many authors and psychologists for a happy life, but here are the five rules that most have agreed upon. To be truly happy an adult must be:

1. Capable of standing on his own feet, taking full responsibility for his own actions

2. Careful to maintain a regard for other persons regardless of their race or religion

3. Able to start work under his own power and not be driven to do a task

4. Mindful of the fact that happiness comes only to those who have a purpose in life

5. Able to take good fortune with a gracious smile and meet misfortune with faith in his ability to overcome it

❧

How Happy are You?

If you were arrested and charged with being a Christian, would there be enough evidence available to convict you?

Your answer will determine how happy you are.

Happiness is the object and the real purpose of our existence.

Happiness is not a product of circumstances or conditions; it does not come with the indulgence of appetites.

Happiness comes with good conduct, sweet relationships with those dear to us, understanding and sensitive relationships with all men, and a measure of confidence in the presence of God.

—*Marion D. Hanks*

❧

Two Ways to be Happy

There are two ways of being happy:

1. Diminish our wants, or

2. Augment our means.

Either will do—the result is the same. And it is for each man to decide for himself, and do that which happens to be easiest.

If you are idle or sick or poor, however hard it may be to diminish your wants, it will be harder to augment your means.

If you are active and prosperous or young or in good health, it may be easier for you to augment your means than to diminish your wants.

But, if you are wise, you will do both at the same time, young or old, rich or poor, sick or well; and, if you are very wise, you will do both in such a way as to augment the general happiness of society.

—Benjamin Franklin

Ten Rules of Happiness

1. Develop yourself by self-discipline

2. Joy comes through creation—sorrow through destruction; every living thing can grow: use the world wisely to realize soul growth

3. Do things which are hard to do

4. Entertain upbuilding thoughts; what you think about when you do not have to think shows what you really are

5. Do your best this hour and you will do better the next

6. Be true to those who trust you

7. Pray for those things such as wisdom, courage, and a kind heart

8. Give heed to God's message through inspiration; if self-indulgence, jealousy, avarice or worry have deadened your response, then pray to the Lord to wipe out these impediments

9. True friends enrich life; if you would have friends, be one

10. Faith is the foundation of all things, including happiness

—David O. McKay

Desiderata

Go placidly amid the noise and haste and remember what peace there may be in silence. As far as possible without surrender, be on good terms with all persons. Speak your truth quietly and clearly; and listen to others, even the dull and ignorant, they, too, have their story.

Avoid loud and aggressive persons, they are vexations to the spirit. If you compare yourself with others, you may become vain and bitter; for always there will be greater and lesser persons than yourself. Enjoy your achievements, as well as your plans.

Keep interested in your own career, however humble; it is a real possession in the changing fortunes of time. Exercise caution in your business affairs, for the world is full of trickery. But let this not blind you to what virtue there is: many persons strive for high ideals, and everywhere, life is full of heroism.

Be yourself. Especially, do not feign affection. Neither be cynical about love: for in the face of all aridity and disenchantment, it is perennial as the grass.

Take kindly the counsel of the years, gracefully surrendering the things of youth. Nurture strength of spirit to shield you in sudden misfortune. But do not distress yourself with imaginings. Many fears are born of fatigue and loneliness. Beyond a wholesome discipline, be gentle with yourself.

You are a child of the universe, no less than the trees and the stars; you have a right to be here. And whether or not it is clear to you, no doubt the universe is unfolding as it should.

Therefore, be at peace with God, and whatever your labors and aspirations, in the noisy confusion of life, keep peace with your soul.

With all its shame, drudgery, and broken dreams, it is still a beautiful world. Be careful. Strive to be happy.

❦

Everybody Can Enjoy a Sunset

Everybody can enjoy a glorious sunset. You would have to pay a great sum for a painting by a skilled artist. Only the wealthy can afford it, but almost any evening, we can look at a brilliant western sky, and each one of us can say, "That's mine." Too few of us appreciate what this means.

Many people have lost the proper sense of values and have sought peace and happiness in vain, in the acquisition of wealth at the expense of spiritual growth.

There are three means of achieving the happy, abundant life:

> 1. Making God the center of one's life,
>
> 2. Using the free agency given to man, and
>
> 3. Rendering service to others.

Wherein then does the secret of happiness lie? The Savior gave us the key to it when he said, "The kingdom of God is within you." The power is within men to choose the right or to choose the wrong. Happiness is not an external condition; it is a state of the spirit and an attitude of the mind.

My experience has taught me that the safe anchor of the soul and, indeed, the security and happiness in life, are founded upon a faith in God, upon a faith in the divinity of Jesus Christ and in the Gospel of peace and life, upon a faith in the efficacy of prayer, and in the power of the priesthood, as bestowed upon the Prophet Joseph Smith and through him conferred upon others, who have been and are worthy to receive this blessed possession.

Such a faith becomes as fixed and constant in its guidance as the polar star. It enables one to overcome trials and discouragements, to face life with courage, to meet disaster with fortitude, and to find true happiness on earth.

—*David O. McKay*

Beauty in a Day's Work

There was once a young man who took an unusual view of work.

He was given a job in a stone quarry, facing with chisel and hammer, the rough blocks that were to form the foundation of a temple.

"You must face ten of these blocks each day," said the foreman, "but you need not be too careful about how they look, since they are to be buried in the earth."

When the young man had finished the first day's work, he stood for a while and looked down on what he had done. The stones were roughly square, to be sure, but every one was ugly and uneven. The youth, loving beauty, seized his hammer and chisel and went to work again, smoothing the rough places and running a straight line along each edge.

Every morning and evening, the youth spent an extra hour or two adding form to blocks that he well knew were to be buried deep in the earth.

Now it happened that the chief architect came one day to the quarry. His trained eye noted the beauty in the pile of foundation stones, and he said to the youth, "I suppose you know that these stones will never be seen again by the eyes of men?"

The youth hung his head, for he thought the great man was angry with him. At last he raised his eyes and said, "The extra work has cost my master nothing. I have done it on my own time and for my own pleasure."

The next day, the architect came again and sat where he could look down into the quarry without being seen. An hour before the other men arrived, the youth came and the ring of his hammer sounded fresh and clear in the crisp dawn. The architect smiled. "Here is a labor of love in the cause of beauty," he said to himself. "The boy is of a noble nature. This day shall he drop his chisel and come with me as an apprentice in the sacred task of temple building."

Years later, when the youth of the stone quarry was fashioning a great amphitheater in a far-distant city, a young man came to him and asked, "Sir, what must I do to succeed? I am about ready to begin my life's work."

The boy of the stone quarry smiled. "There is no recipe for success," he said, "but I can open for you the door to happiness. Add beauty to your day's work, whatever that may happen to be!"

Honesty

To believe in something, and to not live it, is dishonest.
—Mahatma Ghandi

If you tell the truth, then you don't have to remember anything.
—Mark Twain

What a tangled web we weave when first we practice to deceive.

An error which has to be corrected is a heavier burden than the truth.
—Dag Hammarskjold

There are ninety-nine men who believe in honesty for every honest man.
—N. Eldon Tanner

Accuracy is the twin brother of honesty: inaccuracy is a near kin to falsehood.
—Tryon Edwards

This above all: to thine ownself be true, and it must follow as night the day, thou canst not then be false to any man.
—Shakespeare

The trouble with some folks who say there is no harm in telling a "little white lie" is that the tellers usually become progressively color blind.

Every man takes care that his neighbor shall not cheat him. But a day comes when he begins to care that he does not cheat his neighbor. Then all goes well: he has changed his market cart into a chariot of the sun.
—Ralph Waldo Emerson

To the members of the Church everywhere, I say, live honest, sincere lives! Be honest with yourselves, honest with your brethren, honest with your families, honest with those with whom you deal—always honest. The very foundation of all character rests upon the principles of honesty and sincerity.

—*David O. McKay*

Bread and Butter

On the points of good fellowship, a baker and a farmer agreed to exchange goods. The baker would receive from the farmer some butter, and the farmer would receive from the baker some bread.

As time passed, the baker began weighing the butter he had received from the farmer, and noticed that each batch weighed a little less than the previous. The baker let the matter go for some time, then decided to take the farmer to court.

The farmer appeared without hesitancy. When asked by the jury why he had been shorting the butter, he replied, "I weighed my butter by balancing it on the scale with the baker's loaf of bread."

The Little Things

I would like you to come with me to the terrestrial kingdom. Because I'm addressing a group of Mormons, the terrestrial kingdom is probably the best place to tour, since most of you will end up there. You don't believe me! Well, come and see! I want you to meet Jim, a fine man, kind, and pleasant to talk to.

"Jim, I thought you'd be interested in meeting these people. They're Mormons. They've come to hear your story."

"My name is Jim. I was born into a wonderful LDS home. My parents were good Mormons. They lived their religion, and did everything in their power to raise me as a good Mormon. I wasn't too bad. I lived the Word of Wisdom to the best of my ability. I paid a full tithe. I attended all of my Church meetings. Why, I even got up at six every morning to go to seminary. I didn't swear or go with the wrong crowd. I did my best to honor my parents.

"When I was twenty I was called to serve a mission. You should have seen my parents. Boy, were they proud. I worked hard on my mission. I really loved it.

"When I returned home, I became interested in genealogy and began to work very hard at that. And then a wonderful thing happened: I was married in the temple to the most beautiful girl in the world.

"I continued to live the gospel as I always had, and decided I was doing pretty well. I had always been taught to strive for the Celestial Kingdom, and I figured that I was pretty well on the way.

"Most of you are probably thinking, 'He should have made it.'

"Well, after the Lord had appraised my life, he came to me with tears in his eyes and said, 'Jim, I'm sorry, but my kingdom is for completely honest people!'

"I couldn't believe my ears. I was not to be one of the chosen few. But I wouldn't rob a bank or steal a car. I am honest, I thought to myself. Honest, except for:

> Those days in school when I used to look on other people's test papers

> All those pennies and nickels of incorrect change I received and never returned

> My income tax returns—those slight and seemingly unimportant errors

> Being honest with myself

> Those times I didn't try my hardest in my Church assignments

> The time I wasted time watching TV when I could have been studying the scriptures or visiting the sick

"Oh, I had really cheated myself. I could see that now. I was honest—up to a point—that point of division between complete honesty and average honesty; that point of division between God's home and my present one; that point of division between my family's final resting place and mine.

"You know, my kind of dishonesty destroyed our civilization. All those little acts of dishonesty, caused us to rot, to decay, and finally to crumble.

"Bless those few Mormons who understand and are honest in everything. I wish I had been."

—*John Jay Holmes*

Did You Touch?

Today, I saw truth. For a moment, I lived and breathed in the great presence of truth and felt its sweetness plunge deep into my soul.

I am a coach in a junior high school. I work with 500 boys each day. This has been my occupation for more than 20 years. I enjoy it.

Traditionally, I am supposed to be rugged, tough, crusty; yes, even a little severe at times—and yet, underneath this exterior, feeling and understanding must exist if the job is to be done.

Today was test day in climbing the rope. We climb from a standing start to a point 15 feet high. One of my tasks these past few weeks has been to train and teach the boys to negotiate this distance in as few seconds as possible.

The school record for the event is 2.1 seconds, which has stood for three years. Today, this record was broken. But this is not my story. How this record was broken is the important thing here, as it so often is in many an endeavor in this life.

For three years, Bobby Polacio, a 14 1/2-year-old ninth grade Mexican boy, has trained and pointed and, I suspect, dreamed of breaking this record. It has been his consuming passion; it seemed his whole life depended upon owning this record.

In his first of three attempts, Bobby climbed the rope in 2.1 seconds, tying the record. On the second try, the watch stopped at 2.0 seconds flat—a record! But as he descended the rope and the entire class gathered around to check the watch, I knew I must ask Bobby a question. There was a slight doubt in my mind as to whether or not the board at the 15-foot height had been touched. If he missed, it was so very, very close—not more than a fraction of an inch—and only Bobby knew this answer.

As he walked toward me, expressionless, I asked, "Bobby, did you touch?" If he had said, "Yes", the record he had dreamed of since he was a skinny seventh-grader, and had worked for almost daily, would be broken, and he knew I would trust his word.

With the class already cheering him for his performance, the slim, brown-skinned boy shook his head negatively. And in this simple gesture, I witnessed a moment of greatness.

Coaches do not cry. Only babies cry, they say. But as I reached out to pat this boy on the shoulder, there was a small drop of water in each eye. And it was with effort through a tight throat that I told the class, "This boy has not set a record in the rope climb. No, he has set a much finer record for you and everyone to strive for. He has told the simple truth."

I turned to Bobby and said, "Bobby, I'm proud of you. You've just set a record many athletes never attain. Now, in your last try, I want you to jump a few inches higher on the takeoff. You're going to break this record."

After the other boys had finished their next turns, and Bobby came up to the top for his try, a strange stillness came over the gymnasium. Fifty boys and one coach were breathlessly set to help boost Bobby Polacio to a new record. He climbed the rope in 1.9 seconds! A school record, a city record, and perhaps close to a national record for a junior high school boy.

When the bell rang and I walked away, now misty-eyed, from this group of boys, I was thinking, "Bobby, little brown skin, with your clear, bright dark eyes and your straight, trim, lithe body—Bobby, at 14, you are a better man than I. Thank you for climbing so very, very high today."

—*Boys' Life magazine*

My Word of Honor

My friends, I have been asked what I mean by "word of honor". I will tell you. Place me behind prison walls—walls of stone ever so high, ever so thick, reaching ever so far into the ground—and there is a possibility that, in some way or another, I may be able to escape.

But stand me on the floor, draw a chalk line around me, and have me give my word of honor never to cross it.

Can I get out of that circle? No, never! I'd die first!

—*Kurl G. Mueser*

Human Relations

He who slings mud, loses ground.

—William Thackeray

To get nowhere, follow the crowd.

Three may keep a secret, if two are dead.

The greatest fault is to be conscious of none.

—Thomas Carlyle

Don't be down on that which you're not up on.

—Harold B. Lee

If you want to be interesting, become interested.

Apology is often a good way to have the last word.

He who is self-centered travels in very small circles.

—T. Kirkwood Collins

One of the hard things about business is minding your own.

He who accepts the help of a child is helping a child to grow.

Cooperation is doing with a smile what you have to do anyway.

The only way to compel men to speak good of you is to do good.

—Voltaire

Tact is the ability to close your mouth before someone else wants to.

✎

One cannot deny the humanity of another without diminishing his own.

✎

Get someone else to blow your horn and the sound will carry twice as far.
—*Will Rogers*

✎

A man who trims himself to suit everyone will soon whittle himself away.
—*Charles Schwab*

✎

Before you flare up at anyone's faults, take time to count ten—ten of your own.

✎

Social tact is making your guests feel at home, even though you wish they were.

✎

Popularity comes from pleasing people, but greatness comes from pleasing God.

✎

He who cannot forgive others breaks the bridge over which he himself must pass.

✎

The world is a looking glass, and gives back to every man the reflection of his own face.
—*William Thackeray*

✎

Some people are easily entertained: all you have to do is sit down and listen to them.

✎

We easily forget that the way people act toward us may be the result of our own behavior.

✎

If we could take out of our lives what others have put into it, we wouldn't have much left.

✎

There would be fewer arguments if we tried to determine what's right instead of who's right.

❧

God does notice and watch over us, but it is usually through another person that he meets our needs.

—*Spencer W. Kimball*

❧

Speech is to thought what gold is to diamonds: it is needed as a setting, but only a little is required.

—*Voltaire*

❧

When you point the finger of scorn, look at your hand: you will find three fingers pointing back at you.

—*Persian proverb*

❧

Nothing is easier than fault-finding: no talent, no self-denial, no brains, no character are required to set up in the grumbling business.

❧

The art of acceptance is the art of making someone who has done you a small favor wish that he might have done you a greater one.

—*Russell Lynes*

❧

The mass of men worry themselves into nameless graves, while here and there a great unselfish soul forgets himself into immortality.

—*Ralph Waldo Emerson*

❧

The most important part of leadership is to pick good men to lead, and have self-restraint enough not to meddle in what they are doing.

—*Theodore Roosevelt*

❧

Quarrel not at all; no man resolved to make the most of himself can spare time for personal contention; better to give your path to a dog than to be bitten by him.

—*Abraham Lincoln*

❧

Every human being is trying to say something to others, trying to cry out, "I am alive, notice me, speak to me, listen to me, confirm for me that I am important, that I matter."
—*Marion D. Hanks*

If you treat a man as he is, he will remain as he is, but if you treat him as if he were what he ought to be, and could be, then he will become what he ought to be, and should be.
—*Goethe*

Every now and then you run across radiantly attractive people and you're delighted to find they adore you, till you realize that they adore just about everybody—and that's what's made them radiantly attractive.
—*Mignon McLaughlin*

For Whom the Bell Tolls

No man is an island, entire of itself; every man is a piece of the continent, a part of the main. If a clod be washed away by the sea, Europe is the less, as well as if a promontory were, as well as if a manor of thy friend's or of thine own were; any man's death diminishes me, because I am involved in mankind, and therefore never send to know for whom the bell tolls; it tolls for thee.
—*John Donne*

Silence Those Jets

Personal and corporate honesty often pays off in dramatic ways. Donald Douglas, for example, built such a reputation for his aircraft company, and he worked to preserve it.

There was the time when Douglas was competing with Boeing to sell Eastern Airlines its first big jets. Eddie Rickenbacker, who headed Eastern, is said to have told Douglas that his specifications and claims for the DC-8 were close to his competition on everything but noise suppression. He then gave Douglas one last chance to out-promise Boeing on this feature.

After consulting his engineers, Douglas reported back that he did not feel he could make that promise. Rickenbacker replied, "I know you can't. I wanted to see if you were still honest. You just got yourself an order for $135 million. Now go home and learn how to silence those jets!"

The Price of Arrogance

In the year 1884, a young man from America died while visiting Europe. His middle-aged, grieving parents returned with the body.

They were heartbroken: they had loved their son very much. After the funeral, they began to discuss some kind of memorial to him—not a tombstone or an ornate grave, but a living memorial, something that would help other young men like their son.

After considering many alternatives, they decided that something in the field of education would be most appropriate. It would be the kind of memorial that would go on year after year, helping educate young people. That would be the best kind of tribute to their son's memory.

They arranged an appointment with Charles Eliot, then president of Harvard University, and he received the quite ordinary, unpretentious couple in his offices, asking what he could do for them.

They apologized for taking up his valuable time, then told him about the death of their son. They explained that they wanted to establish a memorial to him—something that would help other young men like their son get an education.

Eliot looked at the unprepossessing couple with some impatience and a certain suggestion of aristocratic disdain. "Perhaps you have in mind a scholarship," he said crisply.

"No," said the woman, her mild manner belying the quickness and sharpness of her mind. "We were thinking of something more substantial than that—perhaps a new building..."

"I must explain to you," said Eliot, with what seemed a patronizing air, "that what you suggest costs a great deal of money. Buildings are very expensive." Obviously, Eliot did not think from their appearance that they were capable of that kind of donation.

There was a pause, then the woman rose slowly and said, "Mr. Eliot, what has this entire university cost?"

Eliot shrugged and muttered a figure in the millions.

"Oh, we can do better than that," said the woman, who had now made up her mind. "Come, dear," she motioned to her husband, "I have an idea." And they left.

The following year President Eliot of Harvard learned that the plain, unpretentious couple had contributed $26 million for a memorial to their son: Leland Stanford, Jr. University.

The Face

I saw him on the street only this morning. Already late for work, I cut through Skid Row to my 8:23 commuter. It was a miserable morning, the sky a musky gray made of factory smoke and soot and dirty rain. Even my new coat with its fashionable collar turned up against my face could not hide the dingy alleys covered with broken glass. Scrawny cats pawed through the garbage cans that lined the narrow passageways between the bars

I berated myself for having tried to save time by the shortcut. Lowering my head deeper into my collar, I hurried around the corner, running full tilt into a weaving, lurching man. He fell heavily to the sidewalk in front of me. I stared with horrified fascination at him. His clothes were filthy, and he reeked of garlic and liquor. His unshaven face was clean only where the rain ran down it in tiny streams. His uncombed hair was as black as the eyes that stared fully at me, devoid of any expression. For a second that stretched into an aeon, I stood there, frozen. Then, as he softly called my name, I turned and ran and ran and ran until I saw the familiar station, the people I knew, and the signs and sounds of sanity. But the soft call of my name still sounded in my ears.

Sinking exhausted into my train chair, I closed my eyes to shut out what I had seen. The derelict on Skid Row was not unknown. It was the face of Jim, a boy I had known years earlier in grammar school in the small town where I had been reared.

It was a gossipy little town, closely knit by a common religion and the stand-offish attitude shown those who violated any of its codes. Jim's mother was an alcoholic, and the neighbors could hear his father and mother cursing long into the night. As this news reached the ears of the townspeople, more and more of Jim's playmates were forbidden to play with him. My folks were more lenient and, as the years went by, he came often to our home.

When his father committed suicide while Jim was still in junior high school, the last of his friends drifted away, and he became more lonely, more resentful of society. To fight back at the rules that had excluded him from other groups, he began to cut school, and the boys he associated with were no strangers to police records. Finally, just like all the rest, I turned my back on him.

By leaving him in the alley, I was turning my back on him again. Our town gave him a start toward Skid Row, but I was pushing him the last mile by taking away his last hope of acceptance.

I turned and went back to him. I tried to give him my understanding, my help, and my confidence.

Many years later, I received the following letter from him:

> *Dear Susan:*
>
> *I don't know whether you remember me or not, but I remember you and I always will. You see, you are the one person I will never forget. It has been many years since you used to play badminton with me, and hike up the mountains, and listen to my troubles. It was you who, when I went with you for the first time and tried to get*

fresh, taught me that life is more than sex. You taught me to understand the beauty of a rose. You stimulated me to think about the meaning of life. You were the one person who had faith in me. Three years ago, I got married, and my wife and I now have a beautiful little daughter. With my wife's full approval, we are going to name her after you.

Always,

Jim

※

Shanna's Gift

Robin and Shanna were almost the same age. They lived on the same street and, as little girls, had often played together. But, as they grew, their interests became quite varied, and by the time they reached high school, they had little in common.

Shanna had been born with a birth defect that caused her to walk with difficulty and have poor control over some muscular reflexes. Robin had enjoyed being with Shanna when they were younger, but now she had a new group of friends who would have little to do with Shanna—and, besides, they were interested in things Shanna would never be able to participate in, such as sports and gymnastics.

Robin knew that she was intentionally leaving Shanna out of her life, and felt somewhat guilty over it—because she knew that Shanna still very much wanted to be her friend. She would offer small favors and often ask Robin to walk to school with her, but Robin would decline, offering some excuse or another, telling herself that she didn't want to get up early enough, since Shanna's disabilities caused her to walk so slowly. But deep down, she knew that the real reason was that she was embarrassed to be seen with her.

You see, Shanna was clumsy, and when the girls at school saw her struggle with some obstacle, they giggled and made fun. They didn't mean any harm, and Shanna never noticed—at least, Robin didn't think Shanna noticed. Although Robin never made fun of her, and she really did like her, she told herself that she was more like the other girls and had more in common with them—so she went on leaving Shanna out of her life.

Then one night Robin had a dream.

She saw herself in a beautiful place, in a time she imagined to be before this life. She was a little girl again, surrounded by what seemed to be happiness and love. But she was not alone. She had a playmate with shiny golden hair and deep blue eyes that sparkled when she smiled. They were inseparable, and did everything together. They ran and danced and played little girl games, and Robin marveled at how beautiful and graceful her friend was.

Days joyfully passed, and a time grew near when Robin was going to have to say goodbye—to take her step into this life. Her friend walked with her as far as she dared, and with big tears in her eyes, stood nearby to watch the event unfold.

Robin approached with anticipation and hesitation, and was told at the threshold of her new life on earth that her tiny little body had been injured in some way, and that it was necessary for her to meet a special life-long challenge. Tears flooded her eyes, as she stood, trembling and fearful of what was to come. Her trance-like state was gently interrupted by a familiar and loving touch, and she turned to see her little friend step forward to take her place.

Robin had to be restrained as she called to her friend, and she wept as she saw her friend wave a final, loving goodbye from what seemed to be a long way away. But she could still see the unmistakable evidence of a walk that suddenly became painfully familiar to her. Robin fell sobbing to the ground.

Robin awoke with a start, looked at her clock and, with tears streaming down her face, dressed and left the house without stopping to eat. She knew Shanna would have a head start, but she knew she had to find her. She hurried on with a firm resolve in her aching heart. As she turned the corner, she saw Shanna up ahead. As Robin approached, Shanna dropped an armful of papers on the sidewalk. She was awkwardly bending down to retrieve them when Robin reached her. She knelt to help, and met a startled but pleased expression on Shanna's face.

Robin asked if she could walk with her; Shanna, still a little surprised, said, "Sure!" As they walked on together, Robin thought she detected a familiar sparkle in Shanna's deep blue eyes.

—*Susan Empey*

❧

What Kind of People Live Here?

The story is told of a philosopher who stood at the gate of an ancient city greeting travelers who wished to enter. One of them questioned him, "What kind of people live here?"

The philosopher met the question with a counter question, "What kind of people lived in the city from whence you came?"

"Oh, they were very bad people," answered the traveler, "cruel, deceitful, and devil-worshipping."

"That's the kind of people who live in this city," declared the philosopher.

Another traveler came by and asked the same question, to which the philosopher replied, "What kind of people lived in the city from whence you came?"

"Oh, they were very good people," answered the second traveler, "kind, and truthful, and God-loving."

"That's the kind of people who live in this city," declared the philosopher.

—*Dr. David Goodman*

Do-It-Yourself World

I had to live a long time before I found the courage to admit to myself that we—all of us—make our own world.

I take frequent trips to New York and I had decided that all New York cab drivers were impatient and bad-tempered. Hotel and railroad employees were the same. I found them all difficult to get along with.

Then one day in New York, I came upon the words from Thackeray quoted above. The very same day, when a cabby and I were snarling at each other, this thought occurred to me: Could this whole situation be the result of my own outlook?

I began to live Thackeray's idea. On my next trip east, I encountered not one unpleasant taxi driver, elevator operator, or railroad employee. Had New York changed, or had I? The answer was clear.

To abandon excuses for one's own shortcomings is like journeying to a distant land where everything is new and strange. Here you have to assume the responsibility for failures or difficulties yourself.

Of course, outside pressures do influence our lives, but they don't control them. To assume they do is sheer evasion.

Since that day in New York, I've come to believe that this idea is the basis of all human relationships. The quickest way to correct the other fellow's attitude is to correct our own. Try it. It works. And it adds immeasurably to the fun of meeting people and being alive.

—*King Vidor*

One of the Best

A few months after moving to a small town, a woman complained to a neighbor about the poor service at the local drug store. She hoped the new acquaintance would repeat her complaint to the owner.

Next time she went to the drug store, the druggist greeted her with a big smile, told her how happy he was to see her again, said he hoped she liked their town, and to please let him know if there was anything he could do to help her and her husband get settled. He then filled her order promptly and efficiently.

Later the woman reported the miraculous change to her friend. "I suppose you told the druggist how poor I thought his service was?" she asked.

"Well, no," the woman said. "In fact—and I hope you don't mind—I told him you were amazed at the way he had built up this small-town drug store, and that you thought it was one of the best-run drug stores you'd ever shopped."

The Ten Commandments of Human Relations

1. Speak to people: there is nothing as nice as a cheerful greeting

2. Call people by name: the sweetest music to anyone's ears is the sound of his own name

3. Have humility: there is something to be learned from every living thing

4. Be friendly: if you would have a friend, be one

5. Be cordial: speak and act as if everything you do is a pleasure

6. Be sincerely interested in others: you can like almost everybody if you try

7. Be generous with praise, cautious with criticism

8. Give your word, then keep it

9. Be considerate of the feelings of others

10. Be alert to give service: what counts most in life is what we do for others

Acting vs. Reacting

I walked with my friend, a Quaker, to the newsstand the other night, and he bought a paper, thanking the newsie politely. The newsie didn't even acknowledge it.

"A sullen fellow, isn't he?" I commented.

"Oh, he's that way every night," shrugged my friend.

"Then why do you continue to be so polite to him?" I asked.

"Why should I let him decide how I act?"

As I thought about this incident later, it occurred to me that the important word was "act". My friend acts toward people; most of us react toward them. His was a sense of inner balance which is lacking in most of us. He knows who he is, what he stands for, how he should behave. He refuses to return incivility with incivility, because then he would not be in command of his own conduct.

Nobody is unhappier than the perpetual reactor. His center of emotional gravity is not rooted within himself, where it belongs, but in the world outside him. His temperature is always being raised or lowered by the social climate around him, and he is a mere creature at the mercy of these elements.

Serenity cannot be achieved until we become the masters of our own actions and attitudes. To let another determine whether we shall be rude or gracious, elated or depressed, is to relinquish control over our own personalities, which is ultimately all we possess. The only true possession is self-possession.

—*Sydney J. Harris*

The Humblest and Lowliest

The principal of a preparatory school received a message from a lawyer requesting him to call.

When the principal arrived, the lawyer announced that he had a four-year college scholarship to bestow on a deserving boy, "I have concluded to let you decide which of your boys is most deserving."

"That is a difficult decision to make," replied the principal, thoughtfully. "Two of my boys will complete their courses this year. Both desire a college education. Neither is able to afford it without assistance. They are so nearly equal that I cannot decide which is the more deserving."

"How do they compare in deportment?" asked the lawyer.

"One boy scrupulously observes the rules as well as the other," came the reply.

"Well," decided the lawyer, "if at the end of the year one boy has not surpassed the other, then send them to me and I will choose between them."

As before, following finals, the boys remained equal, and were directed to the lawyer's office, with no further information.

The lawyer was impressed with the two intelligent, well-bred boys, and began to wonder how he would choose between them.

Just then, the door opened and an elderly woman of peculiar appearance entered. She was well known in that office as being of unsettled mind, possessed with the idea that she had been deprived of a large fortune that was justly hers. As a consequence, she was in the habit of visiting the lawyer, carrying in her hands a package of papers which she wished examined. She was always received with respect, and dismissed with kindly words.

Seeing that the lawyer was already occupied, she seated herself to wait. Unfortunately, the chair she selected was broken, resulting in a fall and a scattering of papers. The lawyer looked quickly at the boys before removing himself a distance to observe their behavior.

Charles, after an amused survey of the fall, turned aside to hide a laugh he could not control. Henry, on the other hand, sprang to the woman's side and lifted her to her feet, then carefully gathered up her papers, and politely handed them to her. Her profuse and rambling thanks served only to increase Charles' amusement.

After the woman told her customary story to the lawyer, to which he listened with great intent, he then escorted her to the door, and she departed.

Then he turned to the boys, expressed pleasure at making their acquaintances, and dismissed them.

The next day, the principal was informed of the incident and told that the scholarship would be given to Henry, remarking, "No one so well deserves to be fitted for a position of honor and influence as he who feels it is his duty to help the humblest and lowliest."

The Art of Getting Along

Sooner or later, a man, if he is wise, discovers that life is a mixture of good days and bad, victory and defeat, give and take.

He learns that it doesn't pay to be too sensitive of a soul, that he should let some things go over his head like water off a duck's back.

He learns that he who loses his temper usually loses out.

He learns that all men have burnt toast for breakfast now and then, and that he shouldn't take the other fellow's grouch too seriously.

He learns that carrying a chip on his shoulder is the easiest way to get into a fight.

He learns that the quickest way to become unpopular is to carry tales and gossip about others.

He learns that buck-passing always turns out to be a boomerang, and that it never pays.

He comes to realize that the business could run along perfectly well without him.

He learns that it doesn't matter so much who gets the credit so long as the business benefits.

He learns that even the janitor is human and that it does no harm to smile and say "Good morning," even if it's raining.

He learns that most of the other fellows are as ambitious as he is, that they have brains as good or better, and that hard work, not cleverness, is the secret of success.

He learns to sympathize with the youngster coming into the business, because he remembers how bewildered he was when he first started out.

He learns not to worry when he loses an order, because experience has shown that if he always gives his best, his average will break pretty well.

He learns that no man ever got to first base alone, and that it is only through cooperative effort that we move on to better things.

He learns that bosses are no monsters, trying to get the last ounce of work out of him for the least amount of pay, but that they are usually pretty good fellows who have succeeded through hard work and who want to do the right thing.

He learns that folks are not any harder to get along with in one place than in another, and that the "getting along" depends about ninety-eight percent on his own behavior.

—*Wilfred Peterson*

Kindness

Life is not so short but what there is always time for courtesy.
—*Emerson*

Kindness is the golden charm by which society is bound together.

Kindness is like fresh-fallen snow: it makes beautiful everything that it covers.

There is no outward sign of true courtesy that does not rest on a deep moral foundation.
—*Goethe*

If you would do a kindness, it is not wise to wait: you never know how quickly it's going to be too late.

If you want your neighbor to see what the Christ spirit will do for him, let him see what it has done for you.
—*Henry Ward Beecher*

We should be as courteous to a man as we are to a picture, to which we are willing to give the advantage of the best light.
—*Emerson*

The whole of heraldry and chivalry is in courtesy: a man of fine manners shall pronounce your name with all the ornament that titles of nobility could add.
—*Emerson*

A small child was asked to describe loving kindness. He said, "If I'm hungry and my mother gives me some bread and butter, that's kindness. But if she puts lots of jam on it, that's loving kindness!"

I shall pass through this world but once: if, therefore, there be any kindness I can show, or any good thing I can say, it would be now; let me not defer it or neglect it, for I shall not pass this way again.

—*Etienne de Grellet*

The Reverend Henry Ward Beecher, on a very cold day, stopped to buy a newspaper from a ragged youngster who stood shivering on a corner. "Poor little fellow," he said, "aren't you cold standing here?" The boy looked up with a smile and said, "I was sir— before you passed."

You can't get more than you give, anymore than you can take a pint to a well and bring back a gallon. You can't give frowns and get back smiles; you can't give a loud, angry voice and receive gentleness in return. By the same token, you can't plant a kind word, a thoughtful deed, a generous gift, and not reap more of the same from someone, somewhere, sometime.

Surprise Shoes

A university student took a walk one day with his professor, who was popular among the students because of his kindnesses toward them.

While they were walking together, they saw a pair of old shoes lying in their path. The shoes belonged to a poor man employed in a field nearby, a man nearly finished with his day's work.

The student turned to the professor, and said, "Let's play a trick on that man. We'll hide his shoes and conceal ourselves behind those bushes, and watch to see his perplexity when he can't find them!"

"No," said the professor, "we must never amuse ourselves at the expense of the poor. But you are rich, and may give yourself a greater pleasure than amusement by means of this poor man. Put a dollar in each shoe, and then we will hide."

The student did so, and then hid with the professor in the bushes nearby, from a point where they could easily watch the laborer.

The man soon finished his work, and came across the field to the path where he had left his coat and shoes. While he put on his coat, he slipped one foot into a shoe—but, feeling something, stooped down and found the dollar.

Astonishment and wonder swept across his face. He gazed at the dollar, turned it over in his hand, and looked at it again and again. He looked around him, but could see no one. Finally, he put the money in his pocket, and proceeded to put on his other shoe. How great was his surprise when he found the other dollar!

His feelings overcame him. He fell upon his knees, and there uttered aloud a fervent thanksgiving, in which he spoke of his wife—sick and helpless—and his children—without bread—whom this timely bounty from an unknown hand would save from suffering.

The young student stood there, deeply affected, and tears filled his eyes. "Now," said the professor, "aren't you much more pleased than if you had played your intended trick?"

"You have taught me a lesson I shall never forget," answered the youth, "for I know now how much more blessed it is to give than to receive."

～

Information Please

When I was quite young, my family had one of the first telephones in our neighborhood. I remember well the polished wood case fastened to the wall. The shiny receiver hung on the side of the box. I was too little to reach it, but used to listen with fascination when my mother used it.

Then I discovered that somewhere inside the wonderful device lived an amazing person, whose name was Information Please, and there was nothing she didn't know. Information Please could supply anybody's phone number and the correct time.

My first personal experience with this genie-in-the-bottle came one day while my mother was visiting a neighbor.

Amusing myself at the tool bench in the basement, I whacked my finger with a hammer. The pain was terrible, but there didn't seem to be any reason to cry because there was no one home to give sympathy.

I walked around the house sucking my throbbing finger, finally arriving at the telephone! Quickly I ran for the footstool and dragged it to the phone. Climbing up, I unhooked the receiver and held it to my ear. "Information Please," I said into the mouthpiece.

A click or two and a small clear voice spoke into my ear, "Information."

"I hurt my finger," I wailed into the phone. The tears came readily now that I had an audience.

"Isn't your mother home?" came the question.

"Nobody's home but me," I blubbered.

"Are you bleeding?"

"No," I replied. "I hit my finger with the hammer and it hurts."

"Can you open your icebox?" she asked. I could. "Then chip off a little piece of ice and hold it to your finger."

After that I called Information Please for everything. I asked for help with my geography and she told me where Philadelphia was. She helped me with my math. She told me my pet chipmunk would eat fruits and nuts.

And then there was the time that Petey, our pet canary died. I called Information Please and told her the sad story. She listened, then said the usual things grown-ups say to soothe a child. But I was unconsoled. Why is it that birds should sing so beautifully and bring such joy, only to end up as a heap of feathers, feet up on the bottom of a cage?

She must have sensed my deep concern, for she said quietly, "Paul, always remember that there are other worlds to sing in."

Somehow I felt better.

One time I called to ask her how to spell "fix".

All this took place in a small town in the Pacific Northwest. Then when I was nine years old, we moved across the country to Boston.

I missed my friend very much. Information Please belonged in that old wooden box on the wall back home. For some reason, I never thought of trying the shiny new phone that sat on the hall table in our new home.

Yet, as I grew into my teens, the memories of those childhood conversations never really left me. Often, in moments of doubt and perplexity, I would recall the serene sense of security I had back then. I appreciated now how patient, understanding, and kind she was to have spent her time on a little boy.

A few years later, on my way west to college, my plane put down in Seattle. I had about half an hour or so between planes, and I spent 15 minutes of it on the phone with my sister, who lived there now.

Then without thinking what I was doing, I dialed my hometown operator and said, "Information Please."

Miraculously, I heard again the small, clear voice I knew so well, "Information."

I hadn't planned this, but I heard myself saying, "Could you please tell me how to spell fix."

There was a long pause. Then came the soft spoken answer, "I guess that your finger must have healed by now."

I laughed, "So it's really still you," I said. "I wonder if you have any idea how much you meant to me during that time."

"I wonder," she said, "if you know how much your calls meant to me. I never had any children, and I used to look forward to your calls."

I told her how often I had thought of her over the years and asked if I could call her again when I came back to visit my sister.

"Please do. Just ask for Sally."

Just three months later, I was back in Seattle.

A different voice answered Information and I asked for Sally.

"Are you a friend?"

"Yes, a very old friend."

"Then I'm sorry to have to tell you: Sally has been working part-time for the past few years because she was sick. She died five weeks ago."

Before I could hang up, she said, "Wait a minute. Did you say your name was Paul?"

"Yes."

"Well, Sally left a message for you. She wrote it down. Here it is. I'll read it, "Tell him there are other worlds to sing in. He'll know what I mean.""

I thanked her and hung up.

I knew what she meant.

Life

When life falls into a rut, decay begins.

—Arthur Stillwell

❧

Knowledge comes, but wisdom lingers.

—Tennyson

❧

Life is the childhood of our immortality.

—Goethe

❧

Life is for: learning, improving, repenting, serving.

❧

Everything has its beauty, but not everyone sees it.

—Confucius

❧

Making a living is a necessity; making a life is a duty.

❧

Nothing in life is to be feared: it is only to be understood.

—Marie Curie

❧

Begin at once to live, and count each day as a separate life.

—Seneca

❧

It is better to light one small candle than to curse the darkness.

—Confucius

❧

Do not put off living today because this is the only time we have.

❧

He who thinks wisdom is greater than virtue will lose his wisdom.

—Hebrew proverb

❧

The great use of life is to spend it for something that will outlast it.
—*William James*

❧

Life is 10 percent what you make it, and 90 percent how you take it.

❧

As the buds come forth in the spring, so must the petals drop in the fall.

❧

Don't be a hold out, go all out; do this, and life will not hold out on you.

❧

Endeavor to so live that when you die even the undertaker will be sorry.
—*Mark Twain*

❧

What do we live for, if not to make the world less difficult for each other.
—*George Eliot*

❧

Life is like an onion: you peel it off one layer at a time, and sometimes you weep.

❧

Experience keeps a dear school, but fools will learn in no other, and scarce in that.

❧

The Plan of Salvation is designed to make of this earth, a heaven; and of man, a God.
—*Bruce R. McConkie*

❧

Fifty years ago, people finished a day's work and needed rest; today, they need exercise.

❧

It has taken me all my life to understand that it is not necessary to understand everything.

❧

To be what we are, and to become what we are capable of becoming, is the only end of life.

❧

Fear not that your life shall come to an end, fear rather that it shall never have a beginning.

—Newman

&

Before you're baptized, Heavenly Father writes in pencil; after you're baptized, he writes in pen.

&

To one man, the world is barren, dull and superficial; to another, rich, interesting, and full of meaning.

—Arthur Schopenhauer

&

Life is a grindstone; whether it grinds you down or polishes you up, depends on what you are made of.

&

Life is like a one-way street: you are not coming back, and a lot of people on it are going in the wrong direction.

&

A man would do nothing, if he waited until he could do it so well, that no one would find fault with what he had done.

&

Men occasionally stumble over the truth, but most of them pick themselves up and hurry off as if nothing had happened.

—Sir Winston Churchill

&

There are three kinds of people: those who make things happen, those who watch things happen, and those who have no idea what has happened.

&

He who allows his day to pass by without practicing generosity, and enjoying life's pleasures is like a blacksmith's bellows—he breathes but does not live.

—Ancient Sanskrit proverb

&

The greatest blessing one can enjoy in life is to go to bed at night with a clear conscience, knowing that he has lived that day in harmony with the teachings of the Savior, and has accomplished the work assigned him to do.

—N. Eldon Tanner

❧

It is something to be able to paint a particular picture, or to carve a statue, and so to make a few objects beautiful; but it is far more glorious to carve and paint the very atmosphere through which we look—to affect the quality of the day—that is the highest of arts.

—Henry David Thoreau

❧

Finish every day and be done with it. You have done what you could. Some blunders and absurdities have crept in; forget them as soon as you can. Tomorrow is a new day; you will begin it well and serenely, and with too high a spirit to be encumbered by your old nonsense.

—Emerson

❧

Only Two Things

There are only two things to worry about: either you are well, or you are sick.

If you are well, then there is nothing to worry about; if you are sick, then there are only two things to worry about: either you will get well, or you will die.

If you get well, then there is nothing to worry about; if you die, then there are only two things to worry about: either you will go to heaven, or you will go to hell.

If you go to heaven, then there is nothing to worry about; if you go to hell, then you will be so darn busy shaking hands with all your friends that you won't have time to worry.

❧

A Life Worth Living

It is a wonderful thing to realize in one's inner-most heart that each individual is here in this world for a purpose—that is, to use his own highest abilities and endeavors toward making this world a happier and better place, as its Creator planned.

Those who live this philosophy, and have cultivated their capacity to see and enjoy the finest in life, have found the life worth living.

—Esther Baldwin York

Footprints

A man died and went to heaven where he and the Lord were reviewing his life.

The man looked back along his footprints in life and noticed that as he went through the plains, meadows, easy places, and straight places, there were two sets of prints, but in the deserts, mountains, and rocky places, there was only one set.

He turned to the Lord and asked, "When I was traveling over the easy places, I noticed you walked with me, but when it was hard, I walked alone?"

The Lord replied, "When it was hard, I carried you."

Radiation and Absorption

Into the hands of every individual is given a marvelous power for good or for evil, the silent, unconscious, unseen influence of his life.

This is simply the constant radiation of what a man really is, not what he pretends to be.

Every man, by his mere living, is radiating sympathy, or sorrow, or morbidity, or cynicism, or happiness, or hope, or any of a hundred other qualities.

Life is a state of constant radiation and absorption; to exist is to radiate; to exist is to be the recipient of radiation.

—*William George Jordan*

Unconscious Influence

The only responsibility a man cannot evade in this life is the one he thinks of least, his personal influence.

Man's conscious influence, when he is on dress parade, when he is posing to impress those around him is woefully small.

But his unconscious influence, the silent, subtle radiation of his personality, the effect of his words and acts, the trifles he never considers, is tremendous.

Every moment of life he is changing, to a degree, the life of the whole world. Every man has an atmosphere which is affecting every other. So silent and unconsciously is the influence working, that man may forget it exists.

Two Little Buckets

There were two buckets sitting on the edge of a well. One turned to the other with mouth drooping and said, "All I do is go down and come up and go down and come up all day long. No matter how many times I go down and come up, I always go down empty."

The other little bucket smiled brightly, "That's funny. I have the same task. All I do is go down and come up and go down and come up all day long. But no matter how many times I go down and come up, I always come up full."

That's positive thinking. Hope is positive thinking. Hopeful people are happy people who take the changes and chances of life in their stride, worrying not so much about what happens to them as what they do about it. They look for the best in people and make haste to be kind, to help, to appreciate.

❧

Life is a Great Adventure

Life is a great adventure. We have but one chance at it. If we fail, we cannot come back and try it over. To make the most of it, and to get the best out of it, is the major concern of all men. Any plan or formula that will help us to make it happier and more efficient, that will enable us to extract from it more satisfaction, should be eagerly sought after. Here are two suggestions:

1. Live a day at a time. To live each day bravely and courageously as it comes seems possible for each of us. Charles Kingsley said, "Anyone can carry his burdens, however heavy, until night. Anyone can do his work, however hard, for one day. Anyone can live sweetly, benevolently, lovely and pure, until the sun goes down."

   That philosophy has helped many a man through a great crisis. Our lives, whether they be heroic or commonplace, are made up of days, common days. If we live each one well, the sum total will be a successful and victorious life.

2. What are some of the objectives, the worth-while things to seek after? Ester Fronham once wrote. "To stand graciously, to smile sincerely, to love always, and to seek understanding—these are the worthwhile ambitions of a life worth living."

   —*Bryant S. Hinckley*

❧

Tunnels of Life

A man, his wife, and their two-year-old daughter, were traveling by train from Stockholm to southern Sweden. The little girl was anxious to sit on the table and look out the window.

All at once, the train gave a jerk, and the little girl nearly fell to the floor. Her father took hold of her, but she did not like this. She wanted to take care of herself. The mother suggested that he hold the child's dress without her knowing it. This worked splendidly.

Suddenly the train rushed into a tunnel. The father felt two small arms around his neck, a little cheek softly touched his own. Father was near, the child felt safe.

Like this child, we wish to go our own way in life. We put away all authority, or so we think. This goes for a time, until we run into the tunnels of life. Especially in those moments, it is a blessing for us to know that our Heavenly Father is near to assure and help us.

—*Victor Brattstrom*

Just for Today

Just for today, I will try to live through this day only, and not set far-reaching goals in an effort to overcome all my problems at once. I know I can do something for twelve hours that would appall me if I had to keep it up for a lifetime.

Just for today, I will try to be happy. Abraham Lincoln said, "Most folks are about as happy as they make up their minds to be." He was right. I will not dwell on thoughts that depress me. I will chase them out of my mind and replace them with happy thoughts.

Just for today, I will adjust myself to what is. I will face reality. I will try to change those things I can, and accept those things I cannot change.

Just for today, I will try to improve my mind. I will not be a mental loafer. I will force myself to read something that requires effort, thought, and concentration.

Just for today, I will exercise my soul in three ways. I will do a good deed for somebody without letting them know it. (If they find out I did it, it won't count.) I will do at least two things that I know I should do but have been putting off. I will not show anyone that my feelings are hurt; they may be hurt, but today I will not show it.

Just for today, I will be agreeable. I will look as good as I can, dress becomingly, talk softly, act courteously, and speak ill of no one. Just for today, I'll not try to improve anybody except myself.

Just for today, I will have a program. I may not follow it exactly, but I will have it, thereby saving myself from two pests—hurry and indecision.

Just for today, I will have a quiet half hour to relax alone. During this time, I will reflect on my behavior and will try to get a better perspective on my life.

Just for today, I will be unafraid. I will gather the courage to do what is right and will take the responsibility for my own actions. I will expect nothing from the world, but I will realize that as I give to the world, the world will give to me.

A Change in Attitude

Nowhere is this principle better illustrated than in the story of the young bride from the East who, during the last war, followed her husband to an army camp on the edge of the desert in California. Living conditions were primitive at best, and he had advised against it, but she wanted to be with him.

The only housing they could find was a run-down shack near an Indian village. The heat was unbearable in the daytime—115 degrees in the shade. The wind blew constantly, spreading dust and sand all over everything. The days were long and boring. Her only neighbors were Native Americans, none of whom spoke English.

When her husband was ordered farther into the desert for two weeks of maneuvers, loneliness and the wretched living conditions got the best of her. She wrote to her mother that she was coming home—she just couldn't take any more. In a short time, she received a reply which included these two lines: "Two men looked out from prison bars; one saw mud, the other saw stars."

She read the lines over and over again, and began to feel ashamed of herself. She didn't really want to leave her husband. All right, she'd look for the stars.

In the following days, she set out to make friends with her Native American friends. She asked them to teach her weaving and pottery. At first, they were distant, but as soon as they sensed her interest was genuine, they returned her friendship. She became fascinated with their culture, history, everything about them.

She began to study the desert as well, and soon it, too, changed from a desolate, forbidding place to a marvelous thing of beauty. She studied the forms of cacti, the yuccas, and the Joshua trees. She collected sea shells that had been left there millions of years ago when the sands had been an ocean floor. Later, she became such an expert on the area that she wrote a book about it.

What had changed? Not the desert, not her neighbors. Simply by changing her attitude, she had transformed a miserable experience into a highly rewarding one.

❧

To Live Each Day

Parents are never prepared for the day when their children become young men and women. But inevitably, faces that once wore smiles of egg yolk and jam come to us washed and serious, bearing news that is startlingly mature.

With our son Bob, it was his decision to pay his own way through college. He decided his schooling would mean more to him if he earned his own money. When he told me this, I suddenly realized I wasn't speaking to a boy in knee pants any longer. With a scholarship and summer jobs, he is making it on his own.

A similar awareness occurred when our only daughter, Billie Kay, a 15-year-old sophomore, surprised us with the spiritual perceptiveness she revealed in an English paper, entitled "The Last Week of My Life":

"Today I live; a week from today I die.

"If a situation such as this arose, I would probably weep. As soon as I realized, however, all that had to be done, I would regain my composure and begin.

"The first day of my suddenly shortened life, I would see all my loved ones and assure them that I loved them. I wouldn't hint that anything was wrong because I wouldn't want to remember them sorrowing but happy. I would ask God to give me strength to bear the rest of my precious few days and give me his hand to walk with him.

"On the second day, I would awake to see the rising sun in all its beauty that I had so often cast aside for a few extra moments of coveted sleep. I would gather all my possessions and give them to the needy, trying to console them as much as possible and urge them to consult God for courage.

"The third day, I would spend alone in a woods with the presence of God's creations and goodness around me. In the sweetness of nature, I would sit and reminisce my fondest memories.

"On my fourth day, I would prepare my will. The small sentimental things I would leave to my family and friends. This being done, I would go to my mother and spend the day with her. We have always been close, and I would want to reassure her of my love especially.

"Friday would be spent with my bishop. I would speak to him of my spiritual life. I would like to go with him to see those who were ill, and silently be thankful that I knew no pain.

"Saturday, I would spend visiting the shut-ins I had so often put off for another day. On this night before my death, I would probably remain awake, fearing my impending death, while also preparing for it, knowing that God was by my side.

"Upon awakening Sunday, I would make all of my last preparations. Taking my scriptures, I would go to my church to spend my last hours in prayer. I would ask him for the courage to face the remaining hours, that I might die gracefully. I would hope that my life had bearing on someone and had glorified his holy name. My last hours would be spent in perfect harmony with my God."

This is the end of Billie Kay's theme, "The Last Week of My Life", but it is not the end of the story. Billie Kay's English paper, which was dated Friday, March 15, was finished just seven days before her life was snuffed out in an automobile accident.

While returning from a movie with three teen-aged friends, the car in which Billie Kay was riding was struck from the rear, rolled over, then caught fire.

My daughter's three friends were pulled out of the wreckage with injuries from which they have since recovered. Billie Kay was pinned inside, and died instantly.

The last time I saw Billie Kay was earlier that evening when we dropped her off at a church meeting, where she joined friends, laughing and talking.

As I re-read Billie Kay's essay, I find a guide for my own life. I see clearly that I must live each day, not as if I had seven days remaining, but as if today I die.
                                                          —*Betty Bothwell*

The Day We Flew the Kites

"String!" shouted brother, bursting into the kitchen. "We need lots more string."

It was Saturday. As always, it was a busy one, for "Six days shalt thou labor and do all thy work" was taken seriously then. Outside, Father and Mr. Patrick next door were doing chores.

Inside the two houses, Mother and Mrs. Patrick were engaged in spring cleaning. Such a windy March day was ideal for "turning out" clothes closets. Already, woolens flapped on back yard clotheslines.

Somehow, the boys had slipped away to the back lot with their kites. Now, even at the risk of having brother impounded to beat carpets, they had sent him for more string. Apparently, there was no limit to the heights to which kites would soar today.

My mother looked at the sitting room, its furniture disordered for a thorough cleaning. Again her eyes wandered toward the window. "Come on, girls! Let's take string to the boys and watch them fly their kites for a minute."

On the way, we met Mrs. Patrick, laughing guiltily, escorted by her girls.

There never was such a day for flying kites! God doesn't make two such days in a century. We played all our fresh twine into the boys' kites, and still they soared. We could hardly distinguish the tiny, orange-colored specks. Now and then, we slowly reeled one in, finally bringing it dipping and tugging to earth, for the sheer joy of sending it up again. What a thrill to run with them, to the right, to the left, and to see our poor, earth-bound movements reflected minutes later in the majestic sky-dance of the kites! We wrote wishes on slips of paper and slipped them over the string. Slowly, irresistibly, they climbed up until they reached the kites. Surely all wishes would be granted.

Even our fathers dropped hoe and hammer and joined us. Our mothers took their turn, laughing like schoolgirls. Their hair blew out their pompadours and curled loose about their cheeks, their gingham aprons whipped about their legs. Mingled with our fun was something akin to awe. The grown-ups were really playing with us! Once I looked at Mother and thought she actually looked pretty. And her over forty!

We never knew where the hours went on that hilltop day. There were no hours, just a golden sun and a breeze. I think we were all beside ourselves with joy. Parents forgot their duty and dignity; children forgot their spites and combativeness. "Perhaps it's like this in heaven," I thought.

It was growing dark before, drunk with sun and air, we all stumbled sleepily back to the houses. I suppose we had some sort of supper. I suppose there must have been a surface tidying-up, for the house on Sunday looked decorous enough.

The strange thing was, we didn't mention that day afterward. I felt a little embarrassed. Surely none of the others had thrilled to it as deeply as I had. I locked the memory up in that deepest part of me where we keep "the things that cannot be and yet are."

The years went on, then one day I was scurrying about my own kitchen in a city apartment, while my three-year old cried to "go park and see ducks".

"I can't go!" I said. "I have all this to do and, when I'm through, I'll be too tired to go."

My mother, who was visiting us, looked up from the peas she was shelling. "It's a wonderful day," she offered. "Warm, with a fine breeze. It reminds me of that day we flew kites."

I stopped in my dash between stove and sink. The locked door flew open and, with it, a gush of memories. I pulled off my apron. "Come on," I told my little girl, "It's too good a day to miss."

Another decade passed. We were in the aftermath of a great war. All evening we had been asking our returned soldier, the youngest Patrick boy, about his experiences as a prisoner of war. He had talked freely, but now for a long time he had been silent. What was he thinking of, what dark and dreadful things?

"Say!" A smile twitched his lips. "Do you remember—no, of course you wouldn't. It probably didn't make the impression on you that it did on me."

I hardly dared speak. "Remember what?"

"I used to think of that day a lot in POW camp, when things weren't too good. Do you remember the day we flew the kites?"

Winter came, and the sad duty of calling on Mrs. Patrick, recently widowed, with my condolences loomed. I dreaded the visit. I couldn't imagine how Mrs. Patrick would face life alone.

We talked a little of my family and her grandchildren and the changes in the town. Then she was silent, looking down at her lap. I cleared my throat, waiting for the tears.

When she looked up, Mrs. Patrick was smiling. "I was just sitting here thinking," she said. "Henry had such fun that day. Do you remember, Frances, the day we flew the kites?"

—*Frances Fowler*

೪

Twenty-Four Golden Hours

Charlotte had come to a hard time in her life. She was filled with discontent. Everything seemed wrong. Her ambitions were thwarted; her friends were commonplace; her home unattractive; her own personality unlovely, as she was well aware. The problems were too many for Charlotte. She seemed caught in a current of circumstances that was carrying her into an ugly and dissatisfying life, and she could not escape.

She went to the one person who seemed to be leading the kind of life that she very much desired. Margaret Ames, lovely, popular, gifted, and successful, lived in a cottage studio set in a flower garden. There she painted those charming little water colors that were in such demand that they were always sold in advance. Margaret was so kind, so willing to help, that you dared go to her with your problems.

In the charming studio, Charlotte poured out the story of her heartache over her frustrated, unhappy life. She told all the details, the poverty, the ugliness, the disappointment about school, the unsympathetic family, the careless friends, her own lack of charm and beauty.

After a gentle word of sympathy, Margaret said, "You can change all that if you really have the will to do it."

"How? How?" cried Charlotte. "I'll do anything, no matter how hard."

"Will you indeed? It is not hard at all, it only takes time. You see, you must sow the seed for another kind of life, and wait with patience for it to grow. Here is a test to see whether you truly have the will: Live for twenty-four hours as if Christ were right beside you, seeing everything that you do. Then come to me again, and we'll talk. Will you do that?"

Charlotte was a Church member, but she never spoke of Christ like that—almost as if he were a neighbor that one might speak to. Somewhat constrained and doubtful, she answered, "Yes, Mrs. Ames."

"Then come again tomorrow, sometime in the evening, and we'll talk about the change."

It was late afternoon when Charlotte went home. She knew that she was expected to help get supper on the table. She went to the drawer and took out a wrinkled tablecloth. When she spread it on the table, she noticed several spoiled spots. And here she had her first thought of change.

"If Christ were going to eat with us, I wouldn't put on a soiled cloth," she said to herself.

She got a fresh cloth. And with the same thought, she brought in a small bowl of flowers from the yard. She put the butter on a fresh plate, instead of on the soiled one. She cut the bread with care. She mashed the potatoes, and beat them lightly, instead of putting them on plain-boiled. She made her gravy smooth and rich. "If I'd known Christ would be here, I'd have managed something nice for dessert," she thought. She hoped that it was not sacrilegious to think of Christ in connection with desserts.

"Company tonight?" asked Father, peering through his glasses as he came to the table.

"Just you, Daddy," smiled Charlotte. If Christ were present, of course you'd smile at your family and show them your very best manner.

Her mother, worn out and hot, and still dressed in her kitchen clothes, sat down saying, "I don't know what's gotten into her to fix up so just for us. I suppose she's expecting someone to drop in before we're done."

Charlotte bit back a hasty retort. She and Mother hadn't been getting along well lately. It seemed that mother wouldn't try to keep up-to-date, and that she never understood how a girl felt about things. Charlotte kept still until she thought of the proper thing to say in the presence of the unseen guest. "I don't know of anyone I'd rather fix things up for more than my own folks," she said.

The family simply stared for a minute. That wasn't like Charlotte. Then father said, "That's right, daughter. It's too bad we all don't think of that oftener."

But Dick snickered. Charlotte's anger flared. There is nothing more maddening than to be laughed at when one is doing one's best. In another moment a sharp retort would have started a quarrel. But just in time Charlotte said to herself, "Christ is here," and said nothing aloud. There was a short, uncomfortable silence. Dick was ashamed but wouldn't say so. But soon they were all talking quietly again.

"It is better," thought Charlotte, "to keep still when anyone else is exasperating. A quarrel makes mother really ill, and it gives me a headache, besides making me look like a beast. Besides, I think Dick's ashamed. I can tell, because he's so gruff."

"It's your turn to wash the dishes," said Agnes, when the two girls began to clean up.

"All right," said Charlotte. Usually there was a sharp argument over whose turn it was. Charlotte got the water ready and began. Agnes continued to carry dishes out in silence. After a while, she burst out, "It was really my turn, Charlotte. I was very selfish to let you begin. I'll take my turn tomorrow night, and the next."

"It's all right, Agnes. I really don't mind."

To her astonishment Charlotte knew this was true: when you didn't mind washing, it ceased to be a task.

In the living room, Charlotte slipped a magazine out from the bottom of the pile and began to read. She had brought the magazine home herself, and she kept it under cover. After a few minutes, she put it down. It was not a bad publication; indeed, it was considered entirely respectable, but it was trashy, lurid, sentimental, a world removed from the wholesome reading. "I wouldn't be reading this if Christ were standing where he could read with me," she thought. And she carried it out, and put it in the wastepaper basket.

A party was in the making at Lucy's and she was invited to go. Should she go? Oh, yes! Christ went to parties. He seemed to like going, and he helped other people to have a good time. All through the gay evening, Charlotte kept her thought, "Christ is beside me." She didn't think of herself very much. She helped the girls get the hasty snack prepared. She talked to a quiet, shy young man and drew him into the games. She took her turn at stunts and stories without self-consciousness, and she felt a genuine thrill when someone said in the dark ahead of her on the way home, "That Charlotte is a lot of fun, isn't she?" She knew that the crowd hadn't been thinking her much fun lately until she tried this experiment tonight.

The next morning, Charlotte went to work and applied this same experiment at work. Instead of hating her job like she had before, she tried being cheerful, helpful, and smiling through it all. Before long, she was actually enjoying the job that she had been tolerating only long enough to earn the money she needed for college and a decorating course so that she could one day design beautiful clothes. No matter how rude some of the customers were, Charlotte found that a smile will melt even the rudest and unhappiest customers. The whole day, Charlotte met every customer with an eager interest to serve. Closing time came before she knew it.

At eight o'clock, she sat in Margaret Ames' studio again.

"I tried it, Mrs. Ames, just as well as I could, and, well, it made everything so different. I think I can see what you mean. Of course, it didn't change the things that are bothering me. I'm still poor, and can't go to school, and I live in an ugly house, and I don't know the sort of people I'd like to..."

"Ah, my dear! But you only started the seed-sowing twenty-four hours ago. When you first put the seed in, the garden doesn't look different does it? But it's on the way to becoming different. In three months, it will be bright with bloom, not drab with dull, brown earth. That will be the way with you. You say these handicaps in your life haven't changed. But you've started to change them. Can you keep on as you've begun, and wait patiently for the Lord, as the Psalmist tells us? You will cease to be poor, and without opportunity. Friends will be drawn to you. Doors will open before you. Your surroundings will blossom into beauty. You have the magic word. It is Christ. Fretting or even effort doesn't change things very much, but Christ does. Just remember to keep your daily walk very close to him."

"I'm going to do it," said Charlotte.

Love

They do not love, that do not show their love.
—William Shakespeare

❧

Love makes one richer than a mountain of gold.

❧

True love is the most illogical logic in the world.

❧

Love is the master key that opens the gates of happiness.
—Oliver Wendell Holmes

❧

To love someone means to see him as God intended him.

❧

When love and skill work together, expect a masterpiece.

❧

Those who love not their fellow beings, live unfruitful lives.
—Shelley

❧

Always forgive your enemies: nothing annoys them so much.

❧

Duty makes us do things well, but love makes us do things beautifully.

❧

Love may not make the world go around, but it makes the trip worthwhile!

❧

The entire sum of existence is the magic of being needed by just one person.

❧

Not knowing how to love means the loss of the meaning of life and its fulfillment.
—*Pearl Buck*

❧

A smart girl is one who can hold a man at arm's length, and not lose her grip on him.

❧

Love, which is only an episode in the life of man, is the entire history of woman's life.
—*Mad. de Stael*

❧

Love is a special way of feeling, rather it is that which feelings are a rich and intense part.
—*Truman Madsen*

❧

Love is the feeling you feel when you feel you are feeling a feeling you feel you have felt before.

❧

Our love cannot exceed our ability to get along with the person to whom we were initially attracted.

❧

God has placed the genius of women in their hearts, because the works of this genius are always works of love.
—*Lamartine*

❧

The supreme happiness of life is the conviction of being loved for yourself, or more correctly, being loved in spite of yourself.
—*Victor Hugo*

❧

Love is a miracle! It can come to any of us, at any age, at any time, and in any place: all we have to do is reach out and live, reach out and receive.

❧

Love is a journey with your friends, and if you part the way, through choice or circumstance, that love, refined and pure, remains with you; its depth, its warmth, at the speed of thought, are yours forever.

Some Relation

One cold Christmas Eve day, a little boy of six or seven was standing outside in front of a store window. He had no shoes and his clothes were in rags. A young woman passing by saw the little boy, and could read the longing in his pale blue eyes. She took the child by the hand and led him into the store. There she bought him some new shoes and a complete suit of warm clothing. They came back out into the street and the woman said to the child, "Now you go home and have a very Merry Christmas."

The boy looked up at her and asked, "Are you Jesus' momma?"

She smiled down at him and replied, "No, son, I'm just one of his children."

The little boy then said, "I knew you had to be some relation."

❧

Love, Luck, and Riches

Three men stood, one stormy night, at the threshold of a wayside cottage. Their knock at the door was answered by a child, who asked their names and the purpose of their visit.

One of the two spoke saying: "My name is Love; my companions are Luck and Riches. We are seeking places for rest and refreshment. One of us would be pleased to receive the hospitality of this home tonight, and the choice of who it is to be, we leave with you."

The child was bewildered; she ran and called the other members of the family, who gathered quickly to decide which of the three distinguished callers they would receive.

They learned and repeated over and over again the names of their three would-be guests, studied their characters, and listened again to the request that was made.

Wisdom ruled the family's decision, and the choice was soon made. In unison they exclaimed, "We will entertain Love!"

But the family was perplexed to find that Luck and Riches accompanied the invited Love into the proffered room. Observing their astonishment, Love turned to the kind hosts and explained, with a divine smile, "Be not alarmed. Wherever I am made welcome, there my companions also will make their home."

And that home was blessed forever more.

—*A Syrian legend*

❧

Give It to Me

Moses Mendelssohn—the saintly German-Jewish philosopher who was hunchbacked as a result of boyhood curvature of the spine—fell in love with Guggenheim's charming daughter, Fruntje, nearly two hundred years ago in the city of Hamburg.

"Well, you are a philosopher and a wise man," Guggenheim said, "so you will not take it amiss when I tell you that my daughter became frightened when she saw your appearance."

"I thought as much," Mendelssohn nodded, and asked permission to say farewell to the girl. He went upstairs, and found her busy with her needlework.

She avoided looking at him during their conversation, which he skillfully led around to the subject that was on his mind. Finally, she asked him timidly whether he, too, believed that marriages were made in heaven.

"Certainly," he replied, "and something quite unusual happened to me. As you know, they call out in heaven at the birth of a boy, 'This one will get that girl for a wife.' When I was born, my future wife was also thus announced, but it was added, 'She will, alas, have a terrible hump.'

"I shouted, 'Oh, Lord, a girl who is humpbacked will very easily become bitter and hard. A girl should be beautiful. Good Lord, give the hump to me, and let her be handsome and well formed!'"

The girl, deeply moved, stretched out her hand for Mendelssohn's. She became his faithful and loving wife, devoted to him for the rest of his life.

—*Theodor Reik*

❧

The Love of Two Brothers

Abram and Zimri were brothers, who tilled their lands in a happy vale together. The same plow turned the sod of both their farms in the spring, and when autumn came with its fruitful harvest, they shared equally the bounteous harvest of their common labor, and each stored his portion in his barn.

Abram had a wife and seven sons, but Zimri lived alone. One evening as Zimri lay upon his lonely bed, he thought of Abram and his family. Within himself, he said, "There is my brother, Abram. He has a wife and seven sons, for whom he must provide, while I have neither wife nor child, and yet we share our crops alike. Surely this is an injustice to my brother. I will arise, and go down to the fields, and add to my brother's store."

The moon looked out from between the murky clouds, and threw a shimmering light upon the stubbled field, newly reaped. He took a generous third of his sheaves from his own abundant store, and carried them to his brother's pile. He returned to his home with a light heart, and slept soundly.

As Abram lay upon his bed that night, he thought of his brother. Within himself, he said, "There is my brother, Zimri. He is alone. He has no sons to help him. He does his work without assistance, while I have seven lusty sons who bind my sheaves. Yet we divide our gains equally. Surely this is not pleasing in the sight of God. I will arise and go down to the field, and will add to my brother's store."

The trees stood straight in the light of the cold, round moon, and their yellow leaves were shown, then hidden, as the playful moon sported with the clouds. Abram arose and, guided by the doubtful light, stole softly to the fertile field. From his ample store, he took a generous third, and carried it to add to his brother Zimri's pile. He returned to his home with a good heart and slept, for his soul was untormented.

When morning came, and each surveyed his store of sheaves, he wondered how it was that his own store had not decreased, although the night before he had given away a third—but neither of the brothers spoke in explanation. At length, their day's toil was ended, the sun reclined upon its bed covered by the western hills, and the brothers returned to their homes.

Before the generous Zimri slept that night, he arose—and, led by the beneficent thought that Abram's share should be greater than his own, again visited the scene of his exploit the night before. The tall cedars stood up black against the sky, and the moon silvered their high tops with a mellow, slanting light. Again he carried from his sheaves a third, and stored them with his brother Abram's first.

He then retired behind his pile to keep watch. It was not long before Abram came stealing softly down the silent field. He turned now right, now left, as if he wished not to be seen. He took from his sheaves again the third, and placed it in Zimri's store.

The brothers met. Zimri saw it all, but could not speak, for his heart was full. He leaned upon his brother's breast, and wept.

A Boy and His Dog

"When's supper, Mom?" Jamie's dancing blue eyes looked inquisitively up at his mother washing lunch dishes.

"Little boys," she thought, "they can't even get finished with one meal before they're ready for the next one."

She studied his face—the part she could see through the dirt. After all, it had been a whole hour since he washed it. No one would ever know that the blue plaid shirt and Levis had also been clean just this morning. His tennis shoes that were full of holes were sure a lot more comfortable than the new ones Daddy bought last week.

"How do blonde, curly-headed, eight-year-olds get dirty so fast?" she asked him.

Jamie shrugged his shoulders. He hadn't noticed. Besides mothers always found dirt—even behind ears.

"We'll eat as soon as Daddy comes home tonight."

She watched him scamper out the kitchen door, take his big amber-colored collie, Rusty, by the collar, and start off up the lane.

A boy and a dog—and certainly these two were inseparable. They lived for each other. Jamie's first thought every morning was Rusty's breakfast and a good romp in the yard. Often, it made him late for school but, to him, Rusty was first. Now, in the summertime, it was even hard to separate them at bedtime.

She watched the two from the kitchen window as they sauntered up the lane to the fields beyond.

These fields held mystery for Jamie and his friends. He, Ronnie, and Tim spent hours there playing cowboys and Indians, and "exploring", and they always found something new there. The dry, arid ground provided the exact prairie for driving cattle across the plains, and the few dead cows that had been dumped helped to make the game real.

Their playground was perfect—barbed wire fences, ditches, rocks, fallen trees, hills covered with brush—the very imagination of every young boy.

But beyond the highest hill, the one they had never climbed completely over, was a huge canal carrying the irrigation water for the valley farms. The water ran down the mountain in an ominous, but fascinating waterfall. Jamie's parents had warned him never to go farther than the fence, for one step too close to the edge would send him tumbling yards below to sure death.

The field held so much excitement that none of the boys had ever wandered over the hill. They were always deeply involved in their western scenes, and then it was time to go home.

Today, Jamie and Rusty spent hours in the field chasing each other. Rusty certainly didn't like to die when he was shot, but then he was tough. They camped in their dugout and hours passed without being noticed.

As he was chasing his wild horse up the mountain, the horse ran just a little too far. They climbed through the fence and stood there watching the dirty brown water as it rushed swiftly over the side of the hill and tumbled in gallons of foam to the ditch below. Jamie was thoroughly intrigued with the sound of falling water and the patterns of the foam. It reminded him of clouds in the sky.

Rusty barked and ran around in circles. One time around, he knocked Jamie to the ground. Dirt and rocks began to fall and Jamie tried to catch himself, but could find nothing to grab. He was falling. Below him he could see rushing water and sharp rocks and, then, as if by a miracle, he grabbed at a small branch growing from the side of the mountain. He caught it; there was hope. He hung in mid-air trying to regain his senses and looking for some way to climb up. Nothing.

"Rusty," he called. But there was no answer. "Rusty." He was frantic. "Rusty, where are you? Please come." He looked as far as he could both ways, but could see no sign of Rusty. "Maybe he fell," he thought. He looked below, but could see nothing. Two tears trickled down his cheeks and left a muddy path. He thought of all the things they had done together since Rusty had been born two years ago.

Jamie remembered the day Grandpa's collie dog had had puppies and, right from the start, he had made friends with the cutest one. When the puppies were three days old, Jamie took one home and let it sleep in a box behind the kitchen stove. In the morning, he found it in an old can all covered with rust. And ever since, Rusty was Jamie's most trusted companion. And now where was he? Surely he wouldn't leave him there.

It was getting late and Jamie could no longer see the ground below him. He listened for some sound—maybe a doggy whine. But all he could hear was the water as it pounded against the rocks. He was crying out loud but there was no one to hear him—maybe even tough cowboys hanging on mountain sides cried; they'd have to: it was scary. In fact, the surer he was, the harder he cried. It was cold, too. His little arms pulled in their sockets. Any minute now, he was sure he would have to let go.

What seemed like hours passed. The night was getting darker and then Jamie looked up at the branch he hung to so tightly. Slowly pulling out of the mountain, it could last only another few minutes at the most. Jamie was scared—too scared to cry now. But that was good, because he would need to hold very still. So he thought.

He thought about the chicken that Mom had been fixing for supper, and he wondered if his parents had called Ronnie's house yet.

"They'll never think to look past the fence," he thought. "They've told me so many times not to come here." And then the tears came fast, and every inch of his body ached, and he knew any second either he or the branch would let go.

There was a sound—he thought he heard a dog bark. He listened again, but it was only water. And then, the same sound again.

"Rusty, Rusty, where are you?" But no answer. And he knew he had been imagining things. And then, there it was again—and he was sure this time.

"Rusty, where did you go?" He could see his faithful dog on the edge of the cliff.

"Jamie, we're here." He recognized his father's voice and he knew everything would be fine now. He would go home and make a wish with his wishbone that every guy could have a dog just like Rusty.

—*Sharon Miller*

❧

The Power of Love

The night was cold, damp, and forbidding in every sense of the word. It was the kind of night a physician ordinarily would want to forget. Yet, it was a night I shall never forget.

Three months previously, my father had suffered a stroke that had deprived him of the use of his legs and temporarily halted his speech. Although the strength in his legs seemed forever gone, he gradually regained a partial, halting ability to talk.

At the age of 94, Father had lived a full, useful, and successful life as the loving husband of his childhood sweetheart, and as the over-indulgent father of ten devoted children. Yet, in spite of his advanced age, all of his numerous progeny hoped and prayed for a return to the vigorous state of health in which we had always known him.

As the only member of the medical profession within the huge family, I had brought Father from his home in Salt Lake City to a hospital in Ogden, so I could be near him and watch over him with greater care. However, it gradually became apparent that he would never return to his home again. After three months of tender nursing, his once vigorous body told us that, having served him long and well, it was not capable of mending itself: it had earned the right to be laid to rest.

And now, in the middle of this dreary night, Father's pulse weakened to almost imperceptibility. His temperature dropped below normal. His blood pressure began to falter and slowly it fell. His reflexes denoted the ebbing of life as they disappeared one by one. After three months of desperate fighting, his gallant spirit found its body no longer able to respond. My father was dying.

My first thought was that I should not bother my mother, whose state of health, at best, was precarious. She should not have her rest interrupted, nor should she be brought out into the cold night on a forty-mile trip when she might be too late to see Father. And, if she did arrive before my father died, she would find him in a deep coma from which he would not return.

Then it occurred to me that sixty-six years of married life had earned my parents the right to be together during the last moments of my father's life on this earth. Surely this was a sacred right, more important than any earthly reasoning I might entertain. I felt that neither father nor mother would forgive me should I deny them this privilege.

Only with great effort did my mother make the journey from Salt Lake City to Ogden. In haste, she was wheeled to the bedside of her comatose and dying companion. As was her custom when something was important, she had to stand up. She was literally lifted out of the wheel chair and onto her feet. Unsteadily she leaned over the blanched face of my father, tenderly stroking the few gray hairs on his head as she had done thousand of times before. There were no tears, no sobbing from mother. She merely leaned over, kissed him softly on the forehead, then spoke directly into his ear, "Oh, Father, I love you."

Father's last years had been saddened by a gradual loss of hearing—but he had always heard my mother when she spoke to him. And now, something wonderful happened to this dying man. Suddenly, yet slowly, a tear welled up in the corner of his eye. Even as the tear rolled down his cheek, his pulse quickened, his blood pressure began to rise, and his reflexes slowly returned—almost undetectable at first, but finally undeniably, Father began to rouse from his coma.

We all left the room—except for Mother. When we returned, Father had lapsed back into his coma, but mother said, "We had the grandest visit about some very important things."

You don't have to be a physician to know that the only thing on earth powerful enough to bridge the gulf between life and death is love.

—*Lindsay R. Curtis*

છ્જ

My Brother's Keeper

John and Mary had a nice home and two lovely children, a boy and a girl. John had a good job, and had been asked to travel on business to another city. He invited Mary to accompany him, and they hired a reliable woman to care for the children. As it happened, John concluded his business early, and they headed home ahead of schedule.

As they drove into town, they noticed smoke, and veered from their usual route home to see what it was.

They found a home in flames. Mary said, "Oh, well, it isn't our fire. Let's go home."

But John drove closer and exclaimed, "That home belongs to Fred Jones who works at the plant. He's at work. Maybe there's something we can do."

"It's nothing to do with us," protested Mary. "You have your good clothes on. Let's not go any closer."

But John drove up and stopped. Both were horror-stricken to see the whole house in flames. A woman on the lawn was in hysterics, screaming, "The children! Get the children!"

John grabbed her by the shoulders and demanded, "Where are the children?"

"In the basement," sobbed the woman, "down the hall and to the left."

In spite of Mary's protests, John grabbed the water hose, soaked his clothes, put his wet handkerchief on his head, and bolted for the basement, which was scorching hot and filled with smoke.

He found the door and grabbed two children, carrying one under each arm like the football player he once was.

As he left, he could hear more children whimpering.

He delivered the two badly frightened and nearly suffocated youngsters into waiting arms, filled his lungs with fresh air, and started back, asking the woman how many more were down there.

"Two," the woman answered.

Mary grabbed his arm and screamed, "John! Don't go back! It's suicide! That house will collapse any second!"

But he shook her off, and went back, feeling his way down the smoke-filled hallway and into the room.

It seemed an eternity before he found both children and started back. All three were coughing, and he stooped low to reach the available air.

As he stumbled up the endless steps, the thought occurred to him that there was something vaguely familiar about the little bodies clinging to him.

When at last they came out into the sunlight and air, he found that he had rescued his own children.

The baby-sitter had left them at this home while she did some shopping.

❧

When Do I Croak?

The violent grinding of brakes, and the harsh creaking of skidding wheels, gradually died away as the big car came to a stop. Eddie quickly picked himself up from the dusty pavement where he had been thrown, and looked around wildly.

Agnes! Where was the little sister he had been holding by the hand when they started to cross the street? The next moment he saw her under the big car that had run them down, her eyes closed, a dark stain slowly spreading around her head.

With one bound, the boy was under the car, trying to lift the child.

"You'd better not try, son," suggested a man gently. "Someone has called an ambulance."

"She's not dead, is she?" Eddie begged.

The man stooped and felt the limp little pulse. "No, she's not dead."

A policeman came, dispersed the crowd, and carried the unconscious girl into a nearby drug store. Eddie's folded coat made a pillow for her head until the ambulance arrived. He was permitted to ride with her to the hospital. Something about the sturdy, shabbily dressed boy, who could not be more than ten years old, and his devotion to his little sister, touched the hearts of the emergency crew.

"We must operate at once," declared the surgeon after a brief exam. "She's been injured internally, and has lost a great deal of blood." He turned to Eddie who, inarticulate with grief, stood dumbly by. "Where do you live?"

Eddie told him that their father was dead, and that their mother worked.

"We can't wait to find her," decided the surgeon, "it might be too late."

Eddie waited in the waiting room while the surgeon worked. After that seemed like an eternity, a nurse sought him out.

"Eddie," she said kindly, "your sister is very bad, and the doctor wants to do a transfusion. Do you know what that is?" Eddie shook his head. "She has lost so much blood that she cannot live unless someone gives her his blood. Will you do that for her?"

Eddie's wan face grew paler, and he gripped the arms of the chair so hard that his knuckles went white. Only for a moment did he hesitate, then gulping back his tears, he nodded his head and stood up.

"That's a good lad," said the nurse.

She patted his head, and led him to the operating room where Eddie was prepared, then placed on a gurney next to his sister, while the blood transfusion took place. Afterwards, he was rolled into a corner and forgotten.

Two hours later, the surgeon looked up at his operating staff and announced, "I think she'll pull through."

"It's a miracle," whispered a nurse.

The miracles of modern medicine never ceased to amaze any of them.

Eddie slipped off the gurney, approached the surgeon, and tugged his sleeve. The surgeon looked down to see the ragged, pale-faced boy looking steadily up into his face.

"Say, Doc," Eddie asked quietly, "When do I croak?"

Everyone laughed, and the surgeon replied with a smile, "Why, what do you mean, my boy?"

"I thought when they took a guy's blood he croaked," Eddied answered meekly.

The laughing stopped, the smiles faded, and the miracle of modern science paled. This ragged lad had climbed to the very height of nobility and sacrifice and shown them a glimpse of the greatest miracle of all—selfless love!

But Eddie must never know this. The lesson was too poignantly beautiful to be wasted. "I think, after all, you will get well, Eddie," the surgeon answered. "You and little Agnes."

—Arthur Styron

Appointment with Love

Six minutes to six, said the clock over the information booth in New York's Grand Central Station. The tall young Army officer lifted his sunburned face and narrowed his eyes to note the exact time. His heart was pounding with a beat that choked him. In six minutes he would see the woman who had filled such a special place in his life for the past thirteen months, the woman he had never seen, yet whose written words had sustained him unfailingly.

Lt. Blandford remembered one day in particular, the worst of the fighting, when his plane had been caught in the midst of a pack of enemy planes.

In one of his letters, he had confessed to her that he often felt fear, and only a few days before this battle, he had received her answer, "Of course you fear, all brave men do. Next time you doubt yourself, I want you to hear my voice reciting to you, 'Yea, though I walk through the valley of the shadow of death, I shall fear no evil, for Thou art with me.'" He had remembered, and it had renewed his strength. He was going to hear her real voice now. Four minutes to six.

A girl passed close to him, and Lt. Blandford started. She was wearing a flower, but it was not the little red rose they had agreed upon. Besides, this girl was only about eighteen, and Hollis Maynell had told him she was thirty. "What of it?" he had answered, "I'm 32." He was 29.

His mind went back to that book he had read in the training camp, *Of Human Bondage*; throughout the book were notes in a woman's handwriting. He had never believed that a woman could see into a man's heart so tenderly, so understandingly. Her name was on the bookplate: Hollis Maynell. He got hold of a New York City telephone book and found her address. He had written, she had answered. Next day he had been shipped out, but they had gone on writing. For thirteen months, she had faithfully replied. When his letters did not arrive, she wrote anyway, and now he believed he loved her, and she loved him.

But she had refused all his pleas to send him her photograph, explaining, "If your feeling for me had any reality, what I look like won't matter. Suppose I'm beautiful. I'd always be haunted that you had been taking a chance on just that, and that kind of love would disgust me. Suppose I'm plain, (and you must admit that this is more likely), then I'd always fear that you were only going on writing because you were lonely and had no one else. No, don't ask for my picture. When you come to New York, you shall see me and then you shall make your own decision."

One minute to six...he flipped the pages of the book he held. Then Lt. Blandford's heart leaped.

A young woman was coming toward him. Her figure was long and slim, her blond hair lay back in curls from her delicate ears. Her eyes were blue as flowers, her lips and chin had a gentle firmness. In her pale-green suit, she was like springtime come alive.

He started toward her, forgetting to notice that she was wearing no rose, and as he moved, a small, provocative smile curved her lips.

"Going my way, soldier?" she murmured.

He made one step closer to her. Then he saw Hollis Maynell.

She was standing almost directly behind the girl, a woman well past 40, her graying hair tucked under a worn hat. She was more than plump. Her thick-ankled feet were thrust into low-heeled shoes. But she wore a red rose on her rumpled coat. The girl in the green suit was walking quickly away.

Blandford felt as though he were being split in two, so keen was his desire to follow the girl, yet so deep was his longing for the woman whose spirit had truly companioned and upheld his own, and there she stood. He could see that her pale, plump face was gentle and sensible; her gray eyes had a warm twinkle.

Lt. Blandford did not hesitate. His fingers gripped the worn copy *Of Human Bondage* which was to identify him to her. This would not be love, but it would be something precious, a friendship for which he had been and must ever be grateful.

He squared his shoulders, saluted, and held the book out toward the woman although, even while he spoke, he felt the bitterness of his disappointment.

"I'm Lt. Blandford, and you're Miss Maynell. I'm so glad you could meet me. May I take you to dinner?"

The woman's face broadened in a tolerant smile. "I don't know what this is all about, son," she answered. "But that young lady in the green suit," she said, gesturing toward the girl who had just passed, "begged me to wear this rose on my coat. And she said that if you asked me to go out with you, then I should tell you that she's waiting for you in that restaurant across the street. She said it was some kind of a test."

—*S. I. Kishor (reprinted from "Reader's Digest" with permission)*

Opportunity

Opportunities are the offerings of God.

≈

The greatest opportunity in life is life itself.

≈

Opportunity is always dressed in work clothes.

≈

The sign on the door of opportunity reads, "Push".

≈

Opportunity always looks better going than coming.

≈

Opportunity knocks: temptation kicks the door down.

≈

The door of opportunity swings wide for the prepared.

≈

The wise man will make more opportunities than he finds.

≈

There is no security on this earth: there is only opportunity.
—*Douglas MacArthur*

≈

Opportunities are never lost: someone else will take the ones you miss.

≈

Opportunity is as scarce as oxygen; men fairly breathe it and do not know it.
—*Doc Sane*

≈

God supplies us with the opportunity, but he cannot take advantage of it for us.

≈

Do you see difficulties in every opportunity or opportunities in every difficulty?

≈

We make our lives unhappy worrying about the difficulties of our opportunities.

❧

Success: Think big; catch the whole vision; opportunity does not knock, it is created.
—*Paul H. Dunn*

❧

The secret of success in life is for a man to be ready for his opportunity when it comes.
—*Benjamin Disraeli*

❧

When one door closes, another opens; but we often look so long and regretfully at the closed door, that we do not see the one that has opened.

❧

To look is one thing, to see what you look at is another, to understand what you see is a third, to learn from what you understand is still something else, but to act on what you learn is all that really matters.

❧

Education has opened many doors. However, there are still innumerable doors yet unopened. These are the doors of the future. Perhaps one of my children will open one of these doors. I shall help give him the key.

❧

The Woman Who Never Had a Chance

One night in London, at the conclusion of a lecture by the distinguished naturalist, Dr. Louis Agassiz, a woman complained that she "had never had a chance".

In response to her complaint, he replied, "You say, Madame, you never had a chance. What do you do?"

"I am single and help my sister run a boarding house."

"What do you do?" he asked again.

"I skin potatoes."

"Madame, where do you sit during these duties?"

"On the bottom steps of the kitchen stairs."

"Where do your feet rest?

"On the glazed brick?"

"What is a glazed brick?"

"I don't know, sir."

"How long have you been sitting there?"

"Fifteen years."

"Madame, here is my personal card. Would you kindly write to me concerning the nature of a glazed brick?"

She went home and explored the dictionary to discover that a brick was a piece of baked clay. That definition seemed too simple to send to Dr. Agassiz so, after the dishes were washed, she went to the library and in an encyclopedia read that a glazed brick is vitrified kaolin and anhydrous-aluminum silicate. She didn't know what that meant, but she was curious and found out. She took the word vitrified and read all she could find. She visited museums. She moved out of the basement of her life into a wonderful new world on the wings of vitrified and, having started, she took the word anhydrous, studied geology, and went back to the time when God started the world and laid the clay beds.

One afternoon, she went to a brickyard where she found an intelligent watchman who told her the history of more than 120 kinds of bricks and tiles and why there have to be so many. Then she sat down and wrote thirty-six pages on the subject of glazed bricks and tiles. Back came a letter.

> *Dear Madame:*
>
> *This is the best article I have ever seen on the subject. If you will kindly change the three words marked with an asterisk, I will have it published and pay you for it.*
>
> *Louis Agassiz*

A short time later came a letter with $250 in it; on the bottom of this letter was this query:

> *What was under those bricks?*

She had learned the value of time and replied simply, "Ants".

He wrote back and said, "Tell me about the ants", and she began to study ants.

She found there are between 1,800 and 2,500 different kinds. There are ants so tiny that you could put three, head to head, on the head of a pin and have standing room left over. There are ants an inch long that march in solid armies a half mile wide, driving everything ahead of them; ants that are blind; ants that get wings on the afternoon of the day they die; ants that build ant hills so tiny that you can cover one with a lady's silver thimble; peasant ants that keep cows to milk and deliver the fresh milk to the apartment houses of the aristocratic ants of the neighborhood.

After wide reading, much microscopic work, and deep study, she sat down and wrote Dr. Agassiz 360 pages on the subject. He published the book and sent her the money, and she went to visit all the lands of her dreams on the proceeds of her work.

Prayer

Life is fragile: handle with prayer.

❧

Prayer will change the night to day.

❧

Kneeling keeps you in good standing with the Lord.

❧

He who has ceased to pray has lost a great friendship.
—*Richard L. Evans*

❧

He who prays as he ought will endeavor to live as he prays.
—*Owen*

❧

Prayer does not change things: it changes people; people change things.

❧

Practice in life whatever you pray for, and God will give it to you abundantly.

❧

He who rises from prayer a better man, has his prayer answered.
—*George Meredith*

❧

Prayer is the key that opens the day and the lock that guards the night.

❧

And all things whatsoever ye shall ask in prayer, believing, ye shall receive.
—*Matthew 21:22*

❧

He prays well who is so absorbed with God that he does not know he's praying.

❧

Live among men as though God were watching; talk to God as though men were listening.

❧

Pray as though everything depended upon God, and work as though everything depended upon you.

❧

I don't know of a single foreign product that enters this country untaxed except the answer to prayer.

—*Mark Twain*

❧

Henry Ward Beecher told of a woman who prayed for patience, and God sent her a poor cook. The best answers to prayer may be the vision and strength to meet a circumstance or to assume responsibility.

❧

It is the first principle of the gospel to know for a certainty the character of God, [that] we may converse with him as one man converses with another.

—*Joseph Smith*

❧

If the devil says you cannot pray when you are angry, then tell him it is none of his business, and pray until that species of insanity is dispelled and serenity is restored to your mind.

—*Brigham Young*

❧

If you have a special problem, consult someone who has a special knowledge about it—and do it on your knees.

❧

When we pray unto the Father in the name of Jesus for specific personal things, we should feel in the very depths of our souls that we are willing to subject our petitions to the will of our Father in Heaven.

—*Marion G. Romney*

Did I Wind the Clock?

Have you ever knelt down to pray and, after addressing Deity, wondered if you had turned off the lights, wound up the clock, made a certain phone call?

Get up, check your light, make your phone call, wind the clock, and then kneel again, in humility and, when ready, have a heart-to-heart talk with your Father in Heaven.

❧

A Powerful Friend

He who makes a habit of sincere prayer, and prays believing, will find his life noticeably and profoundly enriched and steadied.

He will increase in tranquility and poise; he will have added courage and stamina. His physical, moral, and spiritual attitude will indicate he is aware of the presence of a powerful friend.

❧

Do You Count Sheep?

A man suffering from insomnia asked a friend how he managed to sleep so well every night.

"Do you count sheep?" he asked.

"No," replied the friend, "I talk to the Shepherd."

—*Harold Taylor*

❧

Pray Till You Do

It matters not whether you or I feel like praying: when the time comes to pray, pray!

If we do not feel like it, then we should pray till we do.

You will find that those who wait until the spirit bids them pray, will never pray much on this earth.

—*Brigham Young*

Strangers

The minute a man stops supplicating God for his spirit and direction, he becomes a stranger to him and his works.

When men stop praying for God's spirit, they place confidence in their own unaided reason, and they gradually lose the spirit of God, just the same as a near and dear friend, by never writing to or visiting each other, will become strangers.

—*Heber J. Grant*

The Serene Effort of Prayer

Prayer is a force as real as terrestrial gravity.

As a physician, I have seen men, after all other therapy had failed, lifted out of disease and melancholy by the serene effort of prayer.

Only in prayer do we achieve that complete and harmonious assembly of body, mind, and spirit which gives the frail human its unshakable strength.

—*Dr. Alexis Carrel*

Grinding Machinery

Do you have family prayers in your family? And when you do, do you go through the operation like the grinding of a piece of machinery, or do you bow in meekness and with a sincere desire to seek the blessing of God upon you and your household?

That is the way we ought to do, and cultivate a spirit of devotion and trust in God, dedicating ourselves to him, and seeking his blessings.

—*John Taylor*

Willing to Help

You know that it is one peculiarity of our faith and religion never to ask the Lord to do a thing without being willing to help him all that we are able; then the Lord will do the rest.

I shall not ask the Lord to do what I am not willing to do.

Do not ask God to give you knowledge when you are confident that you will not keep and rightly improve that knowledge.

—*Brigham Young*

I Wasn't Praying to Them

When President Spencer W. Kimball was in Washington, D. C. for the opening of the Washington Temple for public tours, he was invited to give the prayer for the Senate one morning.

Not all of the Senators show up in time for the prayer. The President of the Senate was apologizing to President Kimball for not having many there to hear his prayer. President Kimball's comment: "Oh, that's all right. I wasn't praying to them, anyway."

—*L. Tom Perry*

God Gives

We ask for strength, and God gives us difficulties which make us strong.

We pray for wisdom, and God sends us problems, the solutions of which develop wisdom.

We plead for courage, and God gives us dangers to overcome.

We ask for favors, and God gives us opportunities.

This is the answer.

Not Difficult

It is not a difficult thing to learn how to pray.

It is not the words we use, particularly, that constitute prayer.

True, faithful, earnest prayer consists more in the feeling that rises from the heart, and from the inward desire of our spirits, to supplicate the Lord in humility and faith, that we may receive his blessings.

It matters not how simple the words may be, if our desires are genuine, and we come before the Lord with a broken heart and contrite spirit, to ask him for what we need.

—*Joseph F. Smith*

A Safeguard

I have little or no fear for the boy and the girl, the young man and the young woman, who honestly and conscientiously supplicate God twice a day for the guidance of his Spirit.

I am sure that when temptation comes, they will have the strength to overcome it by the inspiration that shall be given to them.

Supplicating the Lord for guidance of his Spirit places around us a safeguard and, if we earnestly and honestly seek the guidance of the Spirit of the Lord, then I can assure you that we will receive it.

—Heber J. Grant

Homes Without Prayer

I hope the Latter-day Saints will not fail to say their prayers, their secret prayers and their family prayers.

Children who are reared in homes where they do not have family prayers, and secret prayers, lose a great deal, and I fear that, in the midst of the world's confusion, of hurry and bustle, many times, homes are left without prayer, and without the blessings of the Lord.

These homes cannot continue to be happy.

—George Albert Smith

More Than Any Other

I have more faith in prayer before the Lord than almost any other principle on earth. If we have no faith in prayer to God, then we have not much in either him or the gospel. We should pray unto the Lord, asking him for what we want.

Let the prayers of this people ascend before the Lord continually in the season thereof, and the Lord will not turn them away, but they will be heard and answered, and the kingdom of Zion and God will rise and shine. She will put on her beautiful garments and be clothed with the glory of her God, and fulfill the object of her organization here upon the earth.

—Wilford Woodruff

You Can't Pray a Lie

It made me shiver. And I about made up my mind to pray and see if I couldn't try to quit being the kind of boy I was and be better. So I kneeled down. But the words wouldn't come. Why wouldn't they? It warn't no use to try and hide it from Him. I knowed very well why they wouldn't come. It was because my heart warn't right; it was because I warn't square; it was because I was playing double. I was letting on to give up sin, but away inside of me I was holding on to the biggest one of all. I was trying to make my mouth say I would do the right thing and the clean thing...but deep down in me, I knowed it was a lie, and he knowed it. You can't pray a lie—I found that out.
—*Huckleberry Finn*

A Habit of Prayer

To keep God at the center of one's life requires frequent renewal of power through prayer.

But such renewal is not measured by the amount of time it takes, rather by the degree to which one is able, even for a short time, to have relaxed and unhurried communion with God.

One can pray inwardly at any time and anywhere—but one prays best either alone or with understanding friends.

To avoid neglecting to pray, it is best to have a time, a place, a habit. This is so important that it is worth great effort, in spite of the hurry of life and our lack of privacy.
—*Georgia Harkness*

Seek to Know God

We would say to the brethren, seek to know God in your closets; call upon him in the fields.

Follow the directions of the Book of Mormon and pray for your families, your cattle, your flocks, your herds, your corn, and all things that you possess; ask the blessing of God upon all your labors, and everything that you engage in.

Be virtuous and pure; be men of integrity and truth; keep the commandments of God; and then you will be able more perfectly to understand the difference between right and wrong—between the things of God and the things of men; and your path will be like that of the just, which shineth brighter and brighter unto the perfect day.
—*Joseph Smith*

Answers to Prayers

Answers to prayer often come in unexpected ways.

We pray, for instance, for a certain virtue; but God seldom delivers Christian virtues all wrapped in a package and ready for use. Rather he puts us in situations whereby his help we can develop those virtues.

✎

One of the Greatest Prayers

One of the greatest prayers that a man can offer, so far as I understand prayers and their consistency, is that when an elder of Israel stands before the people, he may communicate and tell some thoughts to do the people good, and build them up in the principles of truth and salvation.

Prayers of this kind are as agreeable in the ears of the Lord as any prayers that an elder of Israel can possibly offer.

For when an elder stands before the people, he should do so realizing that he stands before them for the purpose of communicating knowledge, that they may receive truth in their souls and be built up in righteousness by receiving further light, progressing in their education in the principles of holiness.

—Lorenzo Snow

✎

Victory at Gettysburg

I went to my room one day and locked the door and got down upon my knees before Almighty God and prayed to him mightily for victory at Gettysburg.

I told him that this war was his, and our cause his cause, that we could not stand another Fredericksburg or Chancellorsville.

Then and there, I made a solemn vow to Almighty God that if he would stand by our boys at Gettysburg, I would stand by him, and he did stand by you boys, and I will stand by him.

And after that, I don't know how it was, and I cannot explain it, soon a sweet comfort crept into my soul. The feeling came that God had taken the whole business into his own hands, and things would go right at Gettysburg, and that was why I had no fears about you.

—Abraham Lincoln

Heaven is Never Deaf

I cherish, as one of the dearest experiences in life, the knowledge that God hears the prayer of faith.

It is true that the answer may not come as directly, and at the time, or in the manner we anticipate, but it comes, and at a time, and in a manner best for the interests of him who offers the supplication.

On more than one occasion, I have received direct and immediate assurances that my petition was granted. At one time, particularly, that answer came as distinctly as though my Father stood by my side and spoke the words.

These experiences are part of my being, and must remain so as long as memory and intelligence last. They have taught me that "Heaven is never deaf, but when man's heart is dumb."

—*David O. McKay*

A Prayer

Where there is hatred, let me sow love.

Where there is injury, pardon.

Where there is doubt, faith.

Where there is despair, hope.

Where there is darkness, light.

Where there is sadness, joy.

0 Divine Master, grant that I may not so much seek to be consoled as to console;

to be understood, as to understand;

to be loved, as to love.

For it is in giving that we receive;

it is in pardoning that we are pardoned;

and it is in dying that we are born to eternal life.

—*Francis of Assisi*

Never Mind, Lord

Only the top of his head could be seen bobbing up and down between the waves of the boiling, rushing, muddy waters of the river. When the waves lifted him up higher into view, his arms could be seen threshing helplessly as he attempted to pull himself toward the distant shore.

Don had been too brave in standing near this fast-moving stream so soon after the recent rains. The bank of soft dirt he had been standing on had crumbled suddenly beneath his feet, and carried him helplessly into the dirty water. Don was a strong swimmer, but his strength was no match for this powerful, swift current. When he tried to cry out and shout for help, water gushed forcefully into his open mouth, causing him to choke and struggle for air. The stream was carrying him quickly toward the waterfall and rock-strewn rapids below. It looked like no power on earth could save Don now.

Don had never believed in Jesus or in the power of prayer, but right now he had nowhere else to turn. In desperation, he sincerely whispered, "Heavenly Father, please bless me. Help me to reach the shore. I don't want to die!"

Don had hardly finished his prayer when something struck him on his back with such force that it nearly pushed him underwater. A huge log had floated downstream and was pushing against his body. In desperation, he reached for its out-flung branches and, grasping them firmly, with great effort, he pulled himself onto the large floating log. Just as he did so, one end of the log struck the bank of the stream, causing it to turn toward the bank. This allowed Don to quickly and gratefully jump onto the solid earth of the riverbank.

With a sigh of relief, Don said, "Never mind, Lord, I got out by myself. I don't need your help after all."

꒱

The First Thing

When the film "Sister Kenny" was being shot, the famous Australian nurse herself was called in to explain just how she had discovered her treatment for polio.

Sister Kenny said that she had been summoned to a seven-year-old girl who lived far out in the lonely bush country. The child was in extreme pain, had a high fever, and her leg and foot muscles were contracted.

Sister Kenny had never seen this combination of symptoms before. Hurriedly, she sent a rider to the nearest telegraph station, twenty miles away, and an urgent message to Dr. Eneus MacDonald in Toowamba, requesting advice.

Meanwhile, she spent the night comforting the child as best she could.

At dawn the long awaited reply arrived. "The symptoms you describe indicate infantile paralysis," it read. "There is no known cure. Do the best you can."

Sister Kenny was stunned; the case, then, was virtually hopeless.

At this point Rosalind Russell, who was preparing to portray Sister Kenny on the screen, interrupted, "What did you do? What was the first thing you thought of? Did you tear up a blanket for the hot packs?"

"No," Sister Kenny quietly replied. "The first thing I did was kneel down and say a prayer."

Did You Ever See God?

"Did you ever see God?" a scientist asked his Arab guide who prayed in his presence.

"No."

"Did you ever hear God?"

"No."

"Did you ever put out your hand and touch God?"

"No."

"Then you are a great fool to believe in a God you never saw, a God you never heard, and a God you never put out your hand and touched."

The Arab guide said nothing.

They retired, and arose early the next morning, a little before sunrise.

"There was a camel around the tent last night," said the man of science.

The Arab's eyes twinkled. "Did you see the camel?"

"No."

"Did you hear the camel?"

"No."

"Did you put out your hand and touch the camel?"

"No."

"Well, you are a strange man of science to believe in a camel you never saw, a camel you never heard, and a camel you never put out your hand and touched."

"Oh, but," said the scientist, "I can see his footprints all around the tent."

Just then the sun came up in all its oriental splendor and, with a graceful gesture of his hand, the guide said, "Behold, the footprints of the Almighty! Look, and know there is a God."

❧

A Portrait of Prayer

Prayer is a dialogue, not a monologue. It opens a spiritual channel between man and his immortal guide.

President McKay said that prayer is "a message of the soul...the language is not mere words but spirit vibration".

Prayer can predict our progress. If it is a true blueprint of our intent, it will articulate the best of each of us.

Prayer constitutes deep thoughts and institutes deeper ones. It is part of the key to wisdom. The Prophet Joseph was instructed by Moroni, "Forget not to pray, that thy mind may become strong."

Prayer requires faith, and builds it, and permits each of us to experience the feelings of gratitude, humility, and hope.

Prayer provides relief from mundane burdens through sharing the responsibilities of life with another. It is an invigorating prescription, an antidote for unnecessary cares and qualms, a catalyst for further spiritual endeavors.

Prayer provides an individual with an honest analysis of himself. It teaches him the ability to appraise himself realistically and rightly—not as compared to the neighbors next door, the group at the office, or his graduating class—but to himself, and how well he is running the race of life as an individual, evaluated only according to his inherent "talents" and his use of them.

Prayer teaches, indeed admits, the reality of God. It is a testimony of faith, a daily autobiography, a personal portrait.

Prayer can resolve any doubt, remove any fear, guide and inspire, and teach the eternal truths.

Prayer puts us in touch with the greatest power in the universe. It frees our souls from enmities and grudges, and brings us closer to our Heavenly Father and gives us inner peace and happiness.

The trouble with most of our prayers is that we are not honest with ourselves and with God. We must be free of envy, resentment, jealousy, and greed.

Prayer is a conversation with God, but prayer is no substitute for work.

—*Henry D. Moyle*

❧

A Real Prayer

It had been a busy day. So many things to do. When I shut my bedroom door for prayers, my nerves were taut. My mind would not be still. My thoughts jumped about.

"Our Father which art in heaven…"

Wonder if the basement light's still burning…

"Hallowed be Thy name…"

Forgot to sprinkle the luncheon cloth…need it tomorrow…the nursery window…wind from the west tonight…

"Thy Kingdom come. Thy will be done…"

So tired…didn't clean my teeth…

I arose.

What had I been doing? Saying my prayers? Just that and nothing more. Just saying them…all the lovely words of them with my lips.…but not with my mind or heart.

I went to the nursery…put a screen around the west window…took a peek into the crib… to the bathroom…scrubbed my teeth…to the kitchen…checked on the basement light.…sprinkled the luncheon cloth…made a note to call the plumber in the morning…

In my room again, I went back to my prayer, my mind cleared of all the troublesome little things.

"Our Father which art in heaven."

Our Father…my Father…the Father of us all…

"Hallowed be Thy name."

Holy…sacred…be my every thought of Thee…

"Thy Kingdom come."

To my heart…to the hearts of all men everywhere…

"Thy will be done in earth as it is in heaven."

Thy will…thy good be done in the world around us…as it is in our own hearts…

"Give us this day our daily bread."

Give us our bread…our necessities…our needs…not our foolish greeds…

"And forgive us our debts as we forgive our debtors."

Teach me, Father, to deal as justly, as wisely, as forgivingly with others, as you have dealt with me…

"And lead us not into temptation, but deliver us from evil: for Thine is the kingdom, and the power, and the glory, forever, Amen."

There was more to my prayer—my own special thanksgivings and petitions. And as I made my prayer—freed from the burden of "little things"—my heart found peace.
—*Marion Doolan*

Preparation

Dig a well before you are thirsty.

—*Chinese proverb*

❧

He who has no principle draws little interest.

❧

When you fail to prepare, you prepare to fail.

❧

Only a fool would trifle with the souls of men.

—*Joseph Smith*

❧

When the well's dry, they know the worth of water.

❧

Luck is what happens when preparation meets opportunity.

❧

We were born to prepare to live, and we live to prepare to die.

—*Sterling W. Sill*

❧

Opportunity is always within the reach of the arm of preparation.

❧

To be educated is to realize the implications of one's own beliefs.

❧

If you start soon enough, you won't have to run so fast to catch up.

❧

Early to bed, early to rise, until you've learned and earned enough to do otherwise.

❧

Be sure you take an interest in the future: that's where you will spend the rest of your life.

❧

Wisdom is the principal thing; therefore, get wisdom; and, with all thy getting, get understanding.

&

If you were graduated yesterday, and have learned nothing today, then you will be uneducated tomorrow.

&

All who have meditated upon the art of governing mankind have been convinced that the fate of empires depends upon the education of youth.

—*Aristotle*

&

If a man empties his purse into his head, no man can take it away from him; an investment in knowledge always pays the best interest.

—*Benjamin Franklin*

&

There is an urgency in this day for us to prepare for the coming of the Lord. For those who have heeded the warning and continue in their preparations to accumulate the oil of righteousness in their lamps, great blessings are theirs.

—*Marvin J. Ashton*

&

Thinking Ahead

The engineer of an express train, as he rounded a bend, suddenly saw a short distance ahead a freight wreck on the track next to his own. Two cars had buckled over and lay in the path of his train. There was not time to slow down; there was not time to think.

In a flash, the engineer pulled the throttle wide open, and yelled to the fireman to duck down low. The terrific impetus of the express knocked the wrecked cars from the track and amidst the splintered debris, and the express was brought to a stop a half mile on the other side.

As the passengers crowded around the engineer, one asked him how, in such a moment of crisis, he could think quickly enough to make and to act upon the only decision that could have saved his train from wreck.

"I did not think. I did not have to think. I had often thought of such a possibility, and I made up my mind ten years ago, just what I would do if such a situation ever arose. When it did, I acted instinctively."

Halfway to Nowhere

I was in the ninth grade. A year in which it seemed I was halfway to nowhere. Confidence was not part of my nature. My actions were largely controlled by my feelings of inferiority. Perhaps it was the low light of self-doubt that made the following experience such a bright and guiding star.

Third hour, I sat near the back of the classroom. My feet extended as far forward as I could stretch them. By sitting in this manner, I was scarcely visible from where the teacher sat at her desk in the front.

Friday was the day for current events. When the roll was called, each student had two choices—he could either answer "prepared" or "unprepared". If his response was "prepared", then he had to give a talk. If his response was "unprepared", then he didn't have to do anything. I quickly grasped the idea that "unprepared" was the word that would get me off the hook.

As the weeks went by, each time my name was called, I responded almost with dignity, "unprepared". My friends also mastered this word. We all, as a group, made it easier for each of us as individuals.

Once, as I was visiting with the teacher, I noticed my name in the performance roll book, and behind my name was a long series of negative signs. This worried me, but not enough to make me stand up in front of my friends and give a talk. Speaking to a group seemed like the most frightening of all things.

A girl I liked very much sat in front of me. I liked her so much that, on the way to school, I would think of clever things to say to her but, when in her presence, my mind would go blank and I would become almost tongue-tied.

One day when the teacher called the roll and reached my name, I replied, "unprepared". It was then that this girl did me a great favor. She turned around, looked back at me, and said, "Why don't you get prepared?" I was not able to listen to many of the reports that day. I kept thinking of all sorts of wonderful things like, "What does she care, unless she cares?"

I went home, found an article in the newspaper, and read it time and again, until I had finally committed it to memory. I cut the article out, folded it, placed it in my wallet, and carried it with me all week.

The next Friday, I was there in my usual seat in the back. The teacher started to call the roll without looking up. Finally she got to my name, "George." And very quietly I gave a great speech, "Prepared."

She stopped calling the roll and looked up at me. I poked my head up as far as I could and nodded. The girl turned around and smiled. My friends looked over at me like, "traitor".

Then I sat waiting my turn, saying to myself, "What have I done?" I was scared. Then I made a magnificent discovery. It was all right to be afraid, if I didn't let it stop me from doing what I should.

My turn came. I went to the front and started to speak. I remembered every word and, after the last word had crossed my lips, I stood there for just a second, and a priceless thought passed my mind and found its way to my heart. I said to myself, "I like you."

I returned to my seat and sat down. I didn't hear any of the reports but, as my heart pounded within me, I kept feeling over and over again, "This is the only way to live."

—George Durrant

When You Meet a Tiger

Dear Son:

Last night as we were watching television and you asked me a question I did not answer. Since my jet does not land for a couple of hours, I have decided to write a confidential reply.

You'll recall that it was hard to recognize the sly tiger in the jungle program we were watching, and the great power he seemed to have.

As he snarled with that angry, singsong whine and leaped, you turned to me and asked, "Dad, what do you do when you meet a tiger?"

Well, son, when a man meets a tiger he should be prepared for, if he is not, the tiger will destroy him.

If we were living where tigers are feared by man, and by all other animals, because of their viciousness, cruelty, and treachery, I would suggest that you avoid meeting a tiger at night, or where grass and undergrowth stand high.

To meet a tiger, you had best be in a cage, perched on an elephant's back, or with a powerful rifle across your lap. Even then, it is dangerous.

A tiger's terrible claws can slash through even an elephant's thick skin. If a man meets a tiger, he must know what he is doing and have courage.

I doubt that either of us will ever meet an honest-to-goodness live tiger—at least, I hope not.

But there are other kinds of tigers, just as sly and vicious, and as harmful and deadly as the tigers in India.

I call them invisible tigers.

Invisible tigers, like real-life tigers, are treacherous, both night and day. They are hard to recognize, for they too blend into the tall grass and undergrowth of people and their conversations. They damage a man's soul. To fight them, you have to recognize them, and then surround yourself with a protective shield and powerful weapons, including courage.

There are several rules it would be wise to follow when you meet a tiger:

Rule 1: Tag the tiger

To tag tigers, you really need to be sharp. Because you cannot see them, you must depend largely on what you hear. If someone dares you to do something you know is wrong, or calls you "chicken" when you refuse, or assures you "it's really okay", or "everybody's doing it", then you can bet your life that you have met an "invisible tiger". This tiger is temptation. Of the many varieties of invisible tigers, teenagers are most vulnerable to "show-off" tigers, "follow-the-crowd" tigers, tigers of "rebellion", "break the Word of Wisdom" tigers, and "break the law of chastity" tigers. You can be sure that these tigers are lurking close by when you say to yourself such things as "no one will know", or "just once won't hurt".

Rule 2: Turn up the volume

Inside you is a secret place for things you have been taught, and these things play back to you as you go about your day. Sometimes the play back is not very loud. So when you meet a tiger, turn up the volume.

Rule 3: Set your sights

Slaying your invisible tigers is something you have to do. Setting sights is deciding what to do. In these days, it becomes very difficult to set sights, because your friends have greater influence over you than when you were young. They will be unkind to you at times, and will even persecute you by calling you names. It becomes a problem to make up your mind. Invisible tigers do not drop dead from old age or accident, so you need to decide how you are going to handle them. Keep asking questions that need mature answers; weigh one idea against another; listen to your inner promptings, and then decide. As you test and compare and decide, your ability to eliminate invisible tigers will grow in leaps and bounds.

Rule 4: Use your shield

This shield is the protection afforded by your Heavenly Father through prayer. If you will pray to God and seek his guidance, then he will guide you and surround you with protection more effective than a tiger cage. Your Father in heaven loves you, and you need only to seek his help and try your best to do right.

Rule 5: Cap with courage

After you have tagged the tiger, turned up the volume, set your sights, and used your shield, the final rule for meeting a tiger is to slay it with the courage of your convictions. You are certain to have static from some of your friends, but you can claim no fame through inaction, or going with the crowd, or running away. Courage in doing right is its own reward.

You are very choice to your mother and me and we know that you will always have the courage to fight the tigers you meet.

Love,

Dad

Service

Nothing is yours until you give it away.

Ꙭ

He that serves his fellow man, serves God.

—King Benjamin

Ꙭ

Only a life lived for others is a life worthwhile.

—Albert Einstein

Ꙭ

What on earth are you doing for heaven's sake?

Ꙭ

To ease another's heartache is to forget one's own.

—Abraham Lincoln

Ꙭ

Thee lift me, and I lift thee, and together we ascend.

—John Greenleaf Whittier

Ꙭ

In the gospel, most of the blessings lie in the second mile.

Ꙭ

Doing the will of God leaves me no time to dispute his will.

Ꙭ

In the service of the Lord, it is not where but how you serve.

—J. Reuben Clark

Ꙭ

If you cannot do great things, do small things in a great way.

Ꙭ

Our lives are like shoes, to be worn out in the service of God.

—Spencer W. Kimball

Ꙭ

You get more than you give when you give more than you get.

❧

What do we live for, if not to make life less difficult for others?
—*George Eliot*

❧

The most important position in the church is the one you presently hold.
—*Antoine R. Ivins*

❧

You can't lift anybody until you are standing on higher ground than he is.

❧

To know the real joy of service, try helping someone who can't pay you for it.

❧

Those who bring sunshine to the lives of others, cannot keep it from themselves.
—*Sir James Barnei*

❧

The service we render to others is really the rent we pay for our room on this earth.

❧

There is no better exercise for the heart than reaching down and lifting someone up.

❧

The Lord is willing to go half way: he'll take care of me, if I'll take care of his work.

❧

There are those among us who are trying to serve the Lord without offending the devil.

❧

Every man goes down to his grave bearing in his hands only that which he has given away.

❧

Give a man a fish and feed him for a day; teach him how to fish and feed him for a lifetime.

❧

The greatest pleasure is to do a good action by stealth—and to have it found out by accident.

Hands that help are holier than lips that merely pray; the combination, however, is unbeatable.

He who does a good turn should never remember it, but he who receives one should never forget it.

Learn to follow council, serve faithfully, and magnify your calling, for God's kingdom is a kingdom of order.

We begin to live only when we begin to love; and we begin to love only when self dies, and we live to bless others.

The true way to serve the Lord is through service to man; we should be extremely happy when serving in his church.

—*David O. McKay*

What we have done for ourselves alone dies with us: what we have done for others and the world remains and is immortal.

—*Albert Pipe*

You are indeed charitable when you give, and while giving, turn your face away so that you may not see the shyness of the receiver.

—*Gibran*

No man has ever risen to the real stature of spiritual manhood until he has found that it is finer to serve somebody else than it is to serve himself.

—*Woodrow Wilson*

The longer we live, the more we realize that the people who want to help themselves can only do so by helping others: it's a basic law of success.

"No man is an island," wrote John Donne. Yet too many of us still fear the loss of self that comes through serving others. Actually, such service is the only true way to "find" yourself.

❧

Busier than God

Julia Ward Howe, who wrote the "Battle Hymn of the Republic," asked a distinguished Senator to interest himself in the case of a person who needed help.

The Senator answered, "I have become so busy that I can no longer concern myself with individuals."

She replied, "That's remarkable. Even God hasn't reached that stage yet."

❧

The Golden Rule in Business

People who begin by asking how they can find success solely within themselves are doomed from the start: the rewards go to people who have searched diligently for ways to help others.

One of the many successful men who have used this principle was James Cash Penney. Mr. Penney, beginning with a small general merchandise store in Kemmerer, Wyoming in 1902, built a multi-million-dollar business empire on one simple principle—the golden rule.

For years, the Penney stores were called The Golden Rule Stores. And it was Mr. Penney's faith in that principle—always treating a customer as he himself would want to be treated—that made them grow and prosper.

But, perhaps even more important, was Mr. Penney's attitude toward his employees. In the first place, he did not like the word "employee"; he preferred to treat everyone as a partner, so he called them "associates". And he devoted himself to treating them as he would want to be treated were the situations reversed. Most of all, he knew that, by helping them make money, his own success would be assured.

❧

For The Sake of Giving

John Chapman was a nurseryman in Pittsburgh. He loved all the beautiful things in the world. He especially loved his great apple orchards when they were in bloom in the spring, and when they were loaded with luscious fruit in the fall. He wished everyone could have an apple orchard.

He was generous with his young trees and apple seeds. To the many families moving west who came to buy young trees, he gave apples for their journey, and seeds, as well as saplings, for the orchards they would plant in distant prairie lands.

When discouraging letters came back to him, stating that the saplings and seeds did not grow, he felt that it was because the pioneers did not know how to care for their young orchards. This worried him. He thought of the blessings apple orchards would be out in the new country, to homes, to villages, and to the entire new land.

Finally, he decided he must go himself in defense of his trees. It was as if he heard a call to go and plant orchards in the wilds, to give apple trees to the deprived pioneers. So he dedicated the rest of his life to that kind of giving.

He collected all the apple seeds he could buy or beg and made arrangements so that he could send for more. Then he went out into the wilderness, vowing that with God's help, that he would give the flowers and the fruit of a thousand orchards to the discouraged homesteaders.

He endured many hardships and dangers as he traveled about, putting small nurseries next to isolated cabins, small churches, scattered communities. As the orchards grew, they helped to bring love and hope and joy where there had been only bitterness and despair.

As the years went by, the trees in orchard after orchard took root and bore blossoms and fruit. The people, too, took root. He had the satisfaction of knowing that he had given a priceless gift to humanity, to civilization. He said that the only reward he hoped for was that there would be orchards to plant and nurture in heaven. Truly Johnny Appleseed gave for the sake of giving, and he gave of himself.

—*Eleanor Atkinson*

❧

Never Lose Anything by It

An LDS chapel was to be built in a northern California town. The members of the branch there had been looking forward to this time since six years earlier, when a little old woman, one of the most faithful converts, had handed the branch president five dollars and asked that it be used to start a building fund for a branch chapel. From this small beginning, the fund grew—as did the branch.

Now that the time had arrived to start construction of their Church home, the members of the branch presidency and building committee were determined that nothing should happen to delay the speedy completion of it. So they proceeded to consult the building trade unions.

They explained to union officials that they were not asking for donations, although they would not refuse any donations that were offered, but that they wished to do their own work on the building, as far as they could; that most of it would be donation work and much of it evening and Saturday work; they were asked if there were any objections to union members working on the chapel at these times, if they so desired.

No objection was made by any of the building trade unions until an LDS carpenter met with his union to discuss the matter with them. They did not like the idea of carpenter work being done on Saturday, as union carpenters are pledged not to work on Saturday—even for themselves. They told him they would prefer that the work be done on Sunday.

Then Mr. C, a prominent member of the carpenter's union, asked which church it was that was beginning the new building. He was informed that it was the Church of Jesus Christ of Latter-day Saints, the Mormon Church.

Mr. C's attitude changed, and he addressed the entire group. "Brothers," he said, "I would like to tell all of you my experience with the Mormon Church." Mr. C is one of the most respected members of the carpenter's local union, and is a delegate to the central labor council and to the state conventions. When he speaks, they listen.

"A few years ago," he continued, "I was in Casper, Wyoming. The Mormons were remodeling their church building. They were doing it by donation work, and I helped them for two days. They thanked me kindly and gave me a Book of Mormon.

"Sometime later, I was working in Salt Lake City, and I became sick. I was staying in a hotel room and was full of misery. The weather was hot, and it seemed like I couldn't breathe. I opened my door, and a Mormon elder who was going through the hotel came in to see me. When he found out what kind of condition I was in, he said he would report it to his bishop right away. A little later that bishop, who appeared to be a businessman, came to see me. He got me a good doctor, and I was soon on my feet again. That Mormon bishop not only paid my doctor bill, but my hotel bill as well. Don't ever hesitate to help the Mormons, for you will never lose anything by it."

The building of the LDS meetinghouse went ahead speedily with the enthusiastic work of the members.

—*Alvin D. Day*

Standing on Shore

Some young people were sailing down the river toward Niagara Falls.

A man on the shore cried out to them, "Young men, ahoy, the rapids are below you."

They heeded not his warning call until they realized too late that they were in the midst of the rapids.

With all the power at their commands, they failed to turn their boat upstream, "So," said the man who tried to warn them, "shrieking and cursing, over they went."

The lesson left an indelible impression upon me; but today it seems incomplete.

It's one thing to stand on the shore and cry, "Young men, ahoy, there is danger ahead", and it is another thing to row into the stream and, if possible, get into the boat with the young men and, by companionship, by persuasion, by legitimate force when necessary, turn the boat from the rapids.

Too many of us are satisfied to stand on the shore and cry, "There is danger ahead."

The Miracle

There was a girl in one seminary class who seemed to be helpless and almost hopeless. I tried to encourage her and draw her out; I sensed that she wanted desperately to belong and to do something. But when she was asked to respond, give a prayer, or read a scripture, she would struggle for a while, and then start to cry, and then return to her seat. There was some sympathy on the part of the class for her, but it is also true that there were some students who were often brutal in their comments.

She almost never combed her hair, she had very poor clothing, and she frequently wore mismatched socks, if she wore any at all. If she arrived for class a little early, the chairs on either side of her would almost invariably be empty. If she got to class late, she could sit by someone because that would be the only seat open.

I knew enough about her background to understand why she was the way she was. Her mother was a widow with almost no income.

In that class were the student body president of the high school and also a girl who had been elected the beauty queen. Besides being very handsome and intelligent students, they were talented and involved in many activities.

One day, I called the two of them into my office and asked if they would like to perform a miracle. They were interested. I told them some miracles were a little slow in developing, but they were miracles nonetheless. We then talked a little about the girl, and I made assignments.

The student body president was to smile and speak to her every time he saw her around school. That was all. He didn't have to take her on a date; he didn't have to stop and talk to her; he didn't have to associate beyond that, or single her out—merely a happy, encouraging "I think you're great" or a "Hello, how are you today".

The beauty queen accepted the assignment of walking with the girl across the road from the high school to the seminary. That was all. She didn't have to include her in her circle of friends, other than to walk to and from the seminary every day. She would simply hurry to catch up with her, or slow down to wait for her when they were coming across the street, and just talk about whatever she wanted to talk about.

The two of them went about their tasks quietly but enthusiastically, saying not a word to anyone else. The miracle was not long in coming.

One day, I knew there was something different about the girl. It took me most of the class period to figure out what it was. And then I saw what it was. She had combed her hair that day. That was an event.

Over the next month or two, the transformation continued. Our beauty queen became friendly and chatty with her during that time. She could never walk with her alone because she had her own friends following her. And so other girls were included in the group, and soon the girl was surrounded for those few minutes each day with the most popular girls at school.

There are so many interesting details that could be related about the miracle. Our wallflower transformed herself, went to college, found good employment, married in the temple, and those who know her would never believe the ugly duckling of her youth.

—*Boyd K. Packer*

The King's Highway

Once a king had a great highway built for the members of his kingdom. After it was completed, but before it was opened to the public, the king decided to have a contest. He invited as many as desired to participate. Their challenge was to see who could travel the highway best.

On the day of the contest, the people came. Some of them had fine chariots, some had fine clothing, fine hairdos, or great food. Some young men came in their track clothes and ran along the highway.

People traveled the highway all day, but each one, when he arrived at the end, complained to the king that there was a large pile of rocks and debris left on the road at one spot, and this got in their way and hindered their travel.

At the end of the day, a lone traveler crossed the finish line and wearily walked over to the king. He was tired and dirty, but he addressed the king with great respect and handed him a bag of gold, explaining, "I stopped along the way to clear away a pile of rocks and debris that was blocking the road. This bag of gold was under it all, and I want you to return it to its rightful owner."

The king replied, "You are the rightful owner."

The traveler replied, "Oh no, this is not mine. I've never known such money."

"Oh yes," said the king, "you've earned this gold, for you won my contest. He who travels the road best is he who makes the road smoother for those who will follow."

More Than His Best

An Elder was made supervisor of the Aaronic Priesthood and told by his bishop to activate every boy in the priesthood quorums.

After a short time, the Elder had successfully activated every boy, except one.

The following Sunday, he went to the less active boy's house and knocked on the door. The father of the boy answered the door, and the Elder asked if he might take his son to priesthood meeting. The father told him no.

The Elder went back six times, and each time, he received the same answer from the father.

He had done his best, but the bishop hadn't asked him to do his best, he had asked him to activate every boy in the priesthood quorums.

So the Elder went back to the less active boy's house every Sunday for twenty-six straight weeks.

The last time, the father replied, "All right and, if it means that much to you, I would like to go, too."

⮞⮜

My Daily Fun

A committee of prominent Chicago citizens waited in one of the city's railroad stations. They were to welcome one of the greatest men in the world.

He arrived and greeted them in three languages. He was a giant of a man, six feet four inches tall, with bushy hair and a walrus mustache.

The reception committee stood talking about how honored they were to meet him and how the important people of the city were waiting to entertain him. Reporters took down his every word. Flash cameras were busy taking his picture.

Suddenly the giant of a man asked to be excused. He walked rapidly through the crowd on to the station platform. Coming to an old woman who was struggling with heavy suitcases, he scooped up her bags with his great hands. Then he told her to follow him. He worked his way through the throng and took the woman to her coach. After wishing her a good journey, he returned to the committee. "Sorry to have kept you waiting, gentlemen," he said to the astonished group. "I was just having my daily fun."

The distinguished visitor was Albert Schweitzer, famous philosopher-musician-doctor-missionary. "First time I ever saw a sermon walking," said one of the reporters.

A member of the reception committee remarked, "A lot of us stuffed shirts were unstuffed that moment."

Well they might be. A man with a world mission, engaged in writing a profound history of civilization, was demonstrating, in a simple, unaffected way, the love of God for the least individual, and the democracy of true brotherhood.

—James L. Christensen

Two Seas

There are two seas in Palestine.

One is fresh, with fish. Splashes of green adorn its banks. Trees spread their branches over it, and stretch out their thirsty roots to sip of its healing water. Along its shores, the children play as children played when he was there. He loved it. He could look across its silver surface when he spoke his parables. And on a rolling plain not far away, he fed five thousand people.

The River Jordan makes this sea with sparkling water from the hills so it laughs in the sunshine. And men build their houses near to it and the birds build their nests in its trees. And every kind of life is happier because it is there.

The River Jordan flows on south into another sea.

Here there is no splash of fish, no fluttering leaf, no song of birds, no children's laughter. Travelers choose another route unless on urgent business. The air hangs heavy above its waters, and neither man nor beast nor fowl will drink.

What makes this mighty difference in these neighbor seas?

Not the River Jordan: it empties the same good water into both. Not the soil in which they lie. Not the country roundabout.

This is the difference: the Sea of Galilee receives but does not keep the Jordan; for every drop that flows into it, another drop flows out. The giving and receiving go on in equal measure.

The other sea is shrewder, hoarding its income jealously. It will not be tempted into generous impulse. Every drop it gets, it keeps.

The Sea of Galilee gives and lives.

The other sea gives nothing: it is named The Dead Sea.

There are two kinds of people in the world. There are two seas in Palestine.

Success

Well done is better than well said.

❧

Success comes in cans, not in can'ts.

—Dirk van der Lende

❧

No rules for success work unless you do.

❧

All men are born equal, but some outgrow it.

❧

By others' faults, wise men correct their own.

❧

If at first you don't succeed, you'll get a lot of advice.

❧

Aim for service, not success—and success will follow.

❧

It's too bad that success makes failures of so many men.

❧

Success is measured in terms of preparedness for eternity.

❧

Success is not in never falling, but in rising every time you fall.

❧

Success consists of getting up just one more time than you fall.

❧

Remember that TRIUMPH is just a little "umph" added to "try."

❧

Success needs no excuse; failure has all the excuses in the world.

❦

A successful man keeps looking for work after he has found a job.
—*Raymond Duncan*

❦

Good luck is a lazy man's estimate of a hard-working man's success.

❦

To do for the world more than the world does for you—that is success.
—*Henry Ford*

❦

Those who are willing to take steps enough are the ones who reach the top.

❦

Success is the art of making mistakes when no one is around to notice them.

❦

No man has ever climbed the ladder of success with his hands in his pockets.

❦

You're on the road to success when you realize that failure is merely a detour.

❦

Sometimes a noble failure serves the world as faithfully as a distinguished success.

❦

Success usually is a plant of slow growth, although its flowering may seem sudden.
—*B. C. Forbes*

❦

It's not how much you know, but rather, how well you put what you know into action!

❦

A man may fail many times, but he isn't a failure until he begins to blame somebody else.

❦

The hardest thing about climbing the ladder of success is getting through the crowd at the bottom.

❦

Success in life is a matter, not so much of talent or opportunity, as of concentration and perseverance.

—*Charles Wendte*

❦

For success, write down what you want to be; then, every day write down what you did toward that goal.

❦

There is no comparison between that which is lost by not succeeding, and that which is lost by not trying.

—*Francis Bacon*

❦

No age or time of life, no position or circumstance, has a monopoly on success: any age is the right age to start doing.

—*Gerard*

❦

One of the biggest troubles with success these days is that its recipe is about the same as that for a nervous breakdown.

—*Powerfax*

❦

On the plains of hesitation lie the bleached bones of men who, on the dawn of a great victory in their lives, lay down to rest.

❦

The most successful man is the man who holds onto the old just as long as it is good, and grabs the new just as soon as it is better.

❦

The best way to get ahead in the world is by learning to conquer difficulties by hard work and by cooperation with our fellow men.

❦

The men who have accomplished most in the world were persons who had ambition and a goal, and worked long and hard to attain it.

—*Samscripts*

The greatest of human possessions are a well-trained mind, a body to match, and a love of achievement, without which a man is old before his time.

If man is to achieve lasting greatness, he must have a God-centered life. Remember personal achievement is bought at the price of work and sacrifice.

The Lord gave us two ends to use: one to think with, the other to sit on; which one we use will determine how well we do in life; in other words: heads, you win; tails, you lose.

Success is not a matter of position or possessions. It is a frame of mind. It is the satisfied feeling of service rendered and a life spent in a worthwhile way. There have been rich men, important men, whose lives were complete failure. And there have been poor men whom the ages have delighted to honor.

—*Stephen M. Paulson*

Work

The privilege to work is a gift.

The power to work is a blessing.

The love of work is success.

Indolence

It is well to remember that:

An indolent person did not discover the telephone,

An indolent person did not learn to control steam,

An indolent person did not discover the power of gasoline,

nor learn how to harness the great Niagara Falls.

The Family of Success

The father of success is named Work.

The mother of success is named Ambition.

The oldest son is named Common Sense.

Some of the brothers are called Stability, Perseverance, Honesty, Thoroughness, Foresight, Enthusiasm, and Cooperation.

The oldest daughter is named Character.

Some of the sisters are called Cheerfulness, Loyalty, Care, Courtesy, Economy, Sincerity, and Harmony.

The baby is named Opportunity.

Get acquainted with the father of success, and you will be able to get along with the rest of the family.

Effort Brings Success

I realize that it requires a constant effort on the part of each and every one of us to make a success of our lives. It requires no effort at all to roll down a hill, but it does require an effort to climb to the summit. It needs no effort to walk in the broad way that leads to destruction, but it needs an effort to walk in the straight and narrow path that leads to life eternal.

—*Heber J. Grant*

Only Real Way to Achieve Success

I would like to reiterate that I sincerely believe the only real way to achieve success—no matter what business you are in—is through discipline. You must determine what degree of success you are going to obtain and then discipline yourself to working habits that will lead to your goals. If you do this, then everything will fall into place. Enthusiasm will be kindled, ideas will spring up, knowledge will be accumulated, and the sales will roll in.

Success Gained

He has achieved success who has lived well, laughed often and loved much; who has gained the respect of intelligent men, and the love of little children; who has filled his niche and accomplished his task; who has left the world better than he found it, whether by an improved poppy, perfect poem, or a rescued soul; who has never lacked appreciation of earth's beauty, or failed to express it; who has given the best he had; whose life was an inspiration; whose memory, a benediction.

Syndicated Office Boy

One day back in the Gay Nineties, a fourteen-year-old Brooklyn boy sat down on a curb in the New York shipping district. There he put his brain to work on the problem of how an eighth-grade graduate, whose father had just died, could earn a living for himself and his family.

Emmet J. McCormack had been trying to hook on as an office boy, but four successive firms had told him that they didn't have enough work to keep a boy busy.

After considerable thought, young McCormack rose from the curb and went back to the firms, offering each of them one-fourth of an office boy for $1 per week. They hired him.

McCormack later became co-founder of Moore-McCormack Lines, the second-largest American flag shipping company.

But this was his first coup—and, until his death in 1965, he was proud of having been the world's first "syndicated office boy".

⤐

Lord, In My Success I Need Thee

Lord, forgive me that when life's circumstances lift me to the crest of the wave, I tend to forget thee. Yet like an errant child, I have blamed thee with my every failure, even as I credit myself with every success.

When my fears evaporate like the morning mist, then vainly I imagine that I am sufficient unto myself, that material resources and human resources are enough.

I need thee when the sun shines, lest I forget the storm and the dark.

I need thee when I am popular, when my friends and those who work beside me approve and compliment me. I need thee more then, lest my head begin to swell.

0 God, forgive me for my stupidity, my blindness in success, my lack of trust in thee. Be thou now my Savior in success. Save me from conceit. Save me from pettiness. Save me from myself! And take this success, I pray, and use it for thy glory. In thy strength, I pray. Amen.

—The Prayers of Peter Marshall

⤐

An Unusual Success

Michael J. Dowling was a young man who fell from a wagon in a blizzard in Michigan when he was fourteen years of age. Before his parents discovered that he had fallen, he had been frostbitten.

His right leg was amputated almost to the hip; his left leg, above the knee; his right arm was amputated; his left hand was amputated.

Not much of a future for a young lad like that, was there? Do you know what he did? He went to the board of county commissioners and told them that if they would educate him, he would pay back every penny.

He did just that, after he became president of one of the largest banks in St. Paul.

During World War I, Dowling went to Europe to visit the wounded soldiers.

On one occasion, he was in a large hotel in London, addressing wounded soldiers in their wheelchairs. The soldiers were in the lobby, and Dowling was up on the mezzanine level.

As he started to speak, he minimized the seriousness of their wounds: the fact that one had lost an eye, and another had lost a limb were no grounds for complaint. He got the soldiers so wrought up that they started to boo him.

Then he walked over to the stairs and down toward the lobby, telling them as he walked, how fortunate they were. They continued booing.

Finally, he sat down on one of the steps and took off his right leg, while he kept telling them how well off they were.

They calmed down a little bit, but they still resented his remarks.

Then he took off his left leg.

The booing stopped then.

Before he reached the bottom of the stairs, he had taken off his right arm and flipped off his left hand—and there he sat—a stump of a body.

Not only was Michael Dowling a bank president, but he was also a married father of five children.

He died as a result of the strength he exerted in encouraging the wounded soldiers of World War I to live their life to the fullest.

—*Matthew Cowley*

Teaching

That which we learn pleasantly, we retain.

❧

Teach with certainty—live with conviction.

❧

Teach by the spirit and my grace will attend you.

❧

The creation of a thousand forests is in one acorn.
—*Ralph Waldo Emerson*

❧

If a teacher influences but one, his influence never stops.
—*Greek proverb*

❧

Would the boy/girl I used to be follow the teacher I am today?

❧

Education is learning the rules, experience is learning the exceptions.

❧

Nobody cares how much you know until they know how much you care.
—*Fred Babbel*

❧

The object of teaching a child is to enable him to get along without his teacher.
—*Elbert Hufford*

❧

A great teacher is one who, when you are around him, you are at your very best.

❧

You cannot teach a man anything: you can only help him to find it within himself.
—*Galileo*

❧

If you would learn things well, teach them to others; sharing makes our portion sweeter.

✺

Satan cannot tempt little children, but he can surely get his licks in on we who teach them.

✺

Education is the leading of human souls to what is best, and making what is best out of everything.

✺

To deliver a great message, we must be great messengers. Keep the creative channel open between God and yourself.

✺

The worst education that teaches self-control and self-denial is better than the best that teaches everything else and not that.

✺

One of the greatest powers that God has given us is the power to radiate his life and teachings. He has created us, given us life and breath, and also teaches us daily.

✺

Is education worth the price? When the Lord starts out to make a great oak, he takes a hundred years, but when he makes a common squash, he takes only a few weeks.

✺

The basic ingredient of teaching always has been and always will be love. When love comes first, the rest will follow in proper order. Without love, we struggle in vain with all we do.

—*H. Burke Peterson*

✺

I hear, and I forget.

I see, and I remember.

I do, and I understand.

—*Chinese proverb*

University Life

University life is essentially an exercise in thinking, preparing and being. The aim of education is to place in the students the power of self-mastery that he may never be a slave to indulgence or other weaknesses, to develop virile manhood and beautiful womanhood. Education is an awakening love of truth; giving a just sense of duty; opening the eyes of the soul to the great end and purpose of life. It is not so much gaining words as thoughts; or more maxims as living principles. It is not learning to be honest because it is the best policy, but because it is right.

❦

Big Bird

It was on a summer day early in the morning. I was standing near the window. The curtains obstructed me from two little creatures out on the lawn. One was a large bird and the other a little bird, obviously just out of the nest. I saw the larger bird hop out on the lawn, then thump his feet and cock his head. He drew a big fat worm out of the lawn and came hopping back. The little bird opened its bill wide, but the big bird swallowed the worm. There was squawking in protest.

Then I saw the big bird fly up in a tree. He pecked at the bark for a little while and came back with a big bug in his mouth. The little bird opened his beak wide, but the big bird swallowed the bug. There was squawking in protest.

The big bird flew away, and I didn't see it again, but I watched the little bird. After a while, the little bird hopped out on the lawn, thumped its feet, cocked its head, and pulled a big worm out of the lawn.

God bless the good people who teach our children and our youth.

—*Howard W. Hunter*

❦

There Was a Teacher

A little more than fifty years ago, a Johns Hopkins professor gave a group of graduate students this assignment: Go to the slums; take two hundred boys, between the ages of twelve and sixteen, and investigate their background and environment; then predict their chances for the future.

The students, after consulting social statistics, talked to the boys and, compiling much data, concluded that 90 percent of the boys would eventually spend some time in jail.

Twenty-five years later, another group of graduate students was given the job of testing the prediction. They went back to the slums. Some of the boys—now men—were still there; a few had died; some had moved away. But they got in touch with one hundred and eighty of the original two hundred. They found that only four of the group had ever been to jail.

Why was it that these men, who had lived in a breeding place of crime, had such a surprisingly good record? The researchers were continually told, "Well, there was a teacher..."

They pressed further, and found that in 75 percent of the cases, it was the same woman. The researchers went to this teacher, now living in a home for retired teachers. How had she exerted this remarkable influence over a group of slum children? Could she give any reason why these boys should remember her?

"No," she said, "no, I really couldn't." And then, thinking back over the years, she said musingly, more to herself than to her questioners, "I loved those boys..."

❧

Under the Wing of a Teacher

It was his second day of school when the little, brown-eyed, tousle-haired boy in blue overalls came home early. Shuffling his five-year-old feet heavily in the dust, he trudged up the long road to the ranch house near Jackson, Wyoming. Mother, alerted by his untimely return, went to the porch and dropped to her knees beside him.

His lips were tightly shut, but trembling. His cheeks were smeared where there had been tears. The note in his hand was smudged:

> *It is our judgment that your son is uneducable. The impediment in his speech disrupts classroom procedure.*

"Uneducable," the teacher's note said, because he stuttered too much.

But there was in those days another teacher in Jackson, named Martha Marean. Her name was pronounced "Marine," and she was—taunting schoolboys said—built like one.

The boy's distraught mother returned the note to the little log schoolhouse. Her appeal was denied. But big Martha Marean overheard and she, too, refused to accept the verdict as final. She asked permission to work with the boy after school hours. Miss Marean was convinced his stuttering could be controlled, that he could be educated.

And she did work with the boy until, one day, little Cliff was re-enrolled in school, and so began his education. The speech defect was controlled, not cured.

With patience and persistence, dedication and determination, Martha Marean continued to coach the lad. The self-confidence that his stammering had cost needed to be rebuilt. It was. Through her sympathy and understanding, the boy who had been turned away from school as "uneducable" became a superior student.

With Miss Marean's help and his mother's loving patience, the handicap grew progressively less—until one day, long after he had lost touch with his elementary school teacher, Cliff, now a man, was scheduled to make a speech in public...to an audience...of teachers.

With a little searching, he located Martha Marcan. Would she come to Cheyenne to the Wyoming Education Association meeting to hear him speak?

Of course she would.

She was on her way to Cheyenne, the Wyoming Highway Patrol reported, when her car skidded on a rain-slickened curve. Martha Marean was killed.

And so, against a backdrop of tragedy, Cliff made his speech:

"Ladies and gentlemen, I did want for one particular teacher to be here today to hear me speak, because it is largely due to her efforts that I can.

"In an era when we tend to mass-produce education, I wanted to honor, in this small way, this uncommon woman so that all teachers everywhere might be reminded of the awesomeness of their responsibility, the magnitude of their opportunity."

But Martha Marean was not there—or was she?—as the Honorable Clifford Hansen, Governor of Wyoming, paid homage to her name.

—Paul Harvey

❦

The Indispensable Tiger

A powerful old tiger, the leader of the pack, was preparing to go on a hunt. Gathering the other tigers around him, he said, "We must go out into the plains and hunt, for the winter is coming. You young fellows come with me; perhaps you will learn a thing or two."

The young tigers were pleased to hear this, for the old fellow had hitherto shown no interest in them. He usually left them behind when he went foraging, and they were tired of doing nothing but keeping order among the cubs and performing other routine tasks.

The first day out, the old tiger spotted a herd of elephants. "Here's your chance, Bernard," he said to one of the young tigers. "Look at it as a challenge."

But Bernard had no idea how to go about hunting. With a roar, he rushed at the elephants, who ran off in all directions. "It looks as though I'll have to do the job myself," said the leader philosophically. And so he did.

The next day, the tigers came upon a herd of water buffalo. "Suppose you take over now, Jerome," said the old tiger, and Jerome, reluctant to ask silly questions but determined to do his best, crept up on the grazing buffalo. He leaped straight at the largest of them, but the big buffalo tossed him to the ground, and Jerome was lucky to escape in one piece. Mortified, he crept back to the group.

"No, no, no!" said the old tiger. "What's happening to performance around here?"

"But you never taught us how to do it!" cried one of the young tigers. The old tiger was in no mood to listen. "The rest of you stay where you are," he growled, "and I will do the job myself." And so he did.

"I can see," said the old tiger, as the others gathered admiringly about him, "that none of you is yet ready to take my place." He sighed. "Much as I hate to say it, I seem to be indispensable."

Time brought little change. The old tiger sometimes took the younger ones along with him on hunts, and occasionally he let one of them try to make a kill. But having received no instruction, they were unequal to the task. And the old tiger still made no effort to teach the others his tricks; he had forgotten that he himself was a product of tiger-to-tiger coaching.

One day, when he had grown quite old, the tiger met a friend—a wise lion he had known for years. Before long, the tiger was launched on his favorite topic of conversation: the lack of initiative in the younger generation.

"Would you believe it?" he asked the lion. "Here I am, getting a bit long in the tooth, and I still have to do all the hunting for my pack. There seems to be no one of my stripes around."

"That's odd," said the lion. "I find the younger lions in my pack take well to instruction. Some of them are carrying a good bit of responsibility. In fact," he continued, "I'm thinking about retiring next year and letting the younger fellows take over."

"I envy you," said the tiger. "I'd take things easier and relax myself if I only saw a little leadership material around me." The old tiger sighed and shook his head. "You can't imagine," he said, "what a burden it is to be indispensable."

—*The American Management Association*

Out of the Dark

The most important day I remember in all my life is the one on which my teacher, Anne Mansfield Sullivan, came to me. I am filled with wonder when I consider the immeasurable contrast between the two lives that it connects. It was the third of March, 1887, three months before I was seven years old.

On the afternoon of that eventful day, I stood on the porch, dumb, expectant. I guessed vaguely from my mother's signs, and from the hurrying to and fro in the house, that something unusual was about to happen, so I went to the door and waited on the steps.

The afternoon sun penetrated the mass of honeysuckle that covered the porch, and fell on my upturned face. My fingers lingered almost unconsciously on the familiar leaves and blossoms that had just come forth to greet the sweet southern spring. I did not know what the future held of marvel or surprise for me. Anger and bitterness had preyed upon me continually for weeks, and deep languor had succeeded this passionate struggle.

Have you ever been at sea in a dense fog, when it seemed as if a tangible white darkness shut you in, and the great ship, tense and anxious, groped her way toward the shore with plummet and sounding line, and you waited with beating heart for something to happen? I was like that ship before my education began, only I was without compass or sounding line, and had no way of knowing how near the harbor was. "Light! Give me light!" was the wordless cry of my soul, and the light of love shone on me in that very hour.

I felt approaching footsteps. I stretched out my hand, as I supposed, to my mother. Someone took it, and I was caught up and held close in the arms of her who had come to reveal all things to me—and, more than all things else, to love me.

The morning after my teacher came, she led me into her room and gave me a doll. The little blind children at the Perkins Institution had sent it, and Laura Bridgman had dressed it. When I had played with it a little while, Miss Sullivan slowly spelled into my hand the word d-o-l-l. I was at once interested in this finger play, and tried to imitate it. When I finally succeeded in making the letters correctly, I was flushed with childish pleasure and pride. Running downstairs to my mother, I held up my hand and made the letters for doll. I did not know that I was spelling a word, or even that words existed; I was simply making my fingers go in monkey-like imitation.

In the days that followed, I learned to spell in this uncomprehending way a great many words, among them pin, hat, cup, and a few verbs like sit, stand, and walk. But my teacher had been with me several weeks before I understood that everything has a name.

One day, while I was playing with my new doll, Miss Sullivan put my big rag doll into my lap alongside my new doll, spelled d-o-l-l, and tried to make me understand that d-o-l-l applied to both. Earlier in the day we had had a tussle over the words m-u-g and w-a-t-e-r. Miss Sullivan had tried to impress upon me that m-u-g is mug and that w-a-t-e-r is water, but I was persistent in confounding the two. In despair, she had dropped the subject for the time, only to renew it at the first opportunity.

I became impatient at her repeated attempts and, seizing the new doll, I dashed it upon the floor. I was keenly delighted when I felt the fragments of the broken doll at my feet. Neither sorrow nor regret followed my passionate outburst. I had not loved the doll. In the still, dark world in which I lived there was no strong sentiment or tenderness. I felt my teacher sweep the fragments to one side of the hearth, and I had a sense of satisfaction that the cause of my discomfort was removed.

She brought me my hat, and I knew I was going out into the warm sunshine. This thought, if a wordless sensation may be called a thought, made me hop and skip with pleasure.

We walked down the path to the well house, attracted by the fragrance of the honeysuckle with which it was covered. Someone was drawing water, and my teacher placed my hand under the spout. As the cool stream gushed over one hand, she spelled into the other w-a-t-e-r—first slowly, then rapidly. I stood still, my whole attention fixed on the motions of her fingers.

Suddenly I felt a misty consciousness as of something forgotten—a thrill of returning thought. Somehow, the mystery of language was revealed to me. I knew then that w-a-t-e-r meant the wonderful cool something that was flowing over my hand. That living word awakened my soul, gave it light, hope, joy—and set it free! There were barriers still, it is true, but barriers that could in time be swept away.

I left the well house eager to learn. Everything had a name, and each name gave birth to a new thought. As we returned to the house, every object I touched seemed to quiver with life. That was because I saw everything with the strange new light that had come to me.

On entering the door, I remembered the doll I had broken. I felt my way to the hearth and picked up the pieces. I tried vainly to put them together. Then my eyes filled with tears, for I realized what I had done—and, for the first time, I felt repentance and sorrow.

I learned a great many new words that day. I do not remember what they all were, but I do know that mother, father, sister, and teacher were among them—words that were to make the world blossom for me, "like Aaron's rod, with flowers". It would have been difficult to find a happier child than I was as I lay in my crib at the close of that eventful day, living over the joys it had brought me. For the first time, I longed for a new day to come.
—*Helen Keller*

Look, You Can't Do This To Me

At the high school I attended, they gave a medal and a watch to one student who qualified in various fields of activity—scholarship, athletics, leadership, etc.

I learned a few days before graduation that I was a candidate for this honor. This pleased me, of course. I was especially concerned, therefore—knowing that I had a chance, and knowing the other candidates, whom I regarded highly—with the grades I gathered as I went from class to class on that last day.

There was not anything to be done now about activities or leadership, but I knew these final grades would be significant. So, as they came and were satisfactory, I felt good and encouraged, until I reached my last class, which was taught by a marvelous little soul, who had taught my oldest brother and all of the family members in between—I being the last.

Because this was a class in English literature, a field in which I had been particularly interested in my boyhood, and because I had read most of the assigned materials before, I did little to contribute to the class. I showed up occasionally, but often found reasons to be away on athletic or newspaper or student body business.

When the tests came, I passed them all—with good grades. I had had A's throughout the year, hence, I expected my last grade to be the same. But when I received my grade, it was a big fat E. I sat shocked, and then laughed nervously: surely the teacher was playing a little joke on me.

When the class was over and people were showing each other their grade—and I was holding mine back—I found my way to the teacher's desk and said, laughing nervously, "Look, Miss Young, this is MY report card; you made a mistake."

"I know that is your report card," she said. "In fact, I have made a mistake, but it was a deliberate one—I wanted you to think a little. I am not going to fail you in the class; that would put your graduation in jeopardy." She took the report card away from me and superimposed a big C over the E.

I said, "Look, you can't do this to me."

"Oh, yes I can."

I said, "No, no, open your book." She opened it and we went across the page.

"Look at the marks—ninety, this and this—and compare them with the people you gave the A's to. My marks are better all the way. You can't do this."

She said, "Oh, yes I can. I am going to do it."

I asked, "Do you know what this will do to me?"

She answered, "Yes, I know. Let me tell you something. I taught your oldest brother, and I have taught all the ones in between. When I knew you were coming, I was grateful that I would have the last of the Hanks tribe, because I loved every one of them, and I wanted to love you. But you made it very hard. Do you think I'm stupid? Don't you think I knew what has been going on? Don't you think I know the excuses you have made and the unmanly way you have acted in this course? Oh, you made the grades all right. You had read most of the material before; I knew that. But you haven't been fair with me or yourself. I am not going to mark you this month on what you did in comparison with anybody else. I am going to mark you in comparison with what you should have done—and you get the C."

I said again, "Do you know what this is going to do to me?" By now I was pretty close to tears—this seemed so unfair.

She said, "Yes, I know, and I would like you to know that I have been up most of the night thinking about it and that I love you too much not to do it."

"C"—and out I went. Well, I didn't get the medal or the watch. My name is not on the plaque. Another fellow's is. He is a great and good man who deserved it, a better man than I was.

But I lived long enough to stand in front of a group of elderly ladies, of which she was one, and tell them and her to her face that this was the most important lesson that I learned in school. There is not anything in this world worth having that you can get without working for it, without putting out, without doing your best.

—*Marion D. Hanks*

Three Teachers

And it came to pass that three Latter-day Saints went out from their homes and made way to the chapel at the appointed hour, where they had been called to teach. One was a TALKER; the second, an ENTERTAINER; and the third, a TEACHER. All three bore strong testimonies of the gospel and had a sincere desire to build testimonies in their learners.

The TALKER came well prepared, cited scriptures, read from books, and verily beseeched his learners with many words. For a few, the words fell on fertile soil, and they went straightway from the class greatly enriched. For many, the words were not enough, and visions of roasts in the oven, skiing on powdered slopes, and the excitement of bright colors and taffetas, silks, and laces gradually drowned out the words, words, words, until they had comfortably become a part of the background, making way for more pressing matters.

The ENTERTAINER, familiar with the effect of some talkers on some learners, bore testimony; cited scriptures; showed pictures, maps, charts, videos; and played recordings. Surely the learners' interest was captured by the wonders of the instructional media. Roasts, skis, and apparel became of little concern, and the hour of instruction was all too soon over. The learners left the ENTERTAINER and went their various ways only to be dismayed by the proverbial question, "Well, what did you learn today?" They were unable to answer because the instructional materials were used for the wrong reasons and the learners' recollection of the lesson was now without form and void—so much gloss and tinsel, without real substance.

The TEACHER bore no stronger testimony than the others, nor was he any more dedicated to his calling. He just realized that, if his learners didn't actually change their behavior, increase their testimonies, and start living richer and more productive lives, then he had failed. He faced his many communication problems squarely, and he defined his instructional objectives. He used a variety of instructional materials for the right reasons—to overcome the barriers to effective communication, and to reach his objectives. He used recordings to bring General Authorities into his classroom, in order to reach the active and less active members at the same time, for he had both in his class. When appropriate, he used videos to dramatize important ideas, and the chalkboard for key scriptures. In order to communicate with both the learner who attends under social pressure and the class member who is sincerely interested, he used these and other instructional materials to reach the new convert, as well as the returned missionary, for he knew that they would greatly increase learning, as well as interest. And his learners went out into the land for another week, filled with the spirit, their lives enriched, and with a feeling that they really learned, and for the present they were satisfied with their new knowledge and insight.

I Wish I Could Remember

Dear Teacher,

Today at commencement, we had a peach of an address, "The Education I Wish I Might Have Had". It made me think. And I'm going to break loose and tell you about memories some fellows have which I haven't had.

I wish I could remember one morning that you greeted me with a happy smile when I walked into the room. It would have made such a bright beginning for the day.

I know that I wasn't much to look at with my brown freckled face, crowned with a mop of red hair that just wouldn't stay down no matter how often I combed it.

And my ears—that's why they were always so dirty—they were so big, and they stuck straight out catching every particle of dirt that the wind swept by.

My clothes were dirty too, but that wasn't altogether my fault. Mother never did feel well after baby Sally was born, and I could always dirty my clothes faster than she could get around to wash them. I can hear Mother say in her tired voice, "Johnny, how do you ever get so dirty?" She promised me she would wash my trousers after I had gone to bed (I only had one pair), but I guess she was too tired after putting Sally to bed and then tucking in Billy and Bob, the twins, and Mary, Jane, Tommy, and me for the night, before leaving to hunt for Dad who would be in any one of the six taverns.

You can't imagine how much your smile would have meant on some of these mornings that I came to school with only a dry crust of bread for my breakfast. Once or twice I thought you were going to smile—and then, you just said in a stern voice, "Johnny, you're late again—as usual."

That "as usual" always cut like a knife, and that's why I was afraid you wouldn't understand if I told you the real reason why I was late. Baby Sally needed milk, and I used to walk the three miles over to Smith's every morning to get it. He sold us the milk two cents cheaper than Mr. Jones who lived just across the land from us.

I wish I could remember one kind word that you spoke to me directly, or one time when we played games that you joined the circle next to me and took my hand like you did the other boys'.

True, my hands always looked dirty—it's hard to wash in cold well-water with no soap—but if I'd have known there was a chance that you would take hold of my hand, I'd have scrubbed and scrubbed until they were clean.

The only time you seemed to notice me was when I pulled Norma's hair or poked Bonnie with my pencil. No one wanted to play with me, and sometimes I just felt like I had to do something like that to make sure I was still there.

I wish I could remember one time that you included me in the planning of the class work, instead of simply ignoring me. I rebelled at that—not the work itself, as you supposed when I caused a disturbance or did everything except the work I was supposed to do—but because you didn't consider my views or reasons.

I wish I could remember, above all else, just one time that you and I talked together alone discussing my problems, so that you could have had a better understanding of why I had to do some of the things I did. It was always so easy for you to solve any problem that came up in class, and I'm sure that you could have helped me with my own problems and troubles.

Please do not think I am cursed and that I am blaming you. No teacher could have worked harder and had the children's welfare more at heart than you did. No one could have taught me better how to work or set a better example of honesty, industry, and clean living. But you just didn't know that I, too, dirty and late as I was, needed those things that you gave freely to others but withheld from me. You couldn't have been better to me—no teacher could—but surely, you could have been infinitely nearer.

Your one-time pupil

P.S. I can't send this. After all these years you wouldn't understand. But I wish you knew that I'd gladly give my four years of college for the memories I might have had.

—C. J. Wendel

❧

Looking for a Fence

You're doing children a favor when you establish and enforce rules for them to follow and respect.

On the farm where I spent my youth, I noticed that the first thing that the cattle did when they were let out in the spring was to head for the nearest fence. They leaned on it, marched along it, crawled through it, or jumped over it. There was no apparent reason for their action since the other side of the fence was summer fallow—sandy, dry, indigestible summer fallow.

I believe my father correctly psycho-analyzed the action of the cattle. They were looking for a fence. They wanted to find out as quickly as they could just how far they could go. They wanted to find the limitations of their new-found freedom.

After years of teaching, I have come to the conclusion that people, especially young people, have that same natural urge to find the fence. In adults, we call it the urge to explore, and we say it is wonderful.

Most psychologists admire this quality in children, and so do I. But what most psychologists and many parents forget is that there must be a fence to limit the exploration. Cattle will not prosper if they spend their time crawling through a fence or unhappily staring down at dusty summer fallow. They will be as unhappy as the child who can't find the borders of his existence.

How secure it is to look across your yard in the spring and think that from here to there is mine! How happy is the crawling baby to find the comforting four walls of his home! How confident and secure is the youth who can say to himself, "This, this, and this I can do—but that I cannot do!"

How miserably uncomfortable is the child who cannot find his fence! He is the wild young boy who runs away from home. She is the wayward girl who finds her fence too late. He is the juvenile delinquent who gets arrested for stealing cigarettes, cars, and money from milk bottles. He is the "bad boy" who cripples himself (and maybe others) for life going 90 miles an hour down a residential street; who tears trees and flowers from public parks; who breaks into a house and rips up furniture with a knife. He is the delinquent whose only real crime is in not being able to find his fence. In his mind is that horrible turmoil of a picture reaching out to find its frame.

In my classroom, I have students whose parents have all but disowned them. They have given up trying to understand them. Yet, after a week or two, these young people are no trouble at all.

What marvelous pedagogical discovery did I make to accomplish this miracle? I applied a lesson I learned from my father, who had never heard of pedagogy—or psychology, either. He simply electrified the fence.

Within a few days, the cattle knew where the fence was and they stayed away from it. They grazed contentedly and became fat and healthy. At the time, it seemed to be a waste of power to leave the charger running when no animal came near it. My father shut it off and set me to watch.

Within an hour, a steer came up to test the fence. He was looking for security. There was no shock. He looked back at the herd. He was confused. He jumped the fence. Had I not been there, others would have soon followed.

This is why I tell the students on the first day of school what I expect of them and what the rules are. Some try breaking the rules just to see if the fence means anything. When they find that things are as they were told, they forget about breaking the rules. They can now work contentedly and happily, secure in knowing that the rules are there and that they can depend on them.

Now and then, a potential delinquent tests them just to see. So it is most important that the charger stays on. Nothing must happen to break the confidence, the trust, or the security that has been developed.

Do my students object to being in this state of "rigid control that hampers their zeal to explore"?

One boy, who had been in trouble several times, told me, "I wish everybody was as easy to get along with as you."

"Why?"

"Because I feel so solid here. I know what will happen. I feel free to do things."

No one likes to live in a country where there are frequent revolutions and their accompanying insecurity that make the valued things of today the trash of tomorrow. Insecurity is the detriment to all progressive work. A game is ruined when the referee neglects to enforce the rules—just once.

I recall a parent coming to see me after school one afternoon. As the students left the room at the close of the class, she came up to my desk, an expression of amazement on her face.

"How do you do it?"

"Do what?"

"I've seen all those ruffians hanging around the drugstore at night. I've seen them on the street corners. I must confess I'm afraid to let Tommy out at night for fear that he will be just like them. Yet, from the back of the room there, they seemed as nice as you please. They talk but, when it gets too noisy, you look up and they quit just like you had punished them or something. According to my son's references to your strictness, I half expected you to he some sort of tyrant. But this I did not expect. How do you do it?"

"They know where the fence is. Inside the fence they are free. But they know they must not cross that fence."

"Well, it's nice to know that somebody can beat these fellows down."

"I don't think I've 'beaten them down', as you call it. We have a few simple, well-understood rules that keep us from infringing on the rights of others, and that keep us safe and free. I help them follow those rules. There is no 'beating down' in that. Rather, it is an uplifting to equal dignity."

"Maybe," she smiled, "but I did see some of them chewing gum, I didn't think schools tolerated that."

"I used to refuse permission for gum, too, but that was a rule that didn't work too well. When the air was dry and their throats were sore, somehow it didn't seem so wrong to chew gum. So rather than have a useless rule that tempted breaking, we decided to change the rule. But if the chewing annoys anyone, we stop it."

"You say 'we' all the time."

"We, who the rules are for."

"I see," she nodded, and began on her own problem. "You know, Tommy has me worried. Any advice?"

"Tommy' s a fine boy. He has a problem or two of his own, you know. To an adolescent like Tom, life is a business of being halfway to nowhere. It's little else but a period of confusion and doubts. He needs firm, dependable security."

"I agree. From now on, I'm going to use stricter discipline on him. He's going to be in by eight on school nights and nine on weekends."

"I think that would be a mistake. You are fencing him in too much. He will have no alternative but to jump out. That's not strictness. That is constriction. You would rebel, too, if the walls were pushed in on you so close that they stifled."

"I never thought of it that way."

"If I were you, I'd sit down with Tom or, better yet, I'd get your husband and the two of you together…"

"My husband thinks Tommy will grow out of it."

"Maybe he will; but, in the meantime, it will be a very lonesome, unhappy time for him, when it ought to be a happy time. And he may not 'grow out of it' before a lot of harm is done and many bad habits are formed."

"You think both of us should talk with Tommy?"

"Yes, that, in itself, is a pretty good start on a secure fence. Then build the rest of the fence with Tom. Make it comfortable for him—not so big that he gets lost in it and has doubts that it is there, yet not so small that he can't move around and grow. Then it is up to you as parents to simply help him stay within those walls. When he is ready, he will build his own fence and live in peace with the rest of his society."

"How will we know when he is ready?"

"If you have helped him with this fence and, if he has found that staying inside it is good for both comfort and progress, then he will ask you. He will ask because he has learned to trust you as one who helps, rather than detesting you as one who doesn't care where he wanders, or hating you because you have fenced him in too tightly."

"I wish I had thought of this years ago."

"It would have been easier, but it's never too late to build a fence. Of course, it's a little harder to get used to but, within his fence, Tom will grow up to be a secure, confident, well-adjusted young man. He's worth the trouble!"

—*Les Johnson*

❧

Cipher in the Snow

It started with tragedy on a biting cold February morning. I was driving behind the Milford Corners bus as I did most snowy mornings on my way to school. It veered and stopped short at the hotel, which it had no business doing, and I was annoyed as I had come to an unexpected stop. A boy lurched out of the bus, reeled, stumbled, and collapsed on the snow bank at the curb. The bus driver and I reached him at the same moment. His thin, hollow face was white even against the snow.

"He's dead," the driver whispered.

It didn't register for a minute. I glanced quickly at the scared young faces staring down at us from the school bus. "A doctor! Quick! I'll phone from the hotel."

"No use. I tell you he's dead." The driver looked down at the boy's still form. "He never even said he felt bad," he muttered, "just tapped me on the shoulder and said, real quiet, 'I'm sorry. I have to get off at the hotel.' That's all. Polite and apologizing like."

At school, the giggling, shuffling morning noise quieted as the news went down the halls. I passed a huddle of girls. "Who was it? Who dropped dead on the way to school?" I heard one of them half whisper.

"Don't know his name; some kid from Milford Corners," was the reply.

It was like that in the faculty room and the principal's office. "I'd appreciate your going out to tell the parents," the principal told me. "They don't have a phone and, anyway, somebody from school should go there in person. I'll cover your classes."

"Why me?" I asked. "Wouldn't it be better if you did it?"

"I don't know the boy," the principal admitted levelly. "And, in last year's sophomore personalities column, I note that you were listed as his favorite teacher."

I drove through the snow and cold down the bad canyon road to the Evans place and thought about the boy, Cliff Evans. "His favorite teacher," I thought. "He hasn't spoken two words to me in two years!" I could see him in my mind's eye all right, sitting back there in the last seat in my afternoon literature class. He came in the room by himself and left by himself. "Cliff Evans," I muttered to myself, "a boy who never talked." I thought a minute. "A boy who never smiled. I never saw him smile once."

The big ranch kitchen was clean and warm. I blurted out my news somehow. Mrs. Evans reached blindly toward a chair. "He never said anything about hem' ailing."

His stepfather snorted, "He ain't said nothin' about anything since I moved in here."

Mrs. Evans pushed a pan to the back of the stove and began to untie her apron. "Now hold on," her husband snapped. "I got to have breakfast before I go to town. Nothin' we can do now anyway. If Cliff hadn't been so dumb, he'd have told us he didn't feel good."

After school, I sat in the office and stared blankly at the records spread out before me. I was to close the file and write the obituary for the school paper. The almost bare sheets mocked the effort. Cliff Evans, white, never legally adopted by stepfather, five young half-brothers and sisters. These meager strands of information and the list of D grades were all the records had to offer.

Cliff Evans had silently come in the school door in the mornings and gone out the school door in the evenings, and that was all. He had never belonged to a club. He had never played on a team. He had never held an office. As far as I could tell, he had never done one happy, noisy kid thing. He had never been anybody at all.

How do you go about making a boy into a zero? The grade-school records showed me. The first and second grade teachers' annotations read "sweet, shy child", "timid but eager". Then the third grade note had opened the attack; some teacher had written in a good firm, hand, "Cliff won't talk; uncooperative; slow learner". The other academic sheet had followed with "dull", "slow-witted", "low IQ". They became correct. The boy's IQ score in the ninth grade was listed at 83. But his IQ in the third grade had been 196. The score didn't go under 100 until seventh grade. Even shy, timid, sweet children have resilience. It takes time to break them.

I stomped to the typewriter and wrote a savage report pointing out what education had done to Cliff Evans. I slapped a copy on the principal's desk and another in the sad, dog-eared file. I banged the typewriter and slammed the file and crashed the door shut, but I didn't feel much better. A little boy kept walking after me: a little boy with a peaked, pale face; a skinny body in faded jeans, and big eyes that had looked and searched for a long time and then had become veiled.

I could guess how many times he'd been chosen last to play sides in a game, how many whispered child conversations had excluded him, how many times he hadn't been asked. I could see and hear the faces and voices that said over and over, "You're a nothing, Cliff Evans."

A child is a believing creature. Cliff undoubtedly believed them. Suddenly it seemed clear to me: when finally there was nothing left at all for Cliff Evans, he collapsed on a snow bank and went away. The doctor might list "heart failure" as the cause of death, but that wouldn't change my mind.

We couldn't find ten students in the school who had known Cliff well enough to attend the funeral as his friends. So the student body officers and a committee from the junior class went as a group to the church, being politely sad. I attended the services with them, and sat through it with a lump of cold lead in my chest and a big resolve growing through me.

I've never forgotten Cliff Evans nor that resolve. He has been my challenge year after year, class after class. I look up and down the rows carefully each September at the unfamiliar faces. I look for veiled eyes or bodies scrunched into a seat in an alien world. "Look, kids," I say silently, "I may not do anything else for you this year, but not one of you is going to come out of here a nobody. I'll work or fight to the bitter end doing battle with society and the school board, but I won't have one of you coming out of here thinking himself into a zero."

Most of the time—not always, but most of the time—I've succeeded.

—*Jean E. Mizer*

Time

A little too late is much too late.

—*Sir John Lubboc*

Make time serve you, not you it.

One today is worth two tomorrows.

Spare moments are the gold dust of time.

Don't let yesterday use too much of today.

—*Will Rogers*

Better late than never, but better never late.

Time is one gift that is democratically distributed.

If you are going to kill time, try working it to death.

Everything comes to him who hustles while he waits.

—*Thomas Edison*

Tomorrow: One of the greatest labor-saving devices of today.

There is not a single moment in life that we can afford to lose.

—*Edward M. Goulburn*

How you use today will determine how tomorrow will use you.

❧

Waste of time is the most extravagant and costly of all expenses.
—*Theophrastus*

❧

Tomorrow is often the busiest day of the year: do all you can today.

❧

The best example of time well spent is a golden wedding anniversary.

❧

It takes less time to do a thing right than to explain why you did it wrong.
—*Henry Wadsworth Longfellow*

❧

The best preparation for the future is the present well seen to, the last duty well done.
—*George MacDonald*

❧

People who cannot find time for recreation are obliged, sooner or later, to find time for illness.
—*John Wanamaker*

❧

There are things in the future and things in the past: live each moment as though it were your last.

❧

Our days are like identical suitcases—all the same size, but some can pack into them twice as much as others.

❧

Just as your fortune depends upon how your money is invested, so the success of your life depends upon how your time is invested.
—*Leone Kester*

❧

How you spend your time is more important than how you spend your money: money mistakes can be corrected, but time is gone forever.

❧

I can hardly wish any man better, than that he would seriously consider what he does with his time; how and to what ends he employs it; and what returns he makes to God.

—*Benjamin Franklin*

Guard your spare moments: they are like uncut diamonds. Discard them, and their value will never be known. Improve them, and they will become the brightest gems in a useful life.

—*Ralph Waldo Emerson*

Don't be fooled by the calendar. There are only as many days in the year as you make use of. One man gets only a week's value out of a year while another gets a full year's value out of a week.

—*Charles Richards*

Waste is unjustified, and especially the waste of time—limited as that commodity is in our days of probation. One must live, not only exist; he must do, not merely be; he must grow, not just vegetate.

—*Spencer W. Kimball*

Your inheritance is time. It is capital more precious than any lands or stocks or houses you will ever get. Spend it foolishly, and you will bankrupt yourself. Invest it wisely, and you will bless generations to come.

—*Henry B. Eyring*

"For as a man thinketh in his heart, so is he." And so does he. To arrive at what we really want, we must deeply desire. Wherever or whatever we want to be, we ought to be on our way—for time will go—and all there is of it is ours.

—*Richard L. Evans*

High up in the north in the land called Svithjod, there stands a rock. It is a hundred miles high and a hundred miles wide. Once every thousand years a little bird comes to this rock to sharpen its beak. When the rock has thus been worn away, then a single day of eternity will have gone by.

—*Hendrik van Loon*

Own the Day

Write it on your heart that every day is the best day in the year. He only is rich who owns the day, and no one owns the day who allows it to be invaded with worry, fret, and anxiety. Finish every day and be done with it. This day is all that is good and fair. It is too dear to waste a moment on the yesterdays.

❧

A Prayer for Today

This is the beginning of a new day. God has given me this day to use as I will. I can waste it, or use it for good, but what I do today is important, because I am exchanging a day of my life for it! When tomorrow comes, this day will be gone forever, leaving in its place something that I have traded for it. I want it to be gain, and not loss; good, and not evil; success, and not failure; in order that I shall not regret the price that I have paid for it.

—*Dr. Heartsill Wilson*

❧

Lost

Somewhere between sunrise and sunset,

Two golden hours,

Each set with sixty diamond minutes.

No reward is offered

For they are gone forever.

❧

Time Is

Time is money: we have no right to waste it.

Time is power: we have no right to dissipate it.

Time is influence: we have no right to throw it away.

Time is life: we must value it.

Time is a sacred trust from God: we must answer for every moment.

Time is preparation for eternity: we must redeem it.

Enough

In the coming year, may you have:

Enough happiness to keep you sweet.

Enough trials to keep you strong.

Enough sorrow to keep you human.

Enough hope to keep you happy.

Enough failure to keep you humble.

Enough success to keep you eager.

Enough friends to give you comfort.

Enough wealth to meet your needs.

Enough enthusiasm to look forward.

Enough faith to banish depression.

Enough determination to make each day a better day than yesterday.

॰ॐ॰

Take Time

Take time to work: it's the price of success.

Take time to work with love: it is the assurance of success.

Take time to think: it's the source of power.

Take time to think creatively: it is the foundation of wisdom.

Take time to love and be loved: it's God's given privilege.

Take time to love your fellow men: it is the gateway to heaven.

Take time each day for silence: it is the storehouse of God.

Take time to worship God: it is the highway of peace.

Take time to pray: it's the greatest power on earth.

Take time to read: it's the fountain of knowledge.

Take time to play: it's the secret of perpetual youth.

Take time to be friendly: it's the road to happiness.

Take time to laugh: it's the mirror of the soul.

Take time to give: it's ungodly to be selfish.

Take time: it's yours!

Six Steps to Mastering Time

MAKE NOTES. Use a pencil and paper. Many seemingly big problems become progressively smaller when you break them down on a piece of paper. Leave a pad of notepaper at every strategic location in your home and work area. Put a pencil and paper beside your bed, or on the breakfast table, and on the sun visor of your car. Be prepared to "write it down" any time, day or night. Or, better yet, keep your planner near you at all times so that all ideas and details can be kept in one organized place.

REMOVE DISTRACTIONS FROM YOUR WORK AREA. Keep your desk or worktable as clean as possible. Eliminate such temptations to idleness as newspapers, personal letters, and souvenirs. And once a job is completed, get it out of sight and out of the way.

DISCOURAGE INTERRUPTIONS. Set up certain times in every workday when you can't be reached. Eliminate idle conversation when you're transacting business. Storytellers can wreck every deadline you set. And beware of the telephone—it can be either a time saver or a time waster. Only you can control it.

LEARN TO SAY "NO". It's one of the most valuable and effective words in the English language. Don't let yourself be talked into commitments on things or projects in which you have no real interest. Be selective. Remember, it's your time you are spending.

LET THE POSTMAN BE YOUR ERRAND BOY. If running around eats into your valuable time, you can hire a United States postman for just a few cents. The U.S. Postal Service is the most reliable messenger service in the world. Let him deliver magazines and books, make bank deposits, and carry the checks for payment of household bills.

LEARN TO LISTEN CAREFULLY. You won't have to waste time checking back to verify your understanding. Get all of the facts—who, what, when, where, and why—the first time you're exposed to them. Write them in your planner so they don't clutter your mind. Don't dash off to a dental appointment on Tuesday, when it really isn't scheduled until later in the week—all because you didn't listen carefully and make notes when the date was first arranged.

Today and Time

TODAY is here. I will start with a smile and resolve to be agreeable. I will not criticize. I refuse to waste my valuable time.

TODAY in one thing I know I am equal with all others—time. All of us draw the same salary in seconds, minutes and hours.

TODAY I will not waste my time because the minutes I wasted yesterday are as lost as a vanished thought.

TODAY I refuse to spend time worrying about what might happen: it usually doesn't. I am going to spend time making things happen.

TODAY I am determined to study to improve myself, for tomorrow I may be wanted, and I must not be found lacking.

TODAY I am determined to do the things that I should do. I firmly determine to stop doing the things I should not do.

TODAY I begin by doing and not wasting my time. In one week I will be miles beyond the person I am today.

TODAY I will not imagine what I would do if things were different. They are not different. I will make success with what material I have.

TODAY I will stop saying, "If I had time": I know I never will "find time" for anything. If I want time, I must make it.

TODAY I will act toward other people as though this might be my last day on earth. I will not wait for tomorrow. Tomorrow never comes.

❧

There Wasn't Time

Time. It hangs heavy for the bored, eludes the busy, flies by for the young, and runs out for the aged.

We talk about it like it's a manufactured commodity that some can afford, others can't; some can reproduce, others waste.

We crave it. We curse it. We kill it. We abuse it. Is it a friend? Or an enemy? I suspect we know very little about it. To know it at all, and its potential, perhaps we should view it through a child's eyes:

"When I was young Daddy was going to throw me up in the air and catch me and I would giggle until I couldn't giggle anymore, but he had to change the furnace filter, and there wasn't time."

"When I was young, Mama was going to read me a story and I was going to turn the pages and pretend I could read, but she had to wax the bathroom floor and there wasn't time."

"When I was young Daddy was going to come to school and watch me in a play. I was the fourth Wise Man (in case one of the three got sick), but he had an appointment to have his car tuned up and it took longer than he thought and there was no time."

"When I was young, Grandma and Granddad were going to come for Christmas to see the expression on my face when I got my first bike, but Grandma didn't know who she could get to feed the dogs and Granddad didn't like the cold weather and, besides, they didn't have the time."

"When I was young, Mama was going to listen to me read my essay on 'What I Want To Be When I Grow Up', but she was in the middle of the Monday night movie and Gregory Peck was always one of her favorites and there wasn't time."

"When I was older Dad and I were going fishing one weekend, just the two of us, and we were going to pitch a tent and fry fish with the heads on them like they do in the flashlight ads but, at the last minute, he had to fertilize the grass and there wasn't time."

"When I was older, the whole family was always going to pose together for our Christmas card, but my brother had ball practice, my sister had her hair up, Dad was watching the Colts, and Mom had to wax the bathroom floor. There wasn't time."

"When I grew up and left home to be married, I was going to sit down with Mom and Dad and tell them I loved them and I would miss them. But Hank (he's my best man and a real clown) was honking the horn in front of the house, so there wasn't time."
—*Erma Bombeck*

Tithing

It doesn't take money to pay tithing: it takes faith.

—*Robert L. Simpson*

❦

What Is My Tithing?

I have found a great many people who do not know what their tithing is. I have never met people of that kind, but that I believe, if I were in partnership with them, and they had a tenth interest in that partnership, they would know pretty well what part their tenth was. I do not think they would have any difficulty whatever in finding how much I owed them. So, I am inclined to think that if we wanted to, we would have no difficulty in finding out what is one-tenth of our income, and that is what we owe the Lord—no difficulty whatever.

—*Heber J. Grant*

❦

Robbing God

It is generally understood that in figuring one-tenth of one's income, that in certain cases one needs merely to push the decimal point over one place to the left, and he will know the correct amount to pay as a tithe.

In other cases, however, before the tithing is figured, there may be legitimate deductions made from the wages or income, which deductions constitute the actual expenses involved in making the money and thereby producing the increase.

However, if there ever are questions regarding the deductions, favor the Lord over yourself.

By so doing, you are on the safe side. It would be far better to pay a little extra tithing than it would be to be guilty of robbing God.

—*Milton R. Hunter*

❦

God's Money

Let me start out with a story of a great furniture manufacturer in Grand Rapids, Michigan.

He was starting over in life. His first attempted business had not been a success. The tiny string of credit on which he had to depend consisted of the faith of a few close friends, rather than the calculated mathematical confidence of banks.

One day, he walked slowly through the empty rooms of the little factory. He was alone in the building. As yet the machinery was not in place. When he came to a remote corner of one of the upper floors, he knelt, closed his eyes, and prayed. Then he got up and went out into the world again and began his hard business fight.

The machinery came at last, and he started to make furniture. He borrowed; his business successes strengthened his credit.

But there was a mystery about him in the fields of credit.

Just as he started to look more and more like a safe investment to his creditors, he also started to give money away. Whenever he borrowed, he gave.

Sometimes he said "no" to those who asked for financial aid for religious or philanthropic purposes. But when he did say "yes", he said it with an alacrity that astonished the recipient.

He did not give money to foolish ventures or to unsound enterprises, but it was a puzzling thing to the bankers to have him borrow from them, while he was giving money freely to help others who were finding the world a hard place in which to live.

His business grew; within a few years it became well-established; his furniture became known to the trade for its honest quality. His tiny string of credit had become a thousand-stranded cable. He was one of the marked successes in the furniture world. At last, there came a time when borrowing was no longer necessary.

When he died, after a well-rounded life, the mystery of his gifts was explained.

It seemed that during his business career, he had considered the money he had borrowed, the money he had earned, and the money he had given away, as not his money, but as God's.

A clergyman explained, "I have carried a secret about our friend, which I have never been able to reveal until now.

"When he was making his second start in life, he knelt in an empty room in his new factory; and told God that he wanted to make him a partner, and that one-tenth of all the earnings would go to him, and that he would use the money, as if it were God's."

—*Ernest L. Wilkinson*

❧

The Tenth Load

What does it mean to obey the law of sacrifice? The best shall be given to God. He said, "Take of the firstlings of your herds and of your flocks." (Deuteronomy. 12:6) The rest you may have.

With this thought in view, I thank my earthly father for the lesson he gave to two boys in a hayfield at a time when tithes were paid in kind.

We had driven out to the field to get the tenth load of hay, and then over to a part of the meadow where we had taken the ninth load, where there was "wire grass" and "slough grass".

As we started to load the hay, father called out, "No, boys, drive over to the higher ground." There was timothy and redtop there.

One of the boys called back, "No, let us take the hay as it comes!"

"No, David, this is the tenth load and the best is none too good for God."

That is the most effective sermon on tithing I have ever heard in my life, and it touches, I found in later life, this very principle of the law of sacrifice. You cannot develop character without obeying that law.

The man who is honest with the Lord is honest with himself and is blessed exceedingly.
—*David O. McKay*

✎

A Generous Man

One day on the street I met a friend whom I had known since boyhood. I had not visited with him for some time, and I was interested in being brought up to date concerning his life, his problems, and his faith, therefore I invited him to go to a conference in Utah County with me. He drove his fine car (the make of car I was driving had not been received into society at that time). He took his wife, and I took mine.

At conference, I called on him to speak. I did not know what it might do to him, but I thought I would take a chance.

He gave a fine talk. He told of his trips to the east, how he had explained the gospel to the people he had met, and how grateful he was for his heritage. He stated that his opportunities in the world had been magnified and multiplied because his father and mother had joined the Church in the Old World.

As we drove home, he turned to me and said: "My, this has been a wonderful conference. I have enjoyed it."

I thought to myself, he was like one of our sisters who came home from a fast meeting and said to her family, "That is the best meeting I ever attended."

One of the daughters asked, "Why, Mother, who spoke?"

And then her mother replied, "I did."

I thought he had enjoyed it because he himself had participated. I was glad he had.

Then he said, "You know, I have heard many things in this conference, but there is only one thing that I do not understand the way you do."

"What is it?" I asked.

"Well," he said, "it's about paying tithing."

He thought I would ask him how he paid his tithing, but I did not. I thought if he wanted to tell me, he would.

"Would you like me to tell you how I pay my tithing?" he asked.

"If you want to, you may," I replied.

"Well," he said, "if I make ten thousand dollars in a year, then I put a thousand dollars in the bank for tithing. I know why it's there. Then, when the bishop comes and wants me to make a contribution for the chapel, or give him a check for a missionary who is going away, if I think he needs the money, then I give him a check. If a family in the ward is in distress and needs coal or food or clothing or anything else, I write out a check. If I find a boy or a girl who is having difficulty getting through school in the east, I send a check. Little by little I exhaust the thousand dollars, and every dollar of it has gone where I know it has done good. Now, what do you think of that?"

 "I think you are a very generous man with someone else's property," I replied, and he nearly tipped the car over.

"What do you mean?" he asked.

I said, "You have an idea that you have paid your tithing?"

"Yes," he said.

I said, "You have not paid any tithing. You have told me what you have done with the Lord's money. Tithing should be paid to the Church and it's use directed by the Lord. You haven't done that; you have taken your best partner's money, and given it away."

Well, I will tell you there was quiet in the car for some time. We rode on to Salt Lake City and talked about other things.

About a month after that, I met him on the street. He came up, put his arms in mine, and said, "Brother Smith, I am paying my tithing the same way you do."
—*George Albert Smith*

Values

The best things in life are not things.

❧

The beauty seen is partly in he who sees it.

❧

As a society we tend to love things and use people, rather than the reverse.

—*Eric Fromm*

❧

I often think no man is worth his salt until he has lost and won battles for a principle.

—*John Marsh*

❧

Do not spend money for that which is of no worth, nor your labor for that which cannot satisfy.

❧

Better keep yourself clean and bright: you are the window through which you must see the world.

—*George Bernard Shaw*

❧

It is a good thing to have money and the things that money can buy; it is good, too, to check up once in awhile and make sure we haven't lost the things money can't buy.

❧

The Value of Duty, Honor, Country

Duty, honor, country. Those three hallowed words reverently dictate what you ought to be, what you can be, what you will be.

They are your rallying points: to build courage when courage seems to fail, to regain faith when there seems little cause for faith, to create hope when hope becomes forlorn.

They build your basic character, they make you strong enough to know when you are weak, and brave enough to face yourself when you are afraid.

They teach you to be proud and unbending in honest failure, but humble and gentle in success; not to substitute words for actions, nor to seek the path of comfort, but to face the stress and spur of difficulty and challenge; to learn to stand up in the storm, but to have compassion on those who fall; to master yourself before you seek to master others;

to have a heart that is clean, a goal that is high; to learn to laugh, yet never forget how to weep; to reach into the future, yet never neglect the past; to be serious, yet never take yourself too seriously; to be modest so that you will remember the simplicity of true greatness, the open mind of true wisdom, the meekness of true strength.

They give you a temper of the will, a quality of the imagination, a vigor of the emotions, a freshness of the deep springs of life, a temperamental predominance of courage over timidity, an appetite for adventure over love of ease.

They create in your heart the sense of wonder, the unfailing hope of what's next, and the joy and inspiration of life.

—Douglas MacArthur

⇛

Values to Live By

The most interesting thing about any human being is the values by which he or she lives. Unfortunately, most of us never take the time to sit down and really think through the moral precepts that consciously or unconsciously guide our lives. The following "daily dozen" constitute the personal creed of Robert Louis Stevenson:

1. Make up your mind to be happy. Learn to find pleasure in simple things.

2. Make the best of your circumstances. No one has everything, and everyone has something of sorrow intermingled with the gladness of life. The trick is to make the laughter outweigh the tears.

3. Don't take yourself too seriously. Don't think that somehow you should be protected from misfortunes that befall others.

4. You can't please everybody. Don't let criticism worry you.

5. Don't let your neighbor set your standards. Be yourself.

6. Do the things you enjoy doing, but stay out of debt.

7. Don't borrow trouble. Imaginary things are harder to bear than the actual ones.

8. Since hate poisons the soul, do not cherish enmities, grudges. Avoid people who make you unhappy.

9. Have many interests. If you can't travel, read about new places.

10. Don't hold postmortems. Don't spend your life brooding over sorrows and mistakes. Don't be one who never gets over things.

11. Do what you can for those less fortunate than yourself.

12. Keep busy at something. A very busy person never has time to be unhappy.

More Valuable than Jewels

A wealthy lady was one day visited by two who desired to see first-hand of her wealth and riches, the glory of which they had heard many times.

After several minutes of conversation with her in her home, they asked if they might please see some of her most precious jewels.

She excused herself from the room and was gone several minutes. When she returned, she had with her two small children.

She explained, "Of all the gems and all the wealth which it may be my privilege to enjoy, these two jewels are by far my most precious."

❧

The Value of the Senses

I who am blind can give one hint to those who see: Use your eyes as if tomorrow you would be stricken blind.

The same method can be applied to the other senses.

Hear the music of voices, the song of a bird, the mighty strains of an orchestra, as if you would be stricken deaf tomorrow.

Touch each object as if tomorrow your tactile sense would fail.

Smell the perfume of flowers, taste with relish each morsel, as if tomorrow you could never smell and taste again.

Make the most of every sense, glory, and beauty which the world, in all the facets of pleasure, reveals to you, through the several means of contact which nature provides.

But of all the senses, I am sure that sight is the most delightful.
—*Helen Keller*

❧

Twelve Things to Value

1. The gift of time
2. The reward of perseverance
3. The pleasure of working
4. The dignity of simplicity
5. The worth of character
6. The power of kindness
7. The obligation of duty
8. The virtue of patience

9. The wisdom of economy

10. The improvement of talent

11. The joy of originating

12. The influence of example

❧

The Value of Me

When the other fellow takes a long time to do something, he's slow; but, when I take a long time to do something, I'm thorough.

When the other fellow doesn't do it, he's too lazy; but, when I don't do it, I'm too busy.

When the other fellow goes ahead and does something without being told, he's overstepping his bounds; but, when I go ahead and do something without being told, that's initiative.

When the other fellow states his side of a question strongly, he's bullheaded; but, when I state a side of a question strongly, I'm being firm.

When the other fellow overlooks a few rules of etiquette, he's rude; but, when I skip a few rules, I'm original.

When the other fellow does something that pleases the boss, he's polishing the brass; but, when I do something that pleases the boss, that's cooperation.

When the other fellow gets ahead, he sure had the lucky breaks; but, when I manage to get ahead, I worked hard for it.

❧

The Value of Switches

The course of our lives is not determined by great, awesome decisions. Our direction is set by the little day-to-day choices which chart the track on which we run.

Many years ago, I worked in the head office of one of our railroads. One day, I received a telephone call from my counter-part in Newark, New Jersey, who said that a passenger train had arrived without its baggage car. The patrons were angry.

We discovered that the train had been properly made up in Oakland, California, and properly delivered to St. Louis, from which station it was to be carried to its destination on the east coast. But in the St. Louis yards, a thoughtless switchman had moved a piece of steel just three inches.

That piece of steel was a switch point, and the car that should have been in Newark, New Jersey, was in New Orleans, Louisiana, thirteen hundred miles away.

So it is with our lives—a cigarette smoked, a can of beer drunk at a party, a shot of speed taken on a dare, a careless giving in to an impulse on a date.

Each has thrown a switch in the life of a boy that put him on a track that carried him far away from what might have been a great and foreordained calling.

As Nephi said, "Thus the devil cheateth their souls and leadeth them away carefully down to hell." (2 Nephi. 28:21)

—*Gordon B. Hinckley*

The Kite String

While flying a kite, I once asked my father, "Dad, what holds the kite up?"

"The string," he replied.

"No, Dad, the string holds it down, not up."

"If you think so, let go of the string," he said, "and see what happens."

I let go and the kite began to fall! It seems odd that the very thing which seems to keep the kite down is actually what keeps it up.

This is true not only of kites but of life. Those strings that are tied to us, those rules and regulations that seem to hold us down, are actually holding us up.

And certainly in the realm of the spirit, in the field of faith, this same truth holds with even greater force.

The word "religion" is said to come from a Latin root meaning "to hold back" or tie back. This is what religion does. It provides the string to the soaring kite of our spirit; it keeps us from falling; it binds us to great values; it attaches us to great causes; it helps us fly high in the aid of God's truth, and lifts us until our heads touch the stars, and our lives take on the beauty of men and women who are bound closely to God.

Ten Values for Living

1. Develop yourself by self-discipline

2. Joy comes through creation, sorrow through destruction

3. Do things that are hard to do

4. Entertain upbuilding thoughts: what you think about when you do not have to think shows what you really are

5. Do your best this hour, and you will do better the next

6. Be true to those who trust you

7. True friends enrich life; if you would have friends, be one

8. Pray for wisdom, courage, and a kind heart

9. Give heed to God's messages through inspiration; if self-indulgence, jealousy, avarice, or worry have deadened your responses, pray to the Lord to wipe out those impediments

10. Faith is the foundation of all things—including happiness
—David O. McKay

Values to Believe In

I believe in the supreme worth of the individual and in his right to life, liberty, and the pursuit of happiness.

I believe that every right implies a responsibility; every opportunity, an obligation; every possession, a duty.

I believe that the law was made for man and not man for the law; that government is the servant of the people and not their master.

I believe in the dignity of labor, whether with head or hand; that the world owes every man an opportunity to make a living.

I believe that thrift is essential to well-ordered living and that economy is a prime requisite of a sound financial structure, whether in government, business, or personal affairs.

I believe that truth and justice are fundamental to an enduring social order.

I believe in the sacredness of a promise, that a man's word should be as good as his bond; that character—not wealth or power or position—is of supreme worth.

I believe that the rendering of useful service is the common duty of mankind and that, only in the purifying fire of sacrifice, is the dross of selfishness consumed and the greatness of the human soul set free.

I believe in an all-wise and all-loving God, named by whatever name, and that the individual's highest fulfillment, greatest happiness, and widest usefulness are to be found in living in harmony with His will.

I believe that love is the greatest thing in the world; that it alone can overcome hate; that right can and will triumph over might.

—John D. Rockefeller, Jr. (Inscribed on the wall at Rockefeller Center, New York City)

The Value of Appearances

When a merchant had hired an office boy out of fifty applicants who answered his advertisement, a friend asked, "How did you come to select that fellow? He didn't have a single recommendation."

"He had a great many," replied the merchant.

"He wiped his feet when he came in, and he closed the door after him, showing that he is careful.

"He gave up his seat to a lame old man, showing that he is kind and thoughtful.

"He took off his cap when he came in and answered my questions promptly and respectfully, showing that he is polite and gentlemanly.

"He picked up a book which I had purposely laid on the floor and replaced it on the table, while all the rest of the boys stepped over it or shoved it aside.

"And he waited his turn quietly, instead of pushing or crowding.

"When I talked to him, I noticed that his clothes were carefully brushed, his hair in nice order, and his teeth as white as milk.

"When he wrote his name, I noticed that his fingernails were clean, instead of being tipped with jet like those of that handsome little fellow in the blue jacket.

"Don't you call all these things letters of recommendation? I do; and I would give more for what I can tell about a boy by using my eyes for ten minutes than for all the letters of recommendation he can give me."

A mother who is teaching her boy good manners and habits of self-respect may be providing him with a capital more substantial than a bank account.

I have known a good many boys and some men who make fun of those who take care to dress tidily and attractively. Yet, young people who have a little pride in making themselves presentable, and whose faces are often wreathed in loving, happy smiles, are most likely to make friends.

Not long ago, a prominent business firm discharged their manager because he was never tidy in his personal appearance. When they advertised, they received forty applications for the place; yet, only one young man was asked to call again.

"Did you observe his neatly fitting shirt and necktie?" asked one of the partners after the young man had departed. "How nicely his boots were polished, how tidy he was?"

The young man's references were looked up, and he was engaged the next morning. Several of the others might have been better men for the position, but a first impression is lasting.

In this land of opportunity, the cases are very rare where the poorest boy or man ever needs to appear to poor advantage.

A man's clothes may be thread-bare and even patched; but if they are well brushed and, if he is clean himself, he will command the respect of everyone.

The Value of Life

Charlie was the kind of guy who didn't appreciate the delicious feeling of doing some things slowly. He didn't know that some matters scream to be accomplished in a leisurely manner. Things like eating a parfait. Or watching a child at play. Or kissing his wife when he left the house every morning on his way to work. Sure, a lot of people said Charlie got more accomplished than others. He was a moderately successful businessman, with too much of the stuff called nervous energy.

"Slow down, Charlie," a friend would say. "You're forgetting how to live."

What the friend didn't realize was that Charlie had never known how.

Charlie's oldest son was a high school basketball player, but Charlie had seen him play only once.

"Too many meetings that interfere," Charlie apologized.

His eleven-year-old daughter asked him to attend her piano recital. Charlie promised. But he found himself taking an out-of-town business trip on the little girl's big night. A man has to make a living.

One evening after dinner, Charlie felt a pain in his stomach. It wasn't much at first. But it got worse. Betty, Charlie's wife, called the doctor when Charlie's face went gray. When the doctor told Charlie he was going to the hospital, Charlie didn't want to go. The pain got worse about that time, so Charlie didn't argue.

The doctor stuck some wires on various places around Charlie's body and watched as a needle moved up and down a piece of paper. They stuck a needle in Charlie's arm and told him not to even so much as sit up in bed. Charlie thought this was a lot of hogwash, but the pain in his chest...

The next day, Charlie gathered he'd had a heart attack. It was something that would take weeks, maybe months, to get over. He'd have to lie in bed until the heart mended itself. It scared Charlie, so he minded the doctor.

Betty stayed with Charlie during his three weeks in the hospital and, for the first time in their eighteen years of married life, they became pals. They talked about little things. Charlie watched Betty as she went around the room straightening flowers in the vases, and it was like seeing her for the first time. After that, he spent long minutes just looking into her eyes, and Betty blushed. They were like eighteen-year-olds again.

When Charlie came home, he talked over every single play of the basketball season with his son. Often, when he would hear his daughter practicing the piano, he would turn to Betty and, with a note of surprise in his voice, say, "Hey, she's pretty good!"

Charlie's strength came back and he went to work again. When he met friends on the street, they would stop him and invariably say something like, "Hey, Charlie! Good to see you back on the job! Heart attack, eh? Say, that's bad. They tell me there's nothing as painful as having the old elephant on your chest."

And Charlie would smile and invariably reply something like, "Don't feel sorry for me, chum. That heart attack was the best thing that ever happened to me."

❧

Most Important

Most important six words: I admit I made a mistake.

Most important five words: I am proud of you.

Most important four words: What is your opinion?

Most important three words: If you please.

Most important two words: Thank you.

Most important word: We.

Least important word: I

❧

I Am Third

One day, I walked into the office of the Chief of Chaplains of the Far East Command in Tokyo, Japan, to receive an assignment that eventually took me to the battlefields of Korea.

As I sat waiting for the Chief's arrival, my eye caught sight of a doily hanging on his office wall. The doily had three words embroidered upon it: "I am third."

When the Chief walked in, I curiously asked him what the sign meant. With a little smile, he replied that it was his personal creed, his philosophy for a Christian life, a motto that a chaplain might find useful.

The smile left his face as he explained in a more serious tone, "The Lord is first, my fellowmen are second, and I am third. I have a tendency to forget that occasionally. So, every morning, before commencing the day's work, I repeat it several times, in order to remind myself of the relative position of my life, with respect to other lives upon the face of the earth."

This was a familiar concept, though I had never heard it phrased in those exact terms. Nevertheless, his motto impressed me and I asked him if I could borrow it to use in my sermons as a front-line chaplain. He said he would be pleased and flattered.

I used the motto many times during the thirteen months I served in Korea. Many times it came back to me in the form of tremendous feats of heroism performed by our boys in that war-torn land, demonstrating to me that, in action as well as in word, they truly considered themselves third.

Many of our servicemen were cited for unselfish devotion to duty in Korea. One of our boys, however, proved himself so courageous on the battlefield that he was awarded the Congressional Medal of Honor, the highest military award that our nation can bestow upon one of its citizen soldiers. This young man's behavior, it seems to me, exemplifies the true spirit of sacrifice, responsibility, and leadership that the Church of Jesus Christ would like to instill in all of its youth.

Sergeant David Bleak of Shelley, Idaho, served as a medical corpsman during the Korean War. His primary responsibility was to minister to his companions, as they fell wounded in battle. An excerpt from his citation, written by a personal witness, relates the following:

"We left the line of departure at 2:45 a.m. on June 14, 1952, and crossed several enemy-occupied 'figures of land' to get in position for our final assault.

"When we started our assault, we came under intense automatic small arms and grenade fire. As we neared the top of the hill, a hand grenade thrown by the enemy glanced off the helmet of one of our men. Sergeant Bleak, with total disregard for his personal safety, threw his body on top of the struck soldier and absorbed the full force of the concussion (explosion).

"Continuing to the top of the hill, he was fired on by three of the enemy who were in a trench. Realizing that only by passing through the trench could he reach a wounded man, Sergeant Bleak attempted to cross the area, but was immediately confronted by the three enemy soldiers. Engaging the men in intense hand-to-hand combat, Sergeant Bleak killed them in self-defense.

"After clearing the hill, and while withdrawing under heavy artillery and mortar fire, a machine gun pinned us down and wounded three of our squad. Sergeant Bleak, exposing himself to the deadly enemy fire, went over to dress the men's wounds. While doing this, he was wounded in the left leg by machine gun fire. He then came face to face with two of the enemy charging him with fixed bayonets. He grabbed the two with his bare hands and smashed their heads together.

"Disregarding his wounds, and accepting aid from no one, he picked up one of the wounded men and carried him down the hill.

"Sergeant Bleak's dauntless courage and intrepid actions reflect utmost credit upon himself and are in keeping with the honored traditions of the military service."

His actions also seem to be in keeping with the statement uttered by the Apostle John when he said, "Greater love hath no man than this, that a man lay down his life for his friends." (John 15:13)

"What makes your soldiers so outstanding?" I was repeatedly asked by commanding officers along the front lines.

"Faith," I would respond. "Faith in God, faith in their fellow men, and faith in themselves."

All through their basic religious training, they, like Sergeant Bleak, have been taught the Chief of Chaplain's motto: "The Lord is first, my fellowmen are second, and I am third." This is a divine doctrine that cannot be learned too early in the lives of men.

—*Ben F. Mortensen*

The Children's Story

The teacher was afraid, and the children were afraid. All except Johnny. He watched the classroom door with hate. He felt the hatred deep within his stomach. It gave him strength.

It was two minutes to nine.

The teacher glanced numbly from the door and stared at the flag which stood in a corner of the room. But she couldn't see the flag today.

She was blinded by her terror, not only for herself, but mostly for them, her children. She had never had children of her own. She had never married.

In the mists of her mind, she saw the rows upon rows of children she had taught through her years. Their faces were legion. But she could distinguish no one particular face. Only the same face, which varied but slightly. Always the same age or thereabouts. Seven, perhaps a boy, perhaps a girl. And the face always open and ready for the knowledge that she was to give. The same face staring at her, open, waiting, and full of trust.

The children rustled, watching her, wondering what possessed her. They saw not the gray hair and the old eyes and the lined face and well-worn clothes. They saw only their teacher and the twisting hands.

Johnny looked away from the door and watched the other children. He did not understand anything except that the teacher was afraid and, because she was afraid, she was making them all worse, and he wanted to shout that there was no need to fear. "Just because they've conquered us, there's no need for panic fear," Dad had said. "Don't be afraid, Johnny. If you fear too much, you'll be dead even though you're alive."

The sound of footsteps approached and then stopped. The door opened.

The children gasped. They expected an ogre or giant or beast or witch or monster—like the outer-space monsters you think about when the lights are out and momma and daddy have kissed you good night and you're frightened and you put your head under the cover and all at once you're awake and it's time for school.

But instead of a monster, a beautiful young girl stood in the doorway. Her clothes were neat and clean, all olive green—even her shoes. But most important, she wore a lovely smile, and when she spoke, she spoke without the trace of an accent. The children found this very strange, for they were foreigners from a strange country far across the sea. They had all been told about them.

"Good morning, children," the New Teacher said. Then she closed the door softly and walked to the teacher's desk, and the children in the front row felt and smelled the perfume of her—clean and fresh and young. As she passed Sandra, who sat at the end of the first row, she said, "Good morning, Sandra", and Sandra flushed deeply and wondered aghast, with all the other children, "How did she know my name?" and her heart raced in her chest and made it feel tight and very heavy.

The teacher got up shakily, "I, er, I...good morning." Her words were faltering and she, too, was trying to get over the shock. And nausea.

"Hello, Miss Worden," the New Teacher said. "I'm taking over your class now. You are to go to the principal's office."

"Why? What's going to happen to me? What's going to happen to my children?" The words gushed from Miss Worden, and a lank piece of hair fell into her eyes. The children were agonized by the edge to her voice, and one or two of them felt on the edge of tears.

"He just wants to talk to you, Miss Worden," the New Teacher said gently. "You really must take better care of yourself. You shouldn't be so upset."

Miss Worden saw the New Teacher's smile, but she wasn't touched by its compassion. She tried to stop her knees from shaking.

"Good-bye, children," she said. The children made no reply. They were too terrified by the sound of her voice and the tears that wet her face. And, because she was crying, some of the children cried and Sandra fled to her.

The New Teacher shut the door behind Miss Worden and turned back into the room, cradling Sandra in her arms. "Children, children, there's no need to cry," she said. "I know, I'll sing you a song! Listen."

And she sat down on the floor as gracefully as an angel, Sandra in her arms, and she began to sing and the children stopped crying because Miss Worden never, never sang to them, and certainly never sat on the floor, which is the best place to sit, as everyone in the class knew.

They listened spellbound to the happy lilt of the New Teacher's voice and the strange words of a strange tongue which soared and dipped like the sea of grass which was the birthplace of the song. It was about two children who had lost their way and were all alone in the great grass prairies and were afraid, but they met a fine man riding a fine horse and the man told them that there was never a need to be afraid, for all they had to do was to watch the stars, and the stars would tell them where their home was.

"For, once you know the right direction, then there's never a need to be afraid. Fear is something that comes from inside, from inside your tummies," the New Teacher said radiantly, "and strong children like you have to put food in tummies. Not fear."

The children thought about this and it seemed very sensible. The New Teacher sang the song again, and soon all the children were happy and calm once more, except Johnny. He hated her, even though he knew she was right about fear.

"Now," said the New Teacher, "what shall we do? I know, we'll play a game. I'll try and guess your names."

The children, wide-eyed, shifted in their seats. Miss Worden never did this, and often she called a child by another's name. The New Teacher'll never know all our names, never! they thought. So they waited excitedly while the New Teacher turned her attention to Sandra. Oh, yes, somehow she already knew Sandra's name, but how could she possibly know everyone's? They waited, glad that they were going to catch the New Teacher.

But they were not to catch her. The New Teacher remembered every name!

Johnny put up his hand. "How'd you know our names? I mean, well, we haven't had a roll call or anything, so how'd you know our names?"

"That's easy, Johnny," the New Teacher said. "You all sit in the same places every day. Each desk has one pupil. So I learned all your names from a list. I had to work for three whole days to remember your names. A teacher must work very hard to be a good teacher, and so I worked for three days so that I could know each of you the first day. That's very important, don't you think, for a teacher to work hard?"

Johnny frowned and half-nodded and sat down and wondered why he hadn't figured that out for himself before asking, astonished that she had worked three days just to know everyone's names the first day. But still he hated her.

"Johnny, would you tell me something, please? How do you start school? I mean, what do you begin with?"

Johnny stood reluctantly. "We first pledge allegiance and then we sing the song..."

"Yes, but that's after roll call," Sandra said. "You forgot roll call."

"Yes, you forgot roll call, Johnny," Mary said.

"First, we have roll call," Johnny said. Then he sat down.

The New Teacher smiled. "All right. But we really don't need roll call. I know all your names, and I know everyone's here. It's very lazy for a teacher not to know who's here and who isn't, don't you think? After all, a teacher should know. We don't need roll call while I'm your teacher. So should we pledge? Isn't that next?"

Obediently all the children got up and put their hands on their hearts and the New Teacher did the same, and they began in unison, "I pledge allegiance to the flag..."

"Just a moment," the New Teacher said. "What does 'pledge' mean?"

The children were silent.

"Your teacher never explained it to you?"

The children stood open-mouthed; Miss Worden had never interrupted them before. They stood and stared at the New Teacher. Wordless, and silent.

"What does allegiance mean?" the New Teacher asked, her hand over her heart.

The children stood in silence. Then Mary put up her hand. "Well, pledge is, ah, well something like—sort of when you want to do something very good. You sort of pledge you're going to do something like not suck your thumb 'cause that makes your teeth bend and you'll have to wear a brace and go to the dentist, which hurts."

"That's very good, Mary. Very, very good. The pledge means to promise. And allegiance?"

Mary shrugged hopelessly and looked at her best friend, Hilda, who looked back at her and then at the New Teacher and shrugged helplessly, too.

The New Teacher waited, and the silence hung in the room, hurting. Then she said, "I think it's quite wrong for you to have to say something with long words in it if you don't understand what you're saying. So let's sit down and talk about it."

So the children all sat down and waited expectantly.

"What did your other teachers tell you that it meant?"

After a long silence, Danny put up his hand. "She never said nothin', miss."

"One of my teachers at the other school I went to before this one," Joan said in a rush, "well, she sort of said what it all meant, at least she said something about it just before recess one day and then the bell rang and afterwards we had spelling."

Danny said, "Miss Worden…well, she never told us. We just had to learn it and then say it, that's all. Our real teacher didn't say anything at all."

All the children nodded. Then they waited again.

The children thought about this and shook their heads.

All the children shook their heads. "I don't think that was very good—not to explain. You can always ask me anything. That's what a real teacher should do." Then the New Teacher said, "But didn't you ask your daddies and mummies?"

"Not about I pledge. We just had to learn it," Mary said. "Once I could say it, daddy gave me a nickel for saying it good."

"That's right," Danny said. "So long as you could say it all, it was very good. But I never got a nickel."

"Did you ask each other what it meant?"

"I asked Danny once and he didn't know and none of us knowed really. It's grown-up talk, and grown-ups talk that sort of words. We just have ta learn it."

"Once in second grade, Miss Sander said something about it, but it was only once and I forgot it," Johnny said hopefully.

"The other schools I went to," Hilda said, "they never said anything about it. They just wanted us to learn it. They didn't ask us what it meant. We just had ta say it every day before we started school.

"It took me weeks and weeks and weeks to say it right," Mary said.

So the New Teacher explained what allegiance meant, "...so you are promising or pledging support to the flag and saying that it is much more important than you are. How can a flag be more important than a real live person?"

Johnny broke the silence. "But the next thing is...well, where it says 'and for the country for which it stands.' That means its sort of like...like a..." he searched for the word and could not find it. "Like a, well, sort of sign, isn't it?"

"Yes. The real word is symbol." The New Teacher frowned. "But we don't need a sign to remind us that we love our country, do we? You're all good boys and girls. Do you need a sign to remind you?"

"What's 'remind' mean?" asked Mary.

"It means to make you remember. To make you remember that you're all good boys and girls."

Johnny put up his hand. "It's our flag," he said fiercely. "We always pledge."

"Yes," the New Teacher said. "It is a very pretty one." She looked at it for a moment and then said, "I wish I could have a piece of it. Don't you?"

"I've a little one at home," Mary said. "I could bring it tomorrow."

"Thank you, Mary dear, but I just wanted a little piece of this one because it's our own special classroom one."

Then Danny said, "If we had some scissors we could cut a little piece off."

"I've some scissors at home," Mary said.

"There's some in Miss Worden's desk," Brian said.

The New Teacher found the scissors and then they had to decide who would be allowed to cut off a little piece, and the New Teacher said that because today was Mary's birthday ("How did she know that?" Mary wondered), Mary should be allowed to cut the piece off. And then they decided it would be very nice if they all had a piece. The flag is special, they thought, so if you have a piece of it that's better than having just to look at it 'cause you can keep it in your pocket.

So the flag was cut up by the children and they were very proud that they each had a piece of it. But now the flagpole was bare and strange. And useless. The children pondered what to do with it, and the idea that pleased them most was to push it out of the window. They watched excitedly as the New Teacher opened the window and allowed them to throw it out into the playground. They shrieked with excitement as they saw it bounce on the ground. They began to love the strange New Teacher.

When they were all back in their seats the New Teacher said, "Well, before we start our lessons, perhaps there are some questions you want me to answer. Ask me anything you like. That's only fair, isn't it, if I ask you questions?"

Mary said, after a long silence, "We never get to ask our real teacher any questions."

Johnny broke the silence. "But the next thing is...well..."

"You can always ask me anything. That's the fair way—the New way. Try me."

"What's your name?" asked Danny.

She told them her name and it sounded pretty.

Mary put up her hand. "Why do you wear those clothes? It's like a sort of uniform nurses wear."

"We think that teachers should be dressed the same, then you always know a teacher. It's nice and light and easy to press. Do you like the color?"

"Oh, yes," said Mary. "You've got green eyes, too."

"If you like, children, as a very special surprise, you can all have this sort of uniform. Then you won't have to worry about what you have to wear to school everyday. And you'll all be the same."

The children twisted excitedly in their seats. Mary said, "But it'll cost a lot of money, and my momma won't want to spend the money, 'cause we have to buy food and food is expen...well, it sort of costs a lot of money."

"They will be given to you, as a present. There's no need to worry about money."

Johnny said, "I don't want to be dressed like that."

"You don't have to accept a present, Johnny. Just because the other children want to wear new clothes, you don't have to," the New Teacher said.

Johnny slunk back in his chair. "I'm never going to wear their clothes," he said to himself. "I don't care if I am going to look different from Danny and Tom and Fred."

Then Mary asked, "Why was our teacher crying?"

"I suppose she was tired and needed a rest. She's going to have a long rest." She smiled at them. "We think teachers should be young. I'm nineteen."

"Is the war over now?" Danny asked.

"Yes, Danny. Isn't that wonderful? Now all your daddies will be home soon."

"Did we win or did we lose?" Mary asked.

"We—that's you and I and all of us—we won."

The children sat back happily. Then Johnny's hatred burst. "Where's my Dad? What've you done to my Dad?"

The New Teacher got up from her seat and walked the length of the room and the children's eyes followed her, and Johnny stood, knees of jelly. She sat down on his seat and put her hands on his shoulders, and his shoulders were shaking like his knees.

"He's going to a school. Some grown-ups have to go to school as well as children."

"But they took him away and he didn't want to go." Johnny felt the tears close, and he fought back.

The New Teacher touched him gently, and he smelled the youth and cleanness of her, and it was not the smell of home, which was sour and just a little dirty. "He's no different from all of you. You sometimes don't want to go to school. With grown-ups, it's the same—just the same as with children. Would you like to visit him? He has a holiday in a few days."

"Momma said that dad's gone away forever!" Johnny stared at her incredulously. "He has a holiday?"

The New Teacher laughed. "She's wrong, Johnny. After all, everyone who goes to school has holidays. That's fair, isn't it?"

The children shifted and rustled and watched. And Johnny said, "I can see him?"

"Of course, Johnny, I said wrong thoughts—not bad thoughts. There's nothing wrong with that. But it's right to show grown-ups right thoughts when theirs are wrong, isn't it?"

"Well, yes," Johnny said. "But what wrong thoughts did he have?"

"Just some grown-up thoughts that are old-fashioned. We're going to learn all about them in class. Then we can share knowledge, and I can learn from you and you will learn from me. Shall we?"

"Well, perhaps sometime when you wanted to talk about something very important to your dad, perhaps he said, 'Now, now, Johnny,' or 'I'm busy, we'll talk about it tomorrow.' That's a bad thought, not to give time when it's important, isn't it?"

"My momma says that all the time," said Mary.

And the other children nodded and they wondered if all their parents should go back to school and unlearn bad thoughts.

"Sit down, Johnny, and we'll start learning good things and not worry about grown-up bad thoughts. Oh, yes," she said when she sat down at her seat again, brimming with happiness, "I have a lovely surprise for you. You're all going to stay overnight with us. We have a lovely room and beds and lots of food, and we'll all tell stories and have such a lovely time."

"Oh, good!" the children said.

"Can I stay up till eight o'clock?" Mary asked breathlessly.

"Well, as it's our first new day, we'll stay up to eight-thirty. But only if you promise to go right to sleep afterward."

The New Teacher smiled at her. "Of course. Perhaps we should say a prayer now. In some schools that's the custom, too. But let's pray for something very good. What should we pray for?"

"Bless Momma and Daddy," Danny said immediately.

"That's a good idea, Danny. I have one, too. Let's pray for candy. That's a good idea, isn't it?"

They all nodded happily.

So, following their New Teacher, they all closed their eyes and steepled their hands together, and they prayed with her for candy.

The New Teacher opened her eyes and looked around disappointedly. "But where's our candy? God is all-seeing and is everywhere, and if we pray, he answers our prayers. Isn't that true?"

"I prayed for a puppy of my own, lots of times, but I never got one," said Danny.

"Maybe we didn't pray hard enough. Perhaps we should kneel down like it's done in church."

So the New Teacher knelt and all the children knelt and they prayed very hard. But there was still no candy.

Because the New Teacher was disappointed, the children were very disappointed. Then she said, "Perhaps we're using the wrong name." She thought a moment and then said, "Instead of saying, 'God', let's say 'Our Leader'. Let's pray to Our Leader for candy. Let's pray very hard and don't open your eyes till I say."

So the children shut their eyes tightly and prayed very hard, and as they prayed the New Teacher took out some candy from her pocket and quietly put a piece on each child's desk. She did not notice Johnny—alone of all the children watching her through his half-closed eyes.

She went softly back to her desk and the prayer ended, and the children opened their eyes and they stared at the candy and they were overjoyed.

"I'm going to pray to Our Leader every time," Mary said excitedly.

"Me, too," Hilda said. "Could we eat Our Leader's candy now, Teacher?"

"Oh, let's, please, please, please."

"So Our Leader answered your prayers, didn't he?"

"I saw you put the candy on our desks," Johnny burst out. "I saw you! I didn't close my eyes and I saw you. You had 'em in your pocket. We didn't get them with praying. YOU put them there."

All the children, appalled, stared at him and then at their New Teacher. She stood in front of the class and looked back at Johnny and then at all of them.

"Yes, Johnny, you're quite right. You're a very, very wise boy. Children, I put the candy on your desks. So you know that it doesn't matter who you ask, who you shut your eyes and 'pray' to—to God or anyone, even Our Leader. No one will give you anything, only another human being." She looked at Danny. "God didn't give you the puppy you wanted. But if you work hard, I will. Only I or someone like me can give you things. Praying to God or anything or anyone for something is a waste of time."

"Then we don't say prayers? We're not supposed to say prayers?" The puzzled children watched her.

"You can if you want to, children. If your daddies and mommies want you to. But we know, you and I, that it means nothing. That's our secret."

"My dad says it's wrong to have secrets from him."

"But he has secrets that he shares with your mommy, and not with you, doesn't he?" All the children nodded.

"Then it's not wrong for us to have a few secrets from them, is it?"

"I like to have secrets. Hilda and me have lots of secrets," Mary said.

The New Teacher said, "We're going to have lots of wonderful secrets together. You can eat your candy if you want to. And because Johnny was especially clever, I think we should make him monitor for the whole week, don't you?"

They all nodded happily and popped the candy into their mouths; and chewed gloriously. Johnny was very proud as he chewed his candy. He decided that he liked his teacher very much. Because she had told him the truth. Because she was right about God. He'd prayed many times for many things and never got them, and even the one time he did get the skates, he knew his dad had heard him and had put them under his bed for his birthday, and pretended he hadn't heard him. "I always wondered why he didn't listen and all the time he wasn't there," he thought.

Johnny sat back contentedly, resolved to work hard and listen and not have wrong thoughts like Dad.

The Teacher waited for them to finish their candy. This was what she had been trained for, and she knew that she would teach her children well and that they would grow up to be good citizens.

She looked out of the window, at the sun over the land. It was a good land, and vast. A land to breathe in. But she was warmed not by the sun but by the thought that throughout the school and throughout the land all children, all men, and all women were being taught with the same faith, with variations of the same procedures. Each according to his age group. Each according to his need. She glanced at her watch. It was 9:23.

—*James Clavell*

Work

Work is love made visible.

Pray for a crop, but keep hoeing.

The way to be nothing is to do nothing.

—*Nathaniel Howe*

Work is the yeast that raises your dough.

If the devil find a man idle, he'll set him to work.

—*Scottish proverb*

The reward of a thing well done, is to have done it.

—*Emerson*

Laziness travels so slow that poverty soon overtakes it.

There is no virtue in doing only the things you like to do.

The bee that gets the honey doesn't hang around the hive.

There is no future in any job—only in the man who holds it.

If you want to keep ahead of Satan, you have to work like him.

I am a great believer in luck: the harder I work, the more I have.

Make your job important and it is very likely to return the favor.

❧

There are lots of rules for success but none of them work unless you do.

❧

All that is necessary for the triumph of evil is for good men to do nothing.
—*Edmund Burke*

❧

Too many young people itch for what they want without scratching for it.
—*Tim D. Taylor*

❧

Vision without work is daydreaming; and work without vision is drudgery.
—*Thomas S. Monson*

❧

All share-the-wealth plans have precious little to say about sharing the work.
—*T. Kirkwood Collins*

❧

The only things you can be sure of accomplishing are the things you do today.

❧

The work you have accomplished is the only real legacy you can leave the world.
—*David Lloyd George*

❧

I cannot out-play my opponent in a tournament unless I out-work them in practice.

❧

Don't ask the Lord to guide your footsteps unless you're willing to move your feet.

❧

The highest reward for a man's toil is not what he gets for it, but what he becomes by it.

❧

Thomas S. Monson's "W" formula: Work Will Win When Wishy Washy Wishing Won't.

❧

Keep in mind that even if you're on the right track, you'll get run over if you just sit there.

∽

He who complains loudest about the way the ball bounces is very often the one who dropped it.

∽

Let us realize that the privilege to work is a gift, the power to work is a blessing, the love of work is success.

—David O. McKay

∽

He who sits cross-legged with mouth open waiting for roast duck to fly in is going to have a long hunger.

—Confucius

∽

Only those who have the patience to do simple things perfectly will acquire the skill to do difficult things easily.

—Johann Schiller

∽

The work will wait while you show the child the rainbow, but the rainbow won't wait while you do the work.

—Patricia Clafford

∽

We have too many people who live without working, and we have altogether too many who work without living.

—Charles R. Brown

∽

I never did anything worth doing by accident, nor did any of my inventions come by accident: they came by work.

—Thomas A. Edison

∽

Nature gave man two ends—one to sit on and one to think with. A man's success or failure depends on the one he uses the most.

∽

Live neither in the past nor in the future, but let each day's work absorb your entire energies, and satisfy your strongest ambitions.

❧

There are two things needed in these days: first, for rich men to find out how poor men live, and, second, for poor men to find out how rich men work.

—*E. Atkinson*

❧

Let us realize that the privilege to work is a gift, the power to work is a blessing, the love of work is success. Genius undoubtedly is little more than the capacity for hard, sustained work.

—*David O. McKay*

❧

It is a good safe rule to sojourn in every place, as if you meant to spend your life there, never omitting an opportunity of doing a kindness, or speaking a true word, or making a friend.

—*John Ruskin*

❧

The Lord is no respecter of persons, and will give success to all who work for it. If I can only impress upon the minds of the youth of Zion the eloquence, the inexpressible eloquence of work, I shall be fully repaid.

—*Heber J. Grant*

❧

All growth depends upon activity. There is no development physically or intellectually without effort, and effort means work. Work is not a curse: it is the prerogative of intelligence, the only means to manhood, and the measure of civilization.

—*Calvin Coolidge*

❧

Our Heavenly Father loves us so completely that he has given us a commandment to work. This is one of the keys to eternal life. He knows that we will learn more, grow more, achieve more, serve more, and benefit more from a life of industry than from a life of ease.

—*Howard W. Hunter*

❧

Thank God every morning when you get up that you have something to do that day which must be done, whether you like it or not. Being forced to work, and forced to do your best, will breed in you temperance, self-control, diligence, strength of will, and a hundred virtues which the idle never know

—Kingsley

❧

Bring a Basket

A minister in Africa asked the natives to help him harvest his crop. He asked each to bring a basket in which to carry the crop to market. At the end of the day, the minister let each worker fill his basket as his pay. Those who had brought big baskets had a great salary; those who had brought small baskets were disappointed.

❧

Work for Him

If you work for a man, then, for heaven's sake, work for him! Speak well of him and the institution he represents. If you must growl, condemn, and eternally find fault, then resign your position. And when you are on the outside, damn to your heart's content. But as long as you are part of the institution, do not condemn it. If you do, the first high wind that comes along will blow you away—and you will probably never know why. Remember, an ounce of loyalty is worth a pound of cleverness.

❧

Initiative Pays

Three brothers left the family farm to find work in the city. All three were hired by the same company, at the same pay. Some time later, Jim was making $500 a month; Frank, $1,000; and George, $1,500.

The boys' father decided to visit the company to determine the basis for the unequal pay.

The employer listened to the father and replied, "I'll let the boys explain for themselves."

Jim was summoned to the office.

"Jim, I understand that a large transport plane loaded with Japanese goods has just landed at the airport; go to the airport and see what they have that might be of interest to us."

Three minutes later, Jim returned to the office. "According to one of the crew members," Jim said, "there's some Japanese silk on board."

Frank was summoned next and given the same assignment.

An hour later, Frank returned with an inventory, listing a 1,000 bolts of Japanese silk, 500 transistor radios, and 1,000 hand-painted bamboo trays.

George was summoned next and given the same assignment.

Working hours were over when he finally returned. "The transport plane carried 1,000 bolts of Japanese silk," he began. "It was on sale at $60 a bolt, so I took a two-day option on the whole lot. I have wired a designer in New York, offering the silk at $75 per bolt. I expect to have the order tomorrow. I also found 500 transistor radios, which I sold over the telephone at a profit of $2.30 each. There were 1,000 bamboo trays, but they were of poor quality, so I didn't try to do anything with them."

When George left the office, the employer smiled at the father. "You probably noticed," he said, "that Jim doesn't do what he's told, Frank does only what he's told, but George does without being told."

The amount of extra effort you exert can directly affect your chances for advancement. The future is full of promise for the one who shows initiative.

Index

Especially For Mormons Order Form

❏ Please add me to your mailing list for pre-publication notice, and a special discount, of all the new editions of *Especially for Mormons* (*Christmas Especially for Mormons, Especially for Mormon Women, Poetry Especially for Mormons, Especially for Mormon Missionaries,* etc.) as they become available:

Name _____

Street Address_____

City/State/Zip _____

Phone/Fax/Email _____

❏ Using the same address above, please automatically charge my charge card and ship to me each new edition of *Especially for Mormons* as it is published:

Number of copies per title _____

Type of charge card _____

Name on charge card _____

Charge card number _____

Expiration date _____

Authorized signature _____

Please send as gift(s) to (attach separate page, if necessary) _____

With gift card(s) from _____

❏ I would like to submit the enclosed story for inclusion in the upcoming ALL NEW *Especially for Mormons*; following is my information so you can properly credit me in the book:

Date _____

Name _____

City/State/Country _____

Current Church calling _____

Category of story _____

❏ I would be interested in a three-ring binder version of Especially for Mormons with tabs so I can add other pieces; please send more information.

❏ I would be interested in automatically receiving on a regular basis new pieces for the binder/tab version of Especially for Mormons; please send more information.

To avoid removing this page from your book, please copy it before filling it out.

Please mail or fax to:
Especially for Mormons, Inc.
Box 1516
American Fork, UT 84003-6516
(801) 772-0440; 0990 fax

These same options are also available via our website:

www.especiallyformormons.com